P9-BIH-360

PENGUIN AFRICAN LIBRARY AP1

Edited by Ronald Segal

African Profiles

RONALD SEGAL

RONALD SEGAL

African Profiles

GLOUCESTER, MASS.

PETER SMITH

1970

First Published 1962

Reprinted, 1970, by Permission of
Penguin Books, Inc.

Contents

Acknowledgement

Most of the biographies contained in *African Profiles* are based on accounts which were originally published in *Political Africa* (Stevens & Sons Ltd, 1961) by Ronald Segal.

Political Africa contains biographies of over 400 politicians in Africa and gives an account of the development and present position of more than 100 political parties; the book covers the entire continent.

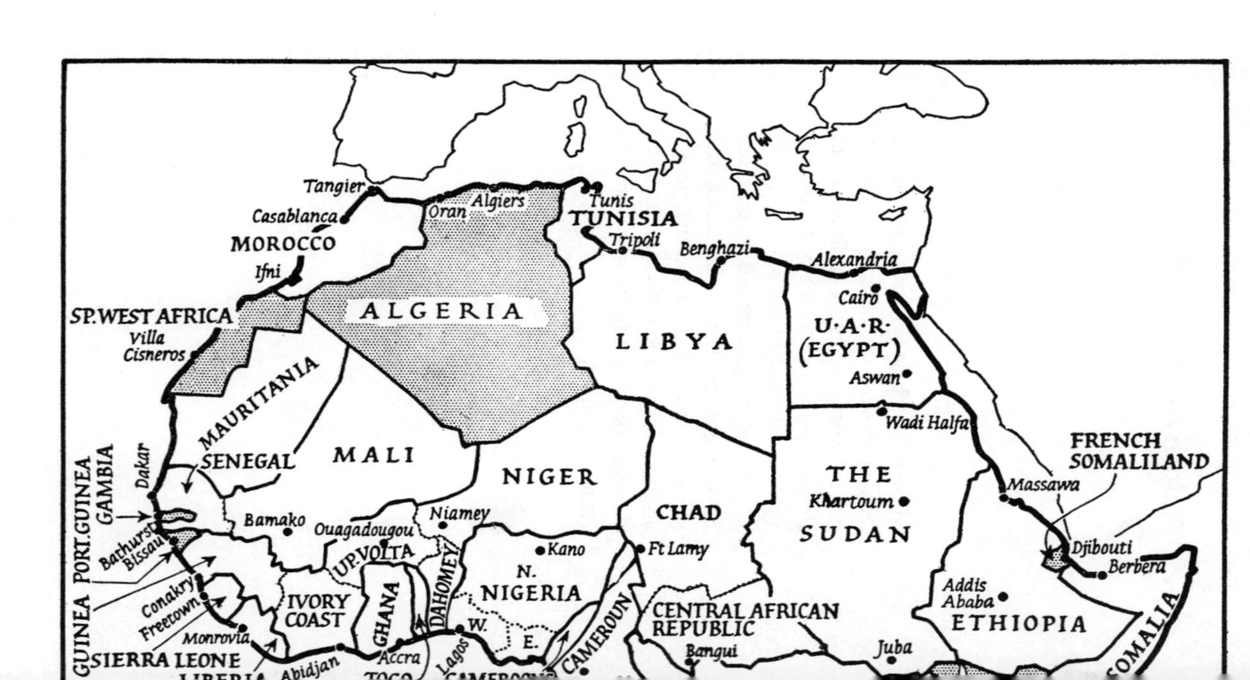
Tangier
Casablanca
MOROCCO
Ifni
SP. WEST AFRICA
Villa Cisneros
Oran
Algiers
ALGERIA
Tunis
TUNISIA
Tripoli
Benghazi
LIBYA
Alexandria
Cairo
U·A·R· (EGYPT)
Aswan
Wadi Halfa
MAURITANIA
SENEGAL
MALI
NIGER
CHAD
THE SUDAN
Khartoum
Massawa
FRENCH SOMALILAND
Djibouti
Berbera
GAMBIA
Dakar
PORT. GUINEA
GUINEA
Bathurst
Bissau
Conakry
Freetown
Monrovia
SIERRA LEONE
Bamako
Ouagadougou
Niamey
UP. VOLTA
IVORY COAST
Abidjan
GHANA
Accra
DAHOMEY
Lagos
W.
E.
N.
NIGERIA
Kano
Ft Lamy
CAMEROUN
CENTRAL AFRICAN REPUBLIC
Bangui
Juba
Addis Ababa
ETHIOPIA
SOMALIA

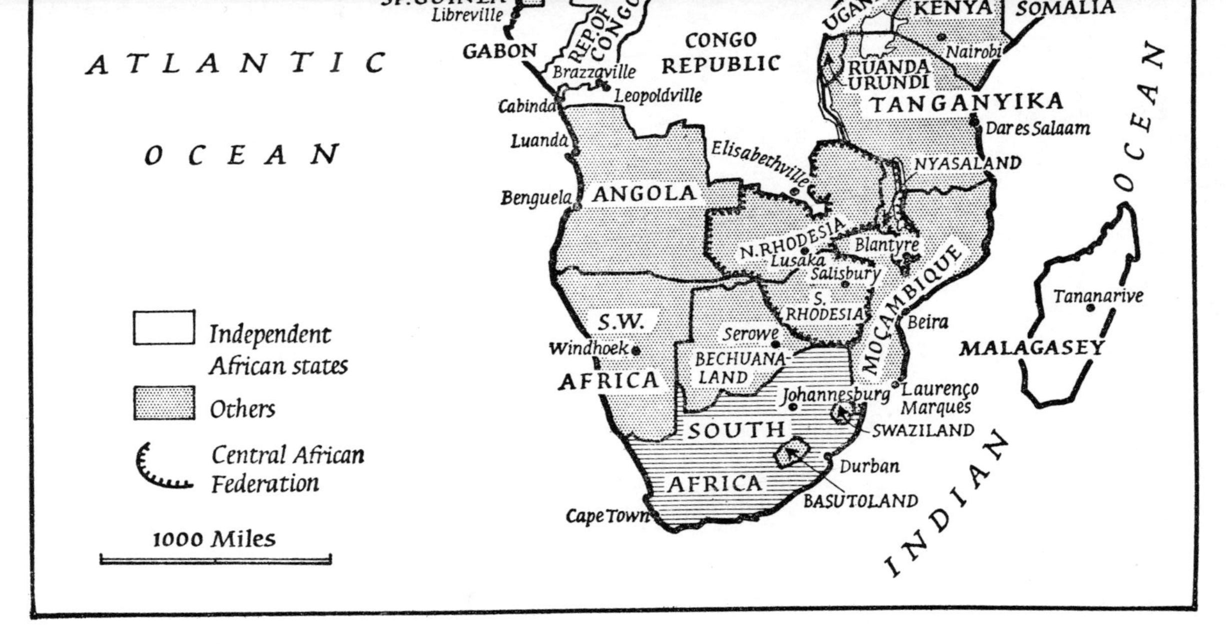
ATLANTIC
OCEAN
SP.GUINEA
Libreville
GABON
REP. OF CONGO
Brazzaville
CONGO
REPUBLIC
Leopoldville
Cabinda
Luanda
Benguela
ANGOLA
Elisabethville
KENYA
SOMALIA
Nairobi
RUANDA
URUNDI
TANGANYIKA
Dar es Salaam
NYASALAND
N.RHODESIA
Lusaka
Blantyre
Salisbury
S.
RHODESIA
MOÇAMBIQUE
Beira
S.W.
AFRICA
Windhoek
Serowe
BECHUANA-
LAND
Johannesburg
Laurenço
Marques
SWAZILAND
SOUTH
AFRICA
Durban
BASUTOLAND
Cape Town
Tananarive
MALAGASEY
INDIAN
OCEAN
Independent
African states
Others
Central African
Federation
1000 Miles

Editorial Foreword

I added the last line to these African profiles on 13 March 1962. No doubt some of the features I have described will have changed their shape by the time the book is published. The speed of change in the world today is nowhere greater or more significant than in Africa. This book merely arrests change at one arbitrary moment for an examination of the past.

In the main, it is an attempt to record the *facts* behind contemporary Africa, the events that have precipitated leaders and policies, the leaders and policies that have precipitated events. The information is as accurate as persistent checking with numerous authorities and alternative sources can assure. But doubtless there are mistakes, and I must ask the reader's pardon for them in advance.

There is *comment* in the text as well, but the comment is nowhere furtive, and those who prefer their facts bare, can ignore the conclusions I have drawn from them. Of course I have my own prejudices. I have yet to read an 'objective' political book on any part of the world or system of government, let alone on a continent as racked by conflict as Africa today.

My prejudices are plain. I believe that domination, foreign or racial, open or clandestine, is wrong, stupid, and inevitably destructive.

It denies to men the control over their own lives that seems to me inseparable from humanity. The white settlers of Southern Rhodesia are wrong fundamentally because they arrogate to themselves the power of choice that belongs to all men of whatever colour, through free and frequent majority decision. Even were they to govern in perfect selflessness – and, of course, they do not – they would be wrong, for they would still be denying the whole human condition.

Domination is stupid because its costs are invariably greater than its receipts. It is a transaction in moral suicide. The struggle of France to retain Algeria has not only been a finally futile one; it has mutilated her political institutions, eroded the freedom of her citizens, and encouraged those ultimate perversions of humanity, terrorism and torture.

Above all, domination disfigures the dominated, turning trust to hatred, reason to violence, aspiration to greed. Savagery may be current coinage in parts of the Congo Republic. For those who have studied the consequences of Portugal's encounter with the Congo kingdom in the fifteenth and sixteenth centuries, the ravages of the slave trade, and the Belgian rule that followed it, such savagery may seem to have been minted more in Europe than in Africa. No one can say with certainty how Africa would have developed on its own, without European penetration. It is possible that the continent would have stagnated in ignorance of electricity, the combine harvester, and penicillin, though commerce might well have existed without conquest. What is at least equally possible is that Africa would have escaped those refinements of Western civilization – the colour bar, compound labour, and the careless corrosions of people and cultures – that accompanied the colonial search for profit and strategic advantages. The achievements of Western dominion are obvious and have been frequently marked. The devastations, of mind as well as body, are less easy to assess and record.

RONALD SEGAL

1 The Colours of Collision: The Republic of South Africa

Born in September 1901 at Amsterdam, DR HENDRIK FRENSCH VERWOERD emigrated to South Africa as a child with his missionary father, who established a grocery shop at Wynberg in Cape Town. Educated successively at Wynberg High School, Milton High School in Bulawayo, and Brandfort High School, he then continued his studies at the University of Stellenbosch. There he was awarded an Abe Bailey Scholarship to Oxford, but, refusing it on the grounds that he preferred to study in Europe, attended instead the Universities of Hamburg, Leipzig, and Berlin. Serving as Professor of Applied Psychology at the University of Stellenbosch from 1927 to 1932, and as Professor of Sociology and Social Work there from 1933 to 1937, he early developed a taste for South Africa's race politics.

In 1936 he was Chief Organizer of the National Conference on the Poor White Problem held at Kimberley, and served as Chairman of its Continuation Commission. It was during this period too that he went with five other Stellenbosch Professors in a deputation to General Hertzog, Prime Minister of the Union, to protest against the government's decision to give asylum in South Africa to a small ship-load of German Jewish refugees. From 1937 to 1948 he was Editor of the Johannesburg Afrikaans daily *Die Transvaler*, in the policy of which he revealed himself as sharply anti-Semitic, anti-British, and sympathetic to the Nazi cause during the Second World War. Attacked in the columns of Johannesburg's English-language newspaper *The Star* for the overt assistance he was giving to Nazi propaganda, he sued for damages in 1943 and lost the case, the judgment of the Witwatersrand Division of the Supreme Court being that 'He did support Nazi propaganda, he did make his paper a tool of the Nazis in South Africa, and he knew it.'

Editorship of *Die Transvaler*, which has for long been the mouthpiece of the National Party in the Transvaal, gave him considerable standing within the dominant political movement of Afrikanerdom, and, though in 1948 he was defeated as Nationalist candidate for the Alberton parliamentary constituency, he was soon afterwards nominated a Government Senator. From 1950 to 1958 he led the National (government) Party in the Senate, becoming, in October 1950, Minister of Native Affairs. He made his department the most crucial in the Cabinet, and was personally responsible for the introduction of much of the apartheid legislation which today controls so minutely every aspect of the African's daily existence.

Though the National Party propagates a policy of apartheid or 'apartness' as its unique political contribution to racial government in South Africa, its leaders have never stated with precision what apartheid really means. The late Dr Jansen, first Minister of Native Affairs in the post-war Nationalist government, described apartheid as 'separate development'. Mr J. G. Strijdom, Nationalist Prime Minister from 1955 to 1958, was less polite.

> Call it paramountcy, 'boss-ship', or what you will, it is still domination. I am being as blunt as I can. I am making no excuses. Either the white man dominates or the black man takes over. . . . The only way the European can maintain supremacy is by domination. . . . And the only way they can maintain domination is by withholding the vote from the non-Europeans. If it were not for that, we would not be here in parliament today.

Dr Verwoerd, speaking in the Senate as Minister of Native Affairs in 1955, was more mystic. He described apartheid as 'a policy of growing from one's own roots through one's own institutions and by one's own powers'. At the intellectual frontier of the party, among the Dutch Reformed Church clergymen and the university professors in the South African Bureau of Racial Affairs, apartheid is 'the territorial separation of European and Bantu, and the provision of areas which must serve as national and political homes for the different Bantu communities and as permanent residential areas for the Bantu population or the major portion of it'. The back-benchers of the party in parliament spontaneously reduce apartheid to the element that the average white voter understands and appreciates – the keeping of the Kaffir in his place.

Dr Verwoerd himself always lent his interminable verbal authority as Minister of Native Affairs to the school of territorial separation, but in practice he energetically pursued the traditional policy of political and social separation, which he accompanied by the fiercely enforced retribalization of the African – even the urban worker – and the stripping from the country's 10,000,000 Africans, 1,500,000 Coloured, and 500,000 Indians of all economic security or political rights. Among other publications, Dr Verwoerd has produced *The Blunting of the Emotions* (*Afstomping van die Gemoedsaandoeninge*) and *An Experimental Study on the Thinking Process*. His career as Minister of Native Affairs certainly revealed him as an accomplished conjurer, who covered his legislative sleight of hand with two- and three-hour expositions in parliament on ethnic differences and his own historical mission.

In 1956 the Tomlinson Commission, appointed by the Malan administration in 1950 to study 'the rehabilitation of the Native Areas', published its report. Urging a clear choice between 'ultimate complete integration', which it opposed, and 'ultimate complete separation between European and Bantu', it recommended a vigorous programme of development for the African areas, so that they might become national homes for the country's Bantu population, and proposed the expenditure of £104 million as a bare minimum for the first ten years. Having rejected almost all the report's major recommendations, the Verwoerd-dominated government voted one-third of the money recommended as essential for the first year and ended up by spending less than that. It became increasingly difficult to escape the conclusion that apartheid as propounded by Verwoerd, the whole concept of a divided South Africa with independent African homelands, was either a fantasy or a deliberate fraud.

In April 1958 Verwoerd won election as Member of Parliament for the Heidelberg constituency in the Transvaal and in September of the same year, after Strijdom's death, was elected leader of the National Party and consequently the new Prime Minister. His candidature did not go uncontested – he defeated his rival, Dr Dönges, now Minister of Finance, by only ninety-eight to seventy-five votes on the second ballot – but his success was assured by the support he commanded within the dominant Transvaal wing of the party and the degree to which the requirements of a rigid race rule had come to control politics.

Though he described himself as a 'democrat' in his first speech as Prime Minister to the House of Assembly, Verwoerd immediately made clear his resolve to promote the policy of white supremacy, whatever the cost, and soon afterwards initiated legislation by which the three white members of parliament representing African interests in the Assembly, and the four representing African interests in the Senate, were expelled. On 21 March 1960, a campaign against the 'pass' laws called by the Pan-Africanist Congress (P.A.C.) was launched at Sharpeville, some forty miles from Johannesburg, by a protest meeting of some 5,000 Africans. Though the crowd was reportedly pacific, police repeatedly fired into it, killing sixty-seven men, women, and children, and wounding over 200 more. A wave of protest swept across the world, the African National Congress (A.N.C.) called for a 'day of mourning' stay-at-home on 28 March, and on 30 March a State of Emergency was declared throughout the country.

The A.N.C. and P.A.C. were both outlawed, and nearly two thousand opposition politicians of all races were detained for several months without charge or trial. On 9 April 1960, while visiting the Transvaal Agricultural Show, Verwoerd was shot twice in the face by a white English-speaking farmer, David Pratt, but he was not seriously injured and recovered within two months. Pratt was committed to an asylum, where he was subsequently reported to have hanged himself.

Verwoerd's intransigence and the personal power he wields were most clearly displayed in his outright rejection of all proposals made by prominent Afrikaner clergymen and politicians for a more liberal policy towards the Coloured people – with their 'white heritage' – at least. Despite mounting rumours that he would first make South Africa a republic and only then submit to pressure within the National Party itself for a relaxation of apartheid policies, he stated on 24 November 1960 that any concessions were out of the question, since they would inevitably lead to further demands.

He announced that the establishment of a republic in South Africa would make no difference at all to the country's membership of the Commonwealth, and he won an all-white referendum on 5 November 1960 by 850,458 votes to 775,878. On 4 March 1961 he arrived in London for the Commonwealth Prime Ministers Conference, and in a statement to reporters at the airport described apartheid as 'a policy of good neighbourliness'. The Prime Minister of India tartly suggested that, in such an event, he was glad he was not one of Dr Verwoerd's neighbours. The twelve million non-whites in South Africa might well have retorted that they involuntarily were, and that they joined Nehru in his scepticism. Despite Verwoerd's vigorously expressed desire to remain within the Commonwealth, and his claim that apartheid was a domestic affair of South Africa, the issue of South Africa's membership became the subject of considerable dispute at the Conference. All attempts at compromise broke down on 15 March, when Dr Verwoerd announced that he would not undertake to permit High Commissioners from African and Asian Commonwealth countries to maintain offices in South Africa, and this reportedly led to rancorous criticism, concluded by his announcement that he was formally withdrawing South Africa's application.

Returning to the Republic, he was met by 20,000 supporters at Jan Smuts airport in Johannesburg, and he immediately informed them that God had willed their country's withdrawal from the Commonwealth. This personal interpretation was widely doubted by opposition opinion in South Africa, and there were hostile demonstrations in various cities. Though the United Party opposition bitterly criticized Dr Verwoerd for his decision, the government itself appeared as rigorously dominated by his leadership as ever.

At last, on 23 January 1962, Dr Verwoerd announced in the House of Assembly the first spectacular steps in the creation of independent Bantu homelands. The Transkei territories, covering some 15,000 square miles and containing an almost exclusively African population of some 1,250,000, were to be given their own parliament. Three days later the government announced that it would spend £57 million in the next five years to develop the African reserves, including £38 million for new villages and housing, £3½ million for irrigation, £5 million for forestry, £2 million for water conservation, and £5 million for fencing – 30,000 miles of it. On the following day Viscount Montgomery, one of Dr Verwoerd's few British admirers, left in a South African Air Force plane for the Transkei 'to see what this independence policy is doing for the black man'.

Large advertisements were inserted in foreign newspapers to emphasize the significance of the government's new policy, films were made available to television networks overseas, and South African government pamphlets rained down on foreign journalists like confetti. The government, however, made no mention of the State of Emergency which had been declared on 30 November 1960 in five districts of Eastern Pondoland, a substantial portion of the Transkei, or of the martial law that had governed the area with sten guns and armoured cars ever since. At the beginning of February the draft constitution for Transkeian self-government was made public. It provided for a Legislative Assembly of 131 members, of whom 95 would be appointed – 68 of them government-salaried tribal chiefs, and 27 their nominees – while 36 would be elected. The government itself would retain control of defence, external affairs, internal security, posts and telegraphs, public transport, immigration, currency, and some other financial matters, including customs and excise. In case, however, the remaining jurisdiction provided the Transkeian Assembly with too much freedom of action, all laws passed in the newly independent Bantu homeland were to be submitted to the President of the Republic for his assent.

But the South African government's new campaign was not entirely wasted. Though international opinion remained assiduously sceptical, Viscount Montgomery promised to 'draw his sword' in defence of the whites, should black Africa combine to oppose them.

Aware of the need for an independent deterrent, the Minister of Justice announced on 16 February an immediate expansion of the country's security police 'because of developments at home and abroad'. Speaking in the Senate, he said: 'Mobile units are now being established and maintained at various centres ... capable of dealing effectively with matters relating to the safety of the state.' Meeting in Addis Ababa, the Pan-African Movement for East, Central, and South Africa described Dr Verwoerd's grant of a new constitution for the Transkei as 'a calculated insult to the African peoples throughout Africa who are demanding complete and genuine freedom and independence in respect of the whole of South Africa'. A resolution called on African states to apply immediate political, economic, diplomatic, and cultural sanctions against South Africa.

As Prime Minister, Dr Verwoerd has ruled his party and the country with a rigid intransigence and an absolute will. Committed to a policy of permanent white supremacy, he is ruthless with resistance, and the years since his election have shown a startling growth in the numbers of Africans imprisoned and killed for opposition to his policies. On 2 August 1961 he appointed, as his new Minister of Justice, Mr B. J. Vorster, who had been interned by the Smuts government during the Second World War as a member of the Nazi-sympathizing Ossewa Brandwag. Invulnerable to criticism, Verwoerd has a fixed conviction about the rightness of his policy and a stated attitude to his mission in saving South Africa that are almost Messianic. After his election as Prime Minister, he stated: 'I believe that the will of God was revealed in the ballot.' He has subsequently referred to the guidance of God on many occasions.

Though dislike of his policies is mounting within the party itself – largely amongst those who are experiencing the expenses of race rule with the flight of capital from the country – he undoubtedly commands the fear and even the awe of those who find his personality distasteful and his obsessions repulsive. Perhaps the answer to the mystery of his dominance is that he alone offers Afrikanerdom an absolute confidence that there is a way out of racial retribution if only his people will follow him, trusting to his vision. Certainly the general election of 18 October 1961 confirmed his white support in the country, while most of those Nationalist parliamentarians whose loyalty he doubted failed to achieve renomination as party candidates in their constituencies. The National Party itself emerged from the elections with 105 seats out of 160, a gain of three, and increased majorities in nearly every constituency.

Where the National Party is the dominant movement of the 1,800,000 Afrikaners, the United Party is that of the 1,200,000 English-speaking South Africans. This linguistic and basically racial division has increasingly over the years reflected a political and economic one, with the National Party canvassing the interests of the farming and white artisan community, and the United Party representing industry and commerce, the mines, and the British connexion. Since its foundation as the South African Party at the time of Union, whether led by General Louis Botha, Field Marshal Smuts, or the latter's inept successors, the United Party has remained as fundamentally attached to the principle of white domination as the most strenuous apostles of apartheid. In 1917, delivering a speech in London, Smuts maintained:

> If we are to solve the Native question, it is useless to try and govern black and white in the same way and subject them to the same forms of legislation. It is hopeless to try that. They are different not only in colour, but almost in soul. They are different in political structure and their political institutions should be different.

In 1945 Smuts said in the House of Assembly:

> There are certain things about which all South Africans are agreed, all parties and all sections, except those who are quite mad. The first is, that it is a fixed policy to maintain white supremacy in South Africa.

The dominance of the National Party has resulted from its clear commitment to Afrikaner nationalism within the traditional framework of white supremacy, the ruthlessness with which it has pursued race rule, and its success in selling to the electorate a picture of the United Party as the creature of British capital and big business.

Born on 8 December 1913, at Sea Point in the Cape Peninsula, the eldest of three sons, SIR DE VILLIERS GRAAFF, present Leader of the United Party, was educated at Diocesan College and at the University of Cape Town, where he gained his Bachelor of Arts degree with distinctions in Constitutional Law and History. Proceeding to Oxford, where he graduated as a Master of Arts and Bachelor of Civil Law, he attended the University of Leyden to continue his studies in Law, and then qualified as a barrister at the Inner Temple in London. Outstanding at sport both at school and at university, he represented Western Province at cricket, won his boxing blue at Oxford, and played cricket for the University.

Joining up on the outbreak of the Second World War, he saw active service as an officer in the Western Desert campaign and was captured with the Second Division at Tobruk. For the rest of the war he was a prisoner in Italy and then in Germany, escaping from Oflag Va at Weinsberg only to be recaptured after seven days. In August 1946 he accepted United Party nomination for the Hottentots Holland constituency and in November claimed at a party meeting that it was 'the policy of the United Party to accord full recognition to the natives as a permanent section of the population'. In May 1948 he won the seat by 571 votes, and in December of the same year was co-opted on to the Action Committee of the party. In September 1949 he was elected Senior Vice-Chairman, and repeatedly from September 1951 Chairman, of the United Party in the Cape. Then, in November 1956, a rebellion within the party unseated J. G. N. Strauss as Leader and consequently as official Leader of the Opposition, and Sir de Villiers Graaff was elected to both posts in his place. The change, however, did not visibly affect the decay in the party's fortunes. In April 1958 Graaff lost the Hottentots Holland seat in the general election, but the Member of Parliament for Rondebosch resigned his own seat, and Graaff won the subsequent by-election in this heartland of English-speaking Cape Town without contest.

At the end of 1960 he visited Britain in an attempt to move opinion there in favour of South Africa's continued membership of the Commonwealth, despite the country's decision in the October referendum to become a republic in May 1961. On 15 March, however, Dr Verwoerd announced at the Commonwealth Prime Ministers Conference that he was withdrawing South Africa's application for readmission to the Commonwealth after becoming a republic, and in the House of Assembly Sir de Villiers Graaff attacked the decision, appealing over Dr Verwoerd's head for a coalition of 'moderate' opinion. This invitation, however, met with no response; it would have been an eccentric white parliamentarian indeed who would have rejected the fruits of government for the ashes of an ever-dwindling opposition.

A gentleman farmer, Sir de Villiers Graaff breeds prize Friesland herds and has substantial family interests in property and finance. Under his leadership, the opposition United Party has failed consistently to oppose, though this has perhaps best suited the mood of a party which campaigns against apartheid under the slogan of 'Discrimination with Justice'.

Mounting clashes between those who wished the party to move even further to the right and those who wanted it to adopt a more liberal policy in order to provide the electorate with the elements of a choice led to the resignation in August 1959 of almost a quarter of the parliamentary group, eleven of whom later formed the Progressive Party while the twelfth decided to sit as an independent in the House of Assembly. Behind the move it was generally believed that the figure of South Africa's most important financier comfortingly rested. Even big business appeared at last to be growing conscious of the United Party's sterility.

HARRY FREDERICK OPPENHEIMER was born in 1908 at Kimberley, the son of a diamond clerk from Germany who rose to control all the diamond mines in South West Africa and then the whole world's diamond market, together with enormous gold and copper interests throughout Central and Southern Africa. Educated at Charterhouse and at Christ Church, Oxford, where he read Politics, Philosophy, and Economics, he went to work in the London office of the Diamond Corporation learning the family business, then returning to South Africa to settle in Kimberley. From 1940 to 1945 he served in the Armoured Car Regiment of the South African forces, and in 1948 he was elected the United Party Member of Parliament for the Kimberley constituency, a seat which his father had held from 1924 to 1938. At first he confined himself to economic affairs in parliamentary debates, but gradually became involved in race relations. He is believed to have financed the United Party to the extent of £250,000 through the United South Africa Trust Fund, but in 1958 he retired from parliament after the death of his father, to concentrate upon his business interests.

In November 1959, when the Progressive Party was formed, he made a public statement supporting it, and served as a member of its Molteno Commission to recommend a bill of rights and franchise programme for South Africa. Associating himself with the Commission's recommendations for a non-racial South African franchise based on educational and/or income qualifications, a Senate with the right to block discriminatory legislation, and a rigid constitution with an entrenched bill of rights, he signed the minority report which proposed a Standard 6 level of schooling as the educational qualification instead of Standard 4. It was the minority report which was shortly afterwards accepted at a special party conference.

Oppenheimer is now the head of a group of companies which includes forty-three assorted mines and other concerns ranging from manufacturing to merchant banking, from ranching to real estate. As Chairman of the Anglo American Corporation (which controls many of the Orange Free State gold mines), De Beers Consolidated Mines Ltd (which controls South Africa's total diamond output as well as – indirectly – the whole world's diamond market), and Rhodesian Anglo American (which controls a substantial slice of the Copperbelt) he presides over interests with a subscribed capital of £336 million and total reserves of £268 million. His enterprises extend from the Cape to the borders of Kenya and cover South West Africa, the Federation of Rhodesia and Nyasaland, Moçambique, Tanganyika, the Congo, and Swaziland, as well as the Republic of South Africa itself. He is responsible for an annual wage bill of £25 million, paid to some 20,000 whites and some 136,000 non-whites.

Indisputably the richest man on the continent and one of the richest in the world, his political influence in the Republic of South Africa is by no means comparable, since the National Party regards him with the suspicion that it directs at all big capital of Jewish ancestry and British connexions. His enemies on the left, however, hold that he could have and can still exercise an enormous economic influence by militant opposition to the government, whatever immediate cost to his South African financial interests this might entail. There is no doubt that his stand has throughout been a moderate one; indeed he has been a great deal less vigorous in his opposition to race discrimination in the Federation than his Copperbelt counterpart, Sir Ronald Prain of Rhodesian Selection Trust. Preferring to back gradualist if small minority groups like the Progressive Party, rather than to associate himself at all with the mass movements of the non-whites, his principal object appears to be the immediate safeguarding and expansion of his financial interests. He accordingly participated prominently in the establishment in 1959 of the South African Foundation, a big business enterprise to protect South Africa's name abroad, though in so doing he unquestionably roused the widespread resentment of South Africa's non-white political leaders. On the principle of apartheid, however, he has always been verbally firm; and in November 1960 he said in London that he felt certain the racial problem would never be settled by separation and partition. The experiment in which the Government was engaging was bound to fail, he claimed, and South Africa would have to turn to a policy of unity on a basis of individual merit, in place of division on a basis of race.

Despite his backing, the Progressive Party has made little real headway with the white electorate in South Africa – it retained only one seat, the opulent Johannesburg suburb of Lower Houghton, in the general election of October 1961 – and every development underlines the inevitability of racial clash. Despite the South African Foundation, South Africa was forced out of the Commonwealth, and despite the sentiments with which Oppenheimer comforts his shareholders, African nationalism continues, ever more vigorously, to demand the establishment of unqualified democracy in South Africa. In his Chairman's statement to the shareholders of Rhodesian Anglo-American Ltd, published on 17 November 1960, he claimed: 'Whether African nationalism is really irresistible in a multi-racial country has . . . yet to be decided. It is quite wrong to think that the majority group in a mixed state is necessarily the most powerful, still less that it is necessarily irresistible.'

PETER BROWN, National Chairman of the South African Liberal Party, would disagree. Born in 1924 in Durban, of a wealthy and old-established Natal family, Peter McKenzie Brown was educated at Michaelhouse, which he left in order to join the army at the age of seventeen. Having seen service in Egypt and Italy, he went to Cambridge after the war and was studying agriculture when he is reported to have been deeply moved by hearing the novelist Peter Abrahams describe conditions on the other side of the colour line in South Africa. Having taken his degree in African Languages and Anthropology at the University of Cape Town, he joined the Natal Health Commission in 1951 and was given the job of editing a non-political newspaper, principally intended for African readers.

In 1952 he opened and ran in Pietermaritzburg the first Natal Y.M.C.A. catering mainly for Africans, and having settled permanently in the town he started an inter-racial discussion group, one of the five which formed the nucleus of the South African Liberal Association. Then in May 1953, when the Association became the Liberal Party, Brown opened its first office in Pietermaritzburg and gave lavishly both of his time and of his money to build up its organization. In 1957 he became the party's Deputy National Chairman and stood unsuccessfully – he lost his deposit – as parliamentary candidate for the seat of Pietermaritzburg District in the general election of 1958. In 1959 he was elected National Chairman of the party, and in March 1960 he was detained under the State of Emergency. Refusing to be released on conditions that would have restricted his movements and speech, he stayed with the bulk of the other detainees until their mass release some four months after their arrest.

A figure of considerable political intelligence and realism, as well as of obvious courage and persistence, he has been substantially responsible for swerving the Liberal Party towards a recognition of the changing demands of political resistance in South Africa. Having backed both the international boycott campaign against South African goods and the change to universal suffrage in the party's franchise policy, he has been a constant advocate of close cooperation with the Congress Alliance, proving himself in the process a better caretaker of his party's career than many of those who brought greater public weight to its founding.

The Congress Alliance is an association of democratic organizations – the African National Congress, South African Indian Congress, South African Coloured People's Congress, the white Congress of Democrats, and the South African Congress of Trade Unions – dedicated to the achievement of a non-racial South Africa, based on equal rights for all. On 26 June 1955, at Kliptown in the Transvaal, some 3,000 delegates of all races, chosen on a regional basis and widely representative especially of the African and Indian urban population, met and adopted the Freedom Charter. This, South Africa's non-racial 'Declaration of Independence', begins: 'We, the people of South

Africa, declare for all our country and the world to know – that South Africa belongs to all who live in it, black and white, and that no government can justly claim authority unless it is based on the will of all the people.' Various clauses then deal with the right of all to adult suffrage, equality before the law, the right to work, security, and education, the nationalization of mineral wealth and banks, freedom of movement, of speech, and of religion.

The history of the dominant organization in the Alliance, the African National Congress, began at least as far back as 1882, with the formation in the Cape of the Native Education Association, which in 1884 made one of the first protests against the 'pass' laws. By 1904 the Natal Native Congress was already making itself felt, and by 1907 so was a similar organization in the Transvaal. In 1909 the National Native Convention met to discuss the implications for Africans of the Act of Union and sent a delegation to Britain in order to protest at the colour bar in the constitution. At last, on 8 January 1912, the South African National Native Congress, which later changed its name to the African National Congress (A.N.C.), was formed at a conference in Bloemfontein. It aimed at the extension of African democratic rights and the recognition of Africans as equal citizens with whites; at the advance of the African people politically, economically, socially, educationally, and industrially; and at 'racial unity and mutual helpfulness'. The Chiefs played a large part in its foundation, and early statements contained warm expressions of loyalty to the Crown.

In 1913, with the passing of the Land Act, which deprived Africans of land rights outside the Reserves, it launched into its first major battle, organized protest meetings in many parts of the country, and sent a deputation to Britain. In 1936, when African voters were removed from the common roll in the Cape and a Native Representative Council was established as a sounding board for African grievances, the A.N.C. permitted its members to serve on the Council despite radical opposition. Dissident A.N.C. members then formed in 1943 the A.N.C. Youth League, which demanded a programme of 'positive action', and by 1946 the A.N.C. itself had decided to boycott the Native Representative Council. The Youth League's Programme of Action was finally adopted by the A.N.C. in 1949, and this led to a new militancy, enforced by the 1950 Suppression of Communism Act, which – with its assault on all organized African opposition – helped to turn the A.N.C. from a talking shop into a movement of vigorous political struggle. The Xuma-Dadoo-Naicker Pact of 1946, signed by the Presidents of the African National, Transvaal Indian, and Natal Indian Congresses, had initiated cooperation between the African National Congress and the South African Indian Congress on matters of common concern in the struggle against white domination, and in 1952 the Defiance of Unjust Laws Campaign was launched by a Joint Planning Council of the two organizations. The campaign was finally brought to an end by the Criminal Laws Amendment Act of 1953, which prescribed severe penalties – including whipping, a fine, and up to five years' imprisonment – for breaking any law by way of protest. Two years later, in 1955, the A.N.C. played the leading part in organizing the Congress of the People and in establishing the inter-racial Congress Alliance.

ALBERT JOHN LUTULI, the President-General of the African National Congress, was born in 1898 near Bulawayo in Southern Rhodesia and grew up first in the Vryheid district of Northern Natal and then in the Groutville Reserve. The son of a Congregationalist mission interpreter and the nephew of the elected reigning Chief of the Abasemakholweni Zulu tribe, he studied at the Groutville mission school, and then proceeded to Adam's College, the American Mission secondary school, where he qualified as a teacher. Staying on there to teach Zulu history and literature, he was comfortably settled in a quiet academic amble when, fifteen years after his appointment, he was petitioned by the elders of his tribe to fill the vacant Chieftaincy. For two years he hesitated, reluctant to return to the close tribal world of petty litigation, Sunday preaching, and the hopeless unending struggle with the exhausted earth. Finally, however, his religion and the allegiance that he felt he owed his people persuaded him to accept.

For seventeen years he governed in Groutville, presiding at the tribal councils and beer drinks, bringing order into the sugar fields and increasing their yield, settling disputes, extracting fines, and enforcing laws. All the while patiently succouring the spirit of his shattered tribe, he himself strengthened his connexion with organized Christianity. In 1938 he travelled to India as a delegate of the Christian Council of South Africa to the International Missionary Council. In 1948 he visited the United States to attend the North American Missionary Conference. In South Africa itself he served as Chairman of the Congregationalist Churches of the American Board, as President of the Natal Mission Conference, and as an Executive Member of the Christian Council of South Africa.

The political resistance movement of the African people, however, was to submerge even the small tribal world of the Abasemakholweni. After a few years of serving on various race relations' committees, in 1946 Lutuli joined the Native Representative Council, which soon afterwards adjourned indefinitely in protest against its political impotence. Symbolically in the same year he joined the African National Congress and rose quickly to the Presidency of the Natal Provincial Division. In 1952 the A.N.C. launched, together with the South African Indian Congress, the Defiance Campaign, and though Lutuli did not himself go to jail, he gave open support to the campaign and encouraged his people to take part in it. A passionate believer in non-violent passive resistance, he felt that Christians should not obey laws which assaulted their essential dignity, and should go to jail submissively rather than meet violence with violence. In October 1952 he was summoned to Pretoria and ordered by the government to resign either from the A.N.C. or from his Chieftaincy.

He refused to do either. And he replied:

> Who will deny that thirty years of my life have been spent knocking in vain, patiently, moderately, and modestly at a closed and barred door? What have been the fruits of moderation? The past thirty years

have seen the greatest number of laws restricting our rights and progress, until today we have reached a stage where we have almost no rights at all. It is with this background and with a full sense of responsibility that, under the auspices of the African National Congress, I have joined my people in the new spirit that moves them today, the spirit that revolts openly and boldly against injustice and expresses itself in a determined and non-violent manner. What the future has in store for me I do not know. It might be ridicule, imprisonment, concentration camp, flogging, banishment, and even death. I only pray to the Almighty to strengthen my resolve so that none of these grim possibilities may deter me from striving, for the sake of the good name of our beloved country, the Union of South Africa, to make it a true democracy and a true union, in form and spirit, of all the communities in the land.

In November 1952 he was deposed from the Chieftaincy by the government and in December elected to succeed Dr Moroka as President-General of the A.N.C. At the same time he was confined by a government ban to his own village for a period of two years. In 1950, as soon as his ban lapsed, he flew to Johannesburg to protest against the Western Areas Removal Scheme, by which Africans lost their remaining freehold land rights in Johannesburg and were forced to leave the suburb of Sophiatown and move themselves to the new government location of Meadowlands. He was, however, prevented from speaking and served with a further two-year ban. In December 1956 he was arrested on a charge of high treason, but released one year later with sixty-four others of the accused. In May 1959 he undertook a speaking tour of the Western Cape, during which he addressed mass meetings that were attended by unprecedentedly large numbers of whites, and straight afterwards he was banished to his village and banned from all gatherings for five years under the Suppression of Communism Act. On 26 March 1960, while in Johannesburg to give evidence at the Treason Trial, he publicly burnt his pass book and called for a national day of mourning on 28 March for those killed by the police the week before during the peaceful protest meeting at Sharpeville. He was himself detained under the State of Emergency declared on 30 March, and assaulted by a policeman while being charged.

At the beginning of February 1961, Social Democrat members of the Swedish Parliament nominated him for the Nobel Peace Prize, and on 23 October 1961 the Nobel Peace Committee announced that it had awarded him the Prize for 1960. *Die Transvaler*, mouthpiece of the Transvaal Nationalists, called the award 'an inexplicable, pathological phenomenon', while *Die Burger*, the Cape Nationalist daily, considered it a 'remarkably immature, poorly considered, and essentially un-Western decision'. The government nonetheless permitted him to travel to Oslo, where he received the Prize on 10 December.

Like Gandhi, whose hold over his people Lutuli's own has in many ways reflected, the Chief – as he is still called by his followers of all races throughout the country – believes in passive resistance not only as a tactic of political opposition but as a spiritual force in itself. Indeed, it has been largely his personal prestige and influence that have restrained mass African protests from turning into a concerted explosion of violence against race rule. During 1959, when African demonstrations against the government broke out in the province of Natal, his repeated appeals for a return to the policy of passive resistance unquestionably prevented the spreading of arson beyond sporadic and individual cases of violence. For the exercise of this restraint he has come under increasing criticism from some of the younger radicals within Congress itself, but the regard in which he is held – by rural and urban Africans alike – has secured his personal position from open assault. Like Gandhi, it is his person, even when it is not his policy, that his people have followed. A figure of great dignity, eloquent and powerful in his resolve, he is in many ways a spiritual leader of the Africans as well as the President of their major political movement.

Not all Africans, however, have retained their allegiance to him and to the movement he leads. From 1957 onwards a few members of the A.N.C., particularly in the Transvaal, began promoting a policy different from that followed by the leadership, acting as a pressure group and calling themselves Africanists. Foremost among them was ROBERT MANGALISO SOBUKWE, who had been born at Graaff-Reinet in the Cape Province in 1924, the youngest of six brothers. Educated at mission schools and at Lovedale, he had proceeded to the University College of Fort Hare, where he had been elected first President of the Students' Representative Council under a new constitution in 1949, and had graduated with a teacher's diploma. A member of the African National Congress Youth League, he had played an active part in its controversy over the direction which the African political resistance movement should take, and early revealed himself as a radical with a restrictively black nationalist approach. After leaving Fort Hare he had become a teacher at Standerton in the Transvaal, but had been dismissed for taking part in the 1952 Defiance Campaign. Then in 1953 he had been appointed Languages Assistant in the Department of Bantu Studies at the University of the Witwatersrand, a post that he held until March 1960, when he resigned.

In 1957 he associated himself with the Africanist group in the A.N.C. and became the editor of *The Africanist*, its mouthpiece. In 1958 he left the A.N.C. altogether, and in April 1959 was elected National President of the Pan-Africanist Congress (P.A.C.), founded by those Africanists who had resigned from the A.N.C. More vigorously than before, he attacked the A.N.C. for what he asserted was its lack of real militancy and above all for its alliance with the white Congress of Democrats, the South African Indian Congress, and the South African Coloured People's Congress, maintaining that the policy of multi-racialism embodied in the Congress Alliance had disfigured the fundamental aspirations of the African people and persistently retarded their resistance.

On 16 March he announced a National Anti-Pass Campaign to begin on 21 March, when his followers would surrender themselves at police stations without their passes, under the slogan – 'no bail, no defence, no fines'. The campaign achieved a substantial response in only two areas, at Sharpeville, where the killing of sixty-seven men, women, and children led to worldwide protests, and in Cape Town, where some 70,000 Africans in the city went on strike for several weeks and were forced back to work only by mass arrests and police assaults.

Sobukwe himself was arrested on the morning of 21 March at Orlando police station, Johannesburg, and later sentenced to three years' imprisonment for incitement. At his trial he refused to recognize the validity of laws passed by an all-white parliament and in this was initially followed by other members of his movement. On 8 November 1960 he lost his appeal against the severity of his sentence, and he is at present in the new prison of Stofberg in the Orange Free State. A man of considerable intellectual vigour, with a stirring eloquence and determination, he enjoys a profound personal allegiance from his followers. His decision not to defend himself in court but rather to deny the validity of the laws, as well as his severe prison sentence, undoubtedly raised his popular prestige amongst many Africans, though his decision to appeal seemed inconsistent and embarrassed several of his admirers.

The Pan-Africanist Congress is a manifestation of the black racialism that has developed in response to the white racialism of apartheid. It takes no account, however, of the degree to which South Africa has become an integrated industrial society, in which African, Indian, Coloured, and white cannot survive without each other. It reflects the easy emotional hysteria of despair, a final disenchantment with the slow process of organized resistance to white supremacy. The movement does not denounce the policy of passive resistance to which the Congress Alliance is committed, and its appeal remains limited to Cape Town and scattered areas of the Transvaal. It embodies, however, a warning to the apostles of white racialism and remains a potential rival to the still overwhelming dominance of the A.N.C. The Congress Alliance, whether driven to violence or not, is essentially a movement of hope, trusting in the possibility of one day creating, whatever the necessary methods, a non-racial democracy in South Africa. Its failure would be the failure of its aspirations.

Recent developments have confirmed the hold of the A.N.C. on militant African opinion, even in the very flouting of the movement's non-violent policy. On 16 December 1961 – a public holiday to commemorate the victory of the Voortrekkers over the Zulu army of Dingaan at the Battle of Blood River in 1838 – four bombs were exploded in Johannesburg, and five in Port Elizabeth. Several buildings were badly damaged, and one African was killed.

On the same day, handbills in English and Zulu appeared in the streets of Johannesburg, announcing the existence of a new organization – Umkonto We Sizwe, or 'Spear of the Nation' – and proclaiming the organization's responsibility for the acts of sabotage. The non-racial tone of the statement, the proclamation of loyalty to the 'national liberation movement', and the slogan – '*Afrika Mayibuye!*' or 'Come Back Africa!' – which concluded the announcement – all marked the new organization as A.N.C. in alignment.

Umkonto We Sizwe is a new independent body formed by Africans. It includes in its ranks South Africans of all races . . . . Umkonto We Sizwe will carry on the struggle for freedom and democracy by new methods, which are necessary to complement the actions of the established national liberation organizations. Umkonto We Sizwe fully supports the national liberation movement, and our members, jointly and individually, place themselves under the overall political guidance of that movement.

It is, however, well known that the main national liberation organizations in this country have consistently followed a policy of non-violence. . . . They have done so because the people prefer peaceful methods of change to achieve their aspirations, without the suffering and bitterness of civil war. But the people's patience is not endless. . . .

We are striking out along a new road for the liberation of the people of this country. The Government policy of force, repression, and violence will no longer be met with non-violent resistance only! The choice is not ours; it has been made by the Nationalist Government, which has rejected every peaceable demand by the people for rights and freedom and answered every such demand with force and yet more force! . . .

In these actions, we are working in the best interests of all the people of this country – black, brown, and white – whose future happiness and well-being cannot be attained without the overthrow of the

Nationalist Government, the abolition of white supremacy, and the winning of liberty, democracy, and full national rights and equality for all the people of this country.

2 An International Trust: South West Africa

To the north-west of South Africa lies the international trust territory of South West Africa, a former German colony surrendered to South African mandate by the League of Nations after the First World War. With an area of 318,099 square miles, its 427,980 Africans, 23,930 Coloured, and 73,154 Europeans are now ruled – in defiance of United Nations General Assembly resolutions and judgments of the International Court – directly by the policy of apartheid, with the white voters – to whom the franchise is limited – represented by six members in the South African House of Assembly. Were international intervention to secure for the territory's non-white inhabitants their fundamental rights, so providing the catalyst for change within South Africa itself, one man more than any other would have been responsible.

Hosea Kutako, Paramount Chief of the Hereros, was born in 1870 at Okahurimehi in the district of Okahandja, his father a clergyman of the Rhenish Mission Church at Omburo. He attended school at Omburo, where he was baptized, and then accompanied his father to Ehuameno.

In 1904 the Herero people rebelled against the German administration and were repressed with great brutality. Chief Hosea fought in the war and was wounded in the leg and later in the cheek. A number of Hereros under Chief Samuel Maharero fled to Bechuanaland, the British Protectorate, while Hosea was detained in a concentration camp at Omaruru and, when released, forced to flee into hiding in the mountains. Then, in 1906–7, when pacification was complete, Hosea was appointed a school-teacher at Omaruru and taught there for two years, after which he left to work in the mines at Tsumeb in the north of the territory.

When pacification began anew on rumours that the Hereros in Bechuanaland were assembling to re-enter South West Africa, Hosea was arrested and imprisoned, but he escaped and lived for some time on wild fruit in the mountains. With the declaration of the First World War, troops from the Union of South Africa entered the territory and defeated the German forces, and in 1917 Hosea was appointed headman of the Hereros. Then in 1919 Chief Maharero in Bechuanaland sent him a letter, asking him to take care of his people, and in 1920 appointed him leader of the Hereros in the territory.

In 1925 the Union Government forced the Hereros out of some of the few areas which the German administration had left them. When they refused to move, their houses were burnt, and bombs were dropped in the vicinity to frighten them away. Chief Hosea was imprisoned in Gobabis with several of his followers, but released after only two days.

In 1939, with the outbreak of the Second World War, the South African government called upon Chief Hosea to persuade the Hereros to enlist in its army. Many of the youth did so, and the people as a whole donated funds for the prosecution of the war. Hardly a year after peace was declared, however, Chief Hosea was ordered in 1946 by the administration to survey the northern part of the territory for possible resettlement, as it had been decided to give the southern and central areas to returning white soldiers and their families. Discovering that the region offered to his people was isolated and far too small, he refused to move or to persuade his followers to do so. In the same year he was asked by the government to accept the incorporation of South West Africa into the Union, and he categorically refused. In the same year he also petitioned the United Nations – work in which he has been engaged for the past fifteen years – to remove the territory from South African administration and govern it towards independence as a United Nations Trust.

In 1957 he instructed the Rev. Michael Scott to give evidence to the United Nations on behalf of the Hereros, and despite the enormous pressures that have been put upon him by the South African government to accept incorporation, he has persistently demanded the independence of the territory. The status of South West Africa has become one of the most explosive international issues of the post-war world. It has stimulated examination of South Africa's race policies and revealed apartheid as a contemporary racial imperialism. Above all, it has emphasized the South African government's defiance of international authority and law, making a head-on collision between the United Nations and South Africa inevitable.

On 26 October 1961 the U.N. South West Africa Committee resolved that South Africa was unfit to administer the mandated territory, demanded the removal of all South African troops from it, and unanimously proposed that the General Assembly assume 'direct or indirect' supervision of the mandate. The collision is close, but Chief Hosea himself is now more than ninety years old. It would be a singular cruelty were he to die – after a lifetime of struggle – before that collision were resolved in a new South West Africa, administered in justice and developed at last towards a society of racial peace and popular government.

3 Fleas in the Queen's Blanket: The High Commission Territories

In the middle of Southern Africa, territorially touching and economically dominated by the Republic of South Africa, are the three British High Commission Territories of Basutoland, Bechuanaland, and Swaziland. Basutoland, with an area of 11,716 square miles, largely mountainous, is completely surrounded by South Africa. In mid-1956 its population was assessed at 641,674.– 638,857 Africans, 1,926 Europeans, 644 Coloured, and 247 Asians; the United Nations estimated its 1959 population at 685,000. The economy relies heavily on the cultivation of crops and the raising of sheep and goats for wool and mohair, but the territory's principal source of income is its export of labour to the gold mines, farms, and factories of the Republic. Indeed, it is officially estimated that some 83,000 men, or forty-three per cent of the total adult male population, work outside this British Protectorate at any given time, while the territory's economy is further tied to the Republic by common customs and currency regulations, and by trade.

The existence of Basutoland as an individual territory dates from the early nineteenth century, when the Basuto Chief Moshoeshoe, commonly known as Moshesh, became Chief of the Bakwana and began to build the Basuto nation. Fearful of white encroachment, Moshoeshoe asked for the protection of Queen Victoria, begging that his people might be considered 'fleas in the Queen's blanket'. His repeated appeals, in 1842, 1861, and 1867, at last received a response, and by Proclamation 14 of 1868 the British government agreed to assume responsibility for the Basuto. In 1871, however, Basutoland was annexed to the Cape Colony over the fiercest protests of the Basuto themselves, and only the eight months' Gun War of 1880 led to the establishment of a separate Basutoland again in 1883. At last, in 1884, the territory was placed under the British High Commission, for the 'peace, order, and good government of the Basuto'.

NTSU MOKHEHLE, President of the Basutoland Congress Party, was born in December 1918 at a small village in the Teyateyaneng district in the north of Basutoland, the son of a sheep-farmer of moderate wealth who was one of the first inspectors of schools in the territory. Educated locally, Mokhehle went in 1935 to the secondary school of St Matthew's at Grahamstown in the Eastern Cape of South Africa, and at the age of nineteen began writing articles for *The Comet*, a Basutoland paper, about the sufferings which the Africans endured as a consequence of their political voicelessness. In 1940 he went to the University College of Fort Hare in the Eastern Cape, but was expelled in 1942 for having planned several strikes. Joining the first modern Basuto national movement, the League of the Common Man – 'Lekhotla La Balo' – he returned to Fort Hare in 1944 to continue his studies and then take his Master of Science degree in Zoology, with a thesis on the parasitology of birds.

Becoming an active member of the African National Congress Youth League in South Africa, he made plans with other Basuto students at Fort Hare to return to Basutoland, despite the low salaries paid there, and take an active part in political life. In 1949 he gained his Education Diploma from Fort Hare and soon afterwards returned home, where he became President of the Basutoland Teachers Association and founded in 1952 – to be elected first President – the Basutoland African Congress. In 1955 he was appointed Principal of the Maseru Primary School, and in the same year founded, together with Bennet Makalo Khaketla, the newspaper *Mohlabani – The Warrior* – which soon exercised a considerable political influence. In 1954 a British Commission headed by Sir Henry Moore had offered district government to the Basuto, but no real control of central power. Under pressure from Congress, the Basuto National Council had rejected the Moore proposals, and in 1955 it appointed a Constitutional Committee which called in Professor D. V. Cowen of the Law Faculty at the University of Cape Town to advise it.

In July 1958 Professor Cowen proposed a Legislative Council of eighty members in place of the Basuto National Council, to deal with all internal matters, as well as an Executive Council – of four British members, four Africans, the Resident Commissioner, and the Paramount Chief – to exercise the powers of a second chamber. He recommended direct elections to the district councils, which would then, sitting as an electoral college, elect the members of the Legislative Council. Both the Basuto National Council and the British government accepted the report, and the Basutoland African Congress agreed to the new constitution as a further stage in political development.

In December 1958 Mokhehle attended the first All-African Peoples Conference in Accra and was elected a member of its Steering Committee. In 1959 he travelled to Ghana and Guinea, where he developed great enthusiasm for the personality and accomplishments of Sékou Touré, and took time off from his political discussions to demonstrate with the Rev. Michael Scott against the exploding of a French atomic bomb in the Sahara.

In January 1960 elections to the district councils in Basutoland took place under the new constitution, and the Basutoland African Congress, now called the Basutoland Congress Party (B.C.P.), won seventy-three seats out of 162, to emerge by far the strongest political group. In the indirect elections that followed, the party won twenty-nine of the forty elected seats in the Legislative Council. Three members of the Executive Council were then elected by the Legislative Council. Both Khaketla, who had become deputy leader of the B.C.P., and Mokhehle himself stood, but only Khaketla was elected, revealing that in the Legislative Council at any rate he had more support than his own leader. During the year disputes between the two men increased, and in December Khaketla finally resigned from Congress to start the Basutoland Freedom Party and continue publishing *Mohlabani* as an advocate of 'constitutional advance'.

Though Mokhehle remains in control of the B.C.P. machine, there have been numerous expulsions and resignations from the party, while discontent continues to simmer at his somewhat authoritarian leadership. Several senior members of the African National Congress in the Republic have sought refuge in the territory and become active within the B.C.P. They have exerted their influence to democratize the B.C.P. leadership, and Mokhehle is reported to have complained of their interference.

At the 10th Annual Conference of the B.C.P., which opened in Maseru on 23 December 1961, an amendment to the constitution was passed which allowed Mokhehle to hold office as President for the next five years, while the Conference empowered the Executive to dissolve any branch whose activities did not comply with the policy of the party.

Paramount Chief of the Basuto and a direct descendant of the great Chief Moshoeshoe, BERENG SEEISO was born in 1939, son of Paramount Chief Seeiso Griffiths by his second wife, Mabereng. Educated at Roma in Basutoland, at Ampleforth, and Corpus Christi College, Oxford, where he was reading Politics, Philosophy, and Economics, he wished to wait until he was twenty-five and had finished his education before succeeding to the Chieftaincy. Growing disputes, however, with the Regent, Paramount Chieftainess Mantsebo Seeiso, led him to demand his immediate installation, and on 4 February 1960 he became Paramount Chief, after his decision to assume the Chieftaincy at once had gained support from the vast majority of Basuto Chiefs.

When required to nominate fourteen members to the Legislative Council, he chose only one from the B.C.P., in the belief that the movement required dilution. He has until now supported the aims of the B.C.P., however, in a recognition that he has to work with the strongest nationalist group in the territory. His personal influence remains considerable and he can do much to accelerate or retard the growth of militant nationalism in the territory.

Since the departure of South Africa from the Commonwealth at the end of May 1961, tension between the British and South African governments over the High Commission Territories has perceptibly increased. On 26 August three African refugees from the Republic, who had taken refuge in Basutoland, are alleged to have been kidnapped, and one of them – Anderson Khumani Ganyile, one time leader of the resistance movement in Pondoland – smuggled out of prison a letter: 'Kidnapped in Basutoland on 26.8.61 at 10.30 p.m. by six policemen from the Union. We know and can identify our kidnappers.' Having denied all knowledge of the incident for several months, the South African government announced the release of Ganyile on 17 January 1962 and apologized to the British government. South Africa's Department of Justice stated that its police, on the night in question, had crossed the Basutoland border in a heavy mist.

Dr Verwoerd told the Orange Free State National Party Congress on 13 September 1961 that talks would take place in the next few months to decide the future relationship between the Republic of South Africa and the British High Commission Territories, and that the country's security would not be sacrificed in the interests of economic advantage. The South African government, said Dr Verwoerd, was aware of the problems involved – cattle theft, liquor smuggling, the difficulty of border control, the free movement of 'agitators', and the influx of 'foreign' Africans into South Africa.

*

Bechuanaland, by far the largest of the three High Commission Territories, is bordered by South West Africa in the west, the Federation of Rhodesia and Nyasaland in the north, and the Republic of South Africa in the east and south. Within an approximate area of 275,000 square miles, it has an estimated population of some 335,000 Africans, 3,200 Europeans, 250 Asians, and 700 Coloured. Mainly a ranching country, only five per cent of its arable land is under cultivation, and its roads and railway system climb along its eastern border, linking the

Republic with Southern Rhodesia, but leaving virtually the whole remainder of the vast territory without adequate communications. Asbestos and manganese are mined in the south, while the Rhodesian Selection Trust is prospecting for coal and other minerals in the Bamangwato Reserve, by a 1959 agreement under which the Bamangwato are to receive twelve and a half per cent of any profits obtained. Much of the cattle farming is geared to providing meat for the markets of the Republic, while the government receives an annual tax revenue of some £55,000 from the labour that the territory exports. All in all some 15,000 or twenty per cent of the adult males are away at any given time in South Africa or in the Federation as migrant workers.

The history of the territory is strongly linked to the Khama family, the royal house of the Bamangwato. In 1876 Chief Khama appealed to Great Britain for protection against Afrikaner penetration and received support from Cecil Rhodes, who wished to annex the territory as part of the road to the north. In 1884 Britain undertook the administration of Bechuanaland and in the following year proclaimed a Protectorate, but the land seemed likely to produce little profit and in 1895 Britain proposed to hand it over to the British South Africa Company. The hostility of the Chiefs, however, who sent three representatives to Britain in order to protest, was successful, and the Company received only a strip of land for its railway.

SERETSE KHAMA, Secretary to the Bamangwato tribe, was born in July 1921, grandson of the great Chief Khama and son of Sekgoma, who for seventeen years himself suffered exile as Seretse was later to do. In 1925, when Sekgoma died, Seretse succeeded to the Chieftaincy and was brought up under the Regency of his uncle, Tshekedi Khama, who treated him as a son.

Educated at Tiger Kloof in Natal, and at Lovedale and the University of Fort Hare in the Eastern Cape of South Africa, he was studying in 1944 at the University of the Witwatersrand in Johannesburg when the Bamangwato approached him to take over the rule of the tribe. He asked, however, for time to continue his studies, and in 1945 went to Balliol College, Oxford, and then to the Middle Temple in order to read Law. While in London he met and became engaged to an English girl, Ruth Williams, and in spite of strong opposition from Tshekedi Khama, he married her.

Returning to Bechuanaland he found the tribe at first very hostile to the marriage, but gradually the elders made it clear that they would rather accept his wife as the Queen Mother than lose their rightful Chief. The whole tribal crisis seemed accordingly to have been settled, but the British government insisted upon holding a judicial inquiry into Seretse's fitness for office – the findings of the inquiry have not been published to this day – and in March 1950 invited him to London for talks.

After meeting with the Secretary of State for Commonwealth Relations in London, Seretse called a press conference to announce that he had been offered £1,100 a year tax free if he would renounce the Chieftaincy and live in Britain. He refused and was thereupon informed that he was banished from Bechuanaland together with his uncle Tshekedi. The reasons why the British government should have decided to act in this way are not yet precisely known, but it is generally believed that the South African government, under Dr Malan, had put the strongest pressure upon it not to permit the rule of an African Chief, married to a white woman, in a neighbouring territory.

The Bamangwato time and again refused, however, to elect another Chief in succession to Seretse, and Rasebolai Kgamane, third in succession after Seretse and Tshekedi, was appointed African Authority by the British government. At last agreeing to surrender all claim to the Chieftaincy for himself and his family, Seretse was permitted to return to Bechuanaland with his wife and children in October 1956, and since then he has lived quietly, working closely with Kgamane in the administration of the tribe.

On 6 December 1960, the British government published a new draft constitution for the territory which provided for the election, on a qualified franchise, of the first Bechuanaland Legislative Council. For the 1960s the new Council can hardly be considered a dramatic constitutional advance. With the

Resident Commissioner as Chairman, it consists of three *ex officio* and seven appointed officials (all white), two appointed (white) unofficial members, and ten (white) members elected by the white population. Two appointed and ten elected African members, with the addition of one Asian to represent the small Asian community, bring the total to thirty-five seats, of which the Africans possess something like one third. The election of the African members is not by adult suffrage, but takes place through the African Councils, meeting as electoral colleges. Seretse Khama himself was, in this fashion, elected as one of the five African members for the Northern Protectorate.

On the same day that the draft constitution was announced, the Bechuanaland People's Party was founded 'to mobilize and organize the political consciousness of the people of Bechuanaland'; to abolish all discrimination on grounds of colour, caste, creed, or class; to protect the citizenship rights of Bechuanaland nationals against 'foreigners and immigrants'; and to promote the integrity and security of the territory. 'Though fully appreciative of the good and opportune service rendered by the ancient institutions of the Chieftainship, a universal phenomenon, to mankind as a focal and rallying point in socialization', the party declared in its constitution that 'in present circumstances of the stage of the social and political evolution of the mass of the people of Bechuanaland, when deference to a chief is almost tantamount to deification, very great caution and circumspection must be exercised in the event of the nomination of a chief, African Authority, or Subordinate African Authority for the office of President or Vice-President or Secretary-General or for a branch chairmanship.'

The President of the B.P.P. is KGALEMAN T. MOTSETE, who was born at Serowe and educated locally. Proceeding to Tiger Kloof in South Africa, he gained his Junior Teacher's Certificate in 1918, took his matriculation, and then went to London University, where he took degrees in Divinity and Arts. Remaining in London to study music, he obtained his teacher's qualifications in the subject and then returned to Bechuanaland, where he ran for a time the Tati Training Institute and then taught at a number of schools in the Republic of South Africa, Nyasaland, and Bechuanaland itself. On 6 December 1960, the very day that the Bechuanaland administration proposed the establishment of a Legislative Council, he formed the Bechuanaland People's Party and became its first President. He appeared on the Northern Protectorate list of ten nominees, from which five Legislative Council Members had to be selected, but he was unsuccessful, and he soon afterwards strongly attacked the new Legislative Council, which he said might be the 'wooden horse' of South African expansionism.

An African commentator in *Fighting Talk*, a periodical supporting the Congress Alliance in South Africa, replied:

> The advent of the Legislative Council and the new constitution for Bechuanaland this year has not been a result of popular pressure, and it is almost true to say that it caught the country unawares. . . . The composition of the Council, with its equal number of seats for Africans and Europeans – out of all proportion to their respective numbers in the country – is only a faint glimmer of true democracy. Its decisions have to be approved by the High Commissioner before becoming law, its African members are largely Chief-approved nominees elected indirectly through Tribal Councils, while its European members are, by and large, an undistinguished body of traders. Nevertheless, it would be a mistake to dismiss the new constitution as a 'sham', as the Bechuanaland People's Party has done. It is undeniably a step forward in the construction of a multi-racial society and presents a vivid contrast to the race-mad Republic with whom it is so closely linked economically.

*

Smallest but richest of the three High Commission Territories is Swaziland, with an area of 6,705 square miles and a population of some 245,000 Africans, 6,000[1] whites, and just under 1,400 Coloured. In 1846 Afrikaner trekkers acquired land concessions from the Swazi Chiefs and increased their pressure until, in 1889, Chief Mbandzeni asked for British protection. The territory was ruled jointly by Great Britain and the South African

1. Current unofficial estimates place the white pop ulation as high as 10,000.

government from 1890, but four years later the Swazis repudiated joint rule, and in 1906 an Order in Council eventually placed Swaziland under the authority of the British High Commissioner. Some three-sevenths of the territory is owned by whites in a patchwork pattern, and Swaziland itself is entirely surrounded by white-controlled territory, to the north, west, and south by the Republic of South Africa, and to the east by Portuguese Moçambique.

Change is rapidly coming to the small population, as the British government and private capital sink money into the territory in order to develop its iron, coal, and wood pulp resources. Mbabane, the administrative capital, and Manzini, formerly called Bremersdorp, now have shiningly efficient automatic telephone exchanges, while tarred roads are linking the towns with the Transvaal border and with Stegi near to the frontier of Moçambique. Everywhere there is talk of the vast new mining projects at Bomvu Ridge in the north-west of the Protectorate, its exploitation by the Anglo-American Corporation, and the sale of its ore to Japan. On 24 October 1961, Britain's Secretary of State for Commonwealth Relations told the House of Commons that some eight million pounds would be spent to construct a railway from western Swaziland to the Mocambique border, a distance of 140 miles, as a link between the iron mines and the port of Lourenço Marques. Britain appears at last to be making a realistic effort to disengage at least one of the three Protectorates from its absolute economic dependance upon South Africa.

SOBHUZA II, the Ngwenyama, Paramount Chief of the Swazis, was born in 1889 of the Dlamini house, the Swazi ruling family which traces back its ancestry for 400 years. Educated at Zombodze school and at Lovedale in the Eastern Cape, he became Paramount Chief in 1921 and has ruled ever since, visiting England only twice, in 1922 and for the coronation of Elizabeth II. In his twenties he spent a great deal of money and effort in challenging through the British Courts the validity of the concessions by which his predecessor, Mbandzeni, had granted large tracts of land to Europeans, and though he took his fight all the way to the Privy Council, he lost. He now believes that nothing should be done in any way to alienate or disturb the European inhabitants, whose presence and participation he feels are so vital to his country. A shrewd ruler, he is well aware of the dangers of enforced incorporation by the Republic of South Africa, and makes every effort to win the Europeans in the Protectorate to his side. In June 1960, however, he stated: 'It is clear to me that both the African and the European seek protection of their rights; and it is therefore necessary not only to assure the European that he will not be ousted from Africa, but also to assure the African that he is not to be kept forever as a subject person.' Traditionalist and patriarchal in attitude, he pays much attention to his ritualistic kingly duties and exercises considerable power over his subjects.

All the Swazilanders, however, do not believe that the future of their country lies most effectively in following the paternalistic prudence of their Paramount Chief. JOHN JUNE NQUKU, founder of the Swaziland Progressive Party, was born in 1899 at Pietermaritzburg in the Republic of South Africa, of Zulu parents. Working as a shepherd boy until 1911, he went to the Loop Street School in Pietermaritzburg and then to the Pholela Institute at Bulwer in Natal. Having qualified as a teacher at St Chad's Training College in Ladysmith, he served from 1920 to 1925 as Principal of the Siyama Government School at Edendale near Pietermaritzburg, and from 1928 to 1929 as Principal of the Impolweni Government School.

In January 1930 he was appointed the first African Inspector of Schools in Swaziland, and settling in the territory he founded in 1934 a vernacular newspaper *Izwi Lama Swazi – The Voice of the Swazi* – serving as Editor until it was taken over by the Bantu Press.

In 1940 he resigned as Inspector and became an active member of the Swazi National Council, the governing council of the Swazi people, to be given charge of coordinating religious and educational policy with control over the expenditure on tribal schools of money provided by the Swazi National Treasury Estimates. In 1945 he became President of the Swaziland Progressive Association, which had been formed in 1929 with the support of the British administration as a social organization for the educated Swazi, and in 1955 he founded and became first editor of the *Swazilander*. During 1957 he travelled widely in Britain, America, and Western Europe, and in 1960 took the initiative in turning the Swaziland Progressive Association into a political movement under the name of the Swaziland Progressive Party, with a policy of self-government, eventual independence, and unequivocal hostility to any incorporation in the Republic of South Africa.

By the end of 1961, however, a split within the leadership of the Swaziland Progressive Party was becoming apparent. Dr Ambrose P. Zwane, Secretary-General, and the youth leader, Clement Dumisa Dhlamini, accused Nquku of regarding the party as his personal property and dictatorially closing meetings of the Executive whenever he found a majority ranged against him. At the end of February 1962, a party conference deposed Nquku as President and elected Dr Zwane in his place. Dhlamini was elected the new Secretary-General.

Born in 1924 at Bremersdorp in Swaziland, AMBROSE ZWANE was educated at Roman Catholic schools in the Protectorate and then at the Inkamana High School in Zululand, South Africa. Studying medicine at the University College of Fort Hare in the Eastern Cape and at the University of the Witwatersrand in Johannesburg, he qualified in 1951 and worked as a houseman at Nquthu Hospital in Zululand. He then returned to Swaziland and worked as a Government Medical Officer for seven years, resigning in April 1960 to engage full-time in politics, and becoming in July Secretary-General of the Swaziland Progressive Party. In January 1962 he was arrested at Zeerust in the Republic of South Africa, while in transit to Bechuanaland, for failing to carry a 'reference book' on his person. After two days in gaol, he was brought to court, charged under a 1952 Act which states that every 'Bantu' in South Africa has to be in possession of a pass, and then released on bail. Dr Zwane made immediate representations to the British High Commissioner's Office in Pretoria, demanding that all those travelling on British passports should be ensured safe passage through South Africa in future.

The crisis within the Swaziland Progressive Party has not been resolved with the change in leadership. Nquku and his followers dispute the election, while the change has clearly received widespread support from the younger members of the party. It remains, however, a crisis of personalities rather than policies, and both groups within the party oppose all attempts to perpetuate the control of tribal traditionalists in any programme of constitutional advance.

When discussions on constitutional reform first began in 1960, Sobhuza II nominated two members of the Swaziland Progressive Party to participate; but it soon became clear that their viewpoint was entirely irreconcilable with that of the Chief's Councillors, and after rancorous disputes the S.P.P. representatives were forced out of the discussions altogether. The party then appointed as its constitutional adviser Professor D. V. Cowen, who had played so prominent a rôle in the shaping of the Basutoland constitution. Interviewed by the Editor of *Contact*, the liberal South African fortnightly, in September 1961, Cowen was clear about what he felt his function to be.

The power of the High Commissioner is out of date. Nowadays no people anywhere in the world are satisfied with a state of affairs where power is given to authorities who are not answerable to the people. People want to rule themselves and, if necessary, to make their own mistakes. Also the power of the Swazi King is out of date. Nowhere in Africa are people content to be ruled on a feudal basis in a purely tribal and traditional system. Two world wars, education, and the pressure of events have produced modern men who wish to be ruled by, and who wish to share in the rule of, governments that are modern.

The scheme apparently favoured by the authorities is one under which approximately half the new legislature would be elected by the white settlers, who number only 10,000 out of a total population of 250,000. This would be an enormous increase in their political power, in addition to the economic power they already have in the territory.

The real clash between the traditionalists and the S.P.P. had arisen from Sobhuza's public suggestion that the Swazis should appoint their own half-share of the new legislature in the traditional way, without elections and the use of political parties, which Sobhuza himself clearly does not believe suitable to African societies. Professor Cowen commented:

What is needed is a compromise which would allow modern democratic elections for all those Swazis who desire them and at the same time allow the traditional system to operate while adjusting itself to modern conditions. . . . The fundamental point on which we will not compromise is the single, non-racial common roll for all. We envisage about sixty per cent of the members of Council being elected by all adults irrespective of race or colour on this roll. Then there might be twenty per cent nominated by the King in the traditional manner. And then there might be another twenty per cent consisting of nominees and officials. This legislature would elect a substantial number of members of an Executive Council which would be an emergent cabinet. The Swazi King would be a constitutional monarch. He would be the constitutional head of the nation, King of all Swazilanders, instead of being, as at present, merely 'Paramount Chief' of the Swazi Africans.

Swaziland is a microcosm of the Union [Republic of South Africa]. It has a sizeable white minority with nearly all the economic power. It has mineral riches and can stand on its own feet. . . . If good relations are maintained it could be a model land, moving smoothly and surely into the modern world. But if a new constitution is introduced which leaves little or no room for the modern man and which jumps the white settlers into a position of power which will allow them to do very much as they like in the territory, then I tremble for the future of Swaziland.

On 1 March 1962, the Constitutional Committee appointed by Sobhuza II recommended a Legislative Council for the Protectorate consisting of a Speaker, four official members, twelve Swazi unofficial members elected by the Swaziland National Council, and twelve unofficial European members elected on a white and Coloured common roll. The National Council would elect its representatives 'by acclamation', while all bills from the Legislative Council would be presented to the

Ngwenyama for his consent. An immediate crisis developed within the Protectorate, and a Swazi tribal gathering to discuss the new constitution broke up in disorder on 3 March. A united front of political parties, trade unions, academic bodies, and the Anglican Church was formed to protest against the racial separation at the core of the proposed constitution, and the various leaders joined in submitting a letter to the Secretary of State for the Colonies. They maintained: 'Separate representation of the Swazis and the white population would propagate the present division of the country along racial lines and would dangerously retard the creation of a unified common society. We believe that the principle of a common roll with universal adult suffrage as its ultimate objective should be the foundation of our constitution.'

On 6 March *The Times*, in a leader on the crisis, commented:

> Any attempt to introduce the western institutions which will diminish the traditional chiefly powers and prerogatives will be resisted by African tribesmen and white settlers alike. Yet it would be wrong for Britain to take the easy path. Swaziland must be given the basic political machinery to enter the modern world and educate itself in so doing. Whatever the safeguards or the time-table – and even at some risk – this means giving the people the right to vote, going to them to sanction policy, and minimizing differences of race, wealth, and social position.

★

Professor Cowen and the Swaziland Progressive Party which he represents are not alone in finding it possible to tremble for the future of the Protectorate. All three High Commission Territories are – and must remain for some time to come – hostages of apartheid, unless the British government makes a dramatic effort to put them economically and politically on their own feet. Section 151 of the Act of Union allows the possibility of their transfer to South Africa after consultations with their inhabitants, and though successive British governments have made it clear that they would regard such consultation as imperative, successive South African governments have made increasingly shrill demands for their absorption.

Recognizing the common dangers which they face, the Basutoland Congress Party, Bechuanaland People's Party, and Swaziland Progressive Party were represented at a joint meeting in Mbabane, Swaziland, on 22–3 January 1962. The leaders resolved on the establishment of a Pan-African Solidarity Conference for the three High Commission Territories, which would co-ordinate their activities and, in particular, their opposition to 'any agreements reached between Britain and South Africa on future relationships with the Protectorates if the people of each territory are not consulted'.

It is one thing for the British government to proclaim its responsibility for the Protectorates. It is quite another for it to sustain its protection against full-scale economic pressures from the Republic of South Africa. Certainly it is difficult to exaggerate the consequences of a move by Dr Verwoerd to close the frontiers between the High Commission Territories and the Republic. And Dr Verwoerd will do precisely that if he should ever decide that he wants the Territories badly enough. Nor, in doing this, will he be infringing the integrity of other states; he will simply be exercising the legal right of his government to control the movement of foreign labour into its territory. Ultimately, in fact, he will only be taking an easy advantage of the failure by successive British governments over the years to develop the Protectorates towards economic self-sufficiency.

There can be few situations in Africa as potentially corrosive of British prestige as the possibilities for economic blackmail against the Protectorates still in the hands of Dr Verwoerd. And the consequences to Britain of having to collapse to such pressures utterly stagger prediction. The three High Commission Territories are small enough – their total population is not much above a million – but their surrender to Dr Verwoerd would have international implications. Certainly, from the abundant claims, moral and political, upon the British Treasury, it is difficult to think of any as pressing as that which requires the rapid economic development of the three High Commission Territories in the pursuit of their viable political independence.

4 Begging is Forbidden: Portuguese Africa

The rains have stopped falling, the dry season has begun, the green vegetation is covered by a thick layer of red dust. The white colonists have taken hope; at Luanda, port and capital, the *Niassa* ceaselessly disembarks troop reinforcements, who can at last be sent to the North now that the roads have become passable again. As everywhere in Africa, one exaggerates to give oneself courage: 'soon there will be 75,000 Portuguese soldiers in the province of Angola'. But in any event, security is assured only until September, only until the coming of the rains. . . .

So the correspondent of *Le Monde* wrote of Angola in June 1961. With September and the coming of the rains, the war for Angola that had already cost some 1,000 Portuguese and 50,000 African lives took on a new guerilla impetus.

Portugal's African empire, with its 794,907 square miles of territory and just under twelve million inhabitants, is the largest of the old colonial empires left in the world and the only one that has survived so far without serious loss the African resurgence of the last fifteen years. Angola on the west coast of Africa, with its 481,352 square miles and estimated 1961 population of 4,500,000 Africans, 200,000 Europeans, and 40,000 Mulattos, exports mainly coffee, diamonds, sugar, and cotton. Directly opposite it, on the east coast, lies Moçambique, with an area of 297,654 square miles and a population of 6,200,000 Africans, 90,000 Europeans, 20,000 Mulattos, and 12,000 Asians – exporting mainly cotton, sugar, sisal, and vegetable oils, and receiving almost half its entire budget from railway and port services, tourism, and the supply of African labour to the mines of South and Central Africa. Through the ports of Moçambique flow the mineral and industrial exports of South Africa and the Federation, while wealthy white Rhodesians and South Africans spend the winter on the sands and in the night clubs of Lourenço Marques.

Portuguese Guinea, with an area of 13,944 square miles, contains 60,000 Africans, 5,000 Cape Verde Creoles, and 2,600 Europeans, while the Cape Verde archipelago has a total area of 1,557 square miles and a population of 180,000 Creoles and 3,200 Europeans. Finally, there are the islands of Sao Thomé and Principe, with an area of 400 square miles, a population of 70,000 Africans and 1,500 Europeans, and an important detention camp for political prisoners whose resistance to the civilizing mission of Portugal has caught the attention of Salazar's secret police.

*

The Angolan war, which now threatens to disrupt the whole Portuguese empire and has already shaken the structure of Salazar's authority in Portugal itself, began on 15 March 1961 at a coffee plantation – Fazenda da Primavera – near to San Salvador do Congo, the ancient capital of the Kingdom of Congo, 100 kilometres from the Congo border. Organized by the União das Populacões de Angola (U.P.A.), an illegal, largely peasant independence movement that had been founded in 1954, the forced labourers on the plantation obeyed a general strike call. Some twenty workers were shot dead, and the remainder overwhelmed their employer. By the morning of 16 March the Portuguese on neighbouring plantations were shooting indiscriminately at their suddenly rebellious Africans.

In retaliation, the Africans organized themselves into groups of two or three hundred men each, armed with sticks, stones, and petrol. They attacked all the Portuguese in the district, killing those they found, and by the beginning of April had spread the uprising across the whole of the Congo Province, south into the neighbouring Provinces of Malange and Luanda, and down to Nova Lisboa and other towns on the Elisabethville-Benguela railway. Military forces withdrew to scattered forts like Maquella and Quibaxi, leaving 900 miles of the Congo frontier and 40,000 square miles in the interior virtually undefended.

A Special Correspondent of the London *Observer*, writing from Leopoldville, described incidents in the terrifying Portuguese repression that had followed the start of the rebellion.

At the village of Sanga on 17 March, jeeps arrived with Angolan soldiers in mufti wearing the badge of the main nationalist party, the Union of Angolan Peoples (U.P.A.), who told the villagers that the struggle had been won. When a crowd had gathered, the soldiers opened fire with machine-guns, and killed eighteen of them.

Two days later, at another village, Tumbi, a car with a loudhailer drove through and announced that 'the king' of the U.P.A. was arriving by aeroplane. A plane actually appeared. When the crowd had assembled, troops converged on the village and killed 300.

At Tomboco, the inhabitants were surrounded in the centre of the village. Mothers with children were allowed to stand to one side. The rest of the population . . . were then shot down.

Later, with the arrival of the first troop and air reinforcements at Mawuela and San Salvador, the Portuguese staged a come-back; families, including the few remaining women and children, organized themselves into armed militia. Mobile columns and increasing air strikes were used to obliterate village after village. . . .

Whatever brutalities may have been committed against the Portuguese colons, they can never justify the wholesale revenge.

Portugal began full-scale emergency measures to deal with the rebellion on 29 April, sending 15,000 trained troops into rebel-held territory, in successive waves. In Luanda itself, a night curfew was imposed in the African suburbs after Europeans had entered them on raids of revenge, shooting Africans on sight and burning their huts. Villages thought to harbour rebels were bombed and strafed by Portuguese aircraft, and any survivors were finished off by paratroops.

An article in the *Economist* of 6 May entitled 'Agony of Angola' claimed:

For the rebels escape is easy; this land of equatorial swamps, seven foot elephant grass, and roads which the rains make impassable, provides a perfect theatre for guerrilla fighting. White and African refugees who managed to flee reached Luanda in a state of stupefaction and horror, and their eye-witness tales induced in the population a mood of hate and fear that bodes ill for the future of race relations in the territory....

The reaction of the Portuguese Government has been as swift as the means allow.... In the absence of any official information, it has been estimated that some 15,000 Angolan and metropolitan troops and police are at present deployed in the territory. Their methods of reprisal are known to be severe to the point of barbarity, but an iron censorship and a complete refusal to allow any journalists (even from the captive local press, whose editors are mere parrots in a locked official cage) to visit the northern province have successfully concealed from the world these draconian measures which are at present the whole of Dr Salazar's Angolan policy.

The wonder is not that Angola exploded with such ferocity, but rather that it took so long to explode in the first place. After more than 400 years of Portuguese rule, there are still less than 250 miles of tarred roads in the territory, while the illiteracy rate – at ninety-eight per cent – is amongst the highest in the world. Outside the main towns and a few mission stations, health services hardly exist, while forced labour is – despite government denials – still widely practised.

A commission of three jurists, appointed by the International Labour Organization to investigate charges by the government of Ghana of forced labour in Portugal's African territories, reported on 5 March 1962 that the Portuguese government had been taking steps to abolish forced labour. But it found that the Diamond Company of Angola was continuing 'to recruit labour through the intermediary of administrative officials and indigenous chiefs in a manner liable to involve compulsion and therefore to constitute forced labour'. The commission also found that the publicly owned railways and ports in Angola were still recruiting labour 'in a manner inconsistent with the requirements of the Abolition of Forced Labour Convention'.

The infant mortality rate in Angola is sixty per cent, and the average wage for Africans some £20 a year. Certainly, the official policy of 'assimilation' has either been conducted with immoderate languor, or is being canvassed merely as a cover for the cruelty and squalor of Portugal's civilizing mission. According to the *Anuario Estatistico do Ultramar* (Lisbon Instituto Nacional de Estatistica, 1959) – hardly a sympathetic source – figures from the 1950 or last available census revealed 30,089 assimilated and 4,006,598 uncivilized Africans in Angola.

In November 1960 Dr Salazar announced to the Portuguese National Assembly:

> We have been in Africa for 400 years, which is rather more than to have arrived yesterday. We carried with us a doctrine, which is not the same as to be carried away by self-interest. We are present there with the policy that authority is steadily effecting and defending, which is not the same as to abandon human destiny to the so-called 'winds of history'.

One hardly requires further commentary on those 400 years than that the percentage of the civilized in Angola should have reached the figure in 1950 of 0·74. The figures for Moçambique (25,149 civilized Africans to 5,646,957 – or 0·44 per cent), and for Portuguese Guinea (1,470 civilized to 502,457 – or 0·29 per cent) are even more revealing.

Despite the ruthless repression, the Angolan insurgents continue to fight, with their leaders organizing from Leopoldville, and the insurgents themselves withdrawing across the borders into the formerly French or formerly Belgian Congo to regroup and then return. *La Voix de la Nation Angolaise*, the organ of the U.P.A., has laid down as the condition for any cease-fire that it should be preceded by official guarantees from the Portuguese government encompassing 'the withdrawal of Portuguese forces from Angola, the establishment of democratic principles, the lifting of press consorship, and the right of free expression and respect for the Angolan personality'. And the insurrection has spread beyond Angola.

Some 200 rebels entered Portuguese Guinea from Senegal on the night of 23–24 July, cutting telephone wires and damaging some villas in Praia Varela, a small seaside resort in the territory. On 25 July Senegal broke off diplomatic relations with Portugal, while on the same day the President of Dahomey gave Portugal a week to evacuate the Fort of John the Baptist. The tiny enclave, which was duly absorbed by Dahomey on 1 August, represented Portugal's first retreat.

Her second retreat, on a somewhat more costly scale, was to follow within five months at the other end of the world. Early in the morning of 18 December 1961, Indian armed forces invaded Goa, Daman, and Diu, Portugal's three enclaves on the west coast of India. Despite the 'fierce fighting' claimed by Lisbon radio, Portuguese troops surrendered on the following day, and an imperial rule that had lasted for 451 years irrevocably vanished.

While Lisbon mourned, the government of Dr Salazar had the future to engage its attention. Though the overall defence budget had been almost doubled, to account for nearly half of the nation's spending, the Angolan rebellion had not been crushed and rumours were rife that Africans from Moçambique, operating from Kenya and Tanganyika, were preparing for an insurrection in their homeland. And discontent with the government was spreading fast within Portugal itself. On 1 January 1962 Captain Varela Gomes, son of an admiral, raised an armed rebellion at Beja in Southern Portugal. The attempt to dislodge Salazar failed. But few in Portugal or the outside world believed that it would be the last.

On 28 August 1961 the Portuguese Minister for the Overseas Provinces, Dr Adriano Moreira, announced a new statute which would give citizenship to every native of Portugal's overseas territories. He also announced, however, that power should always be exercised by those who were most fitted for it, and that the law would therefore define the conditions under which anyone might intervene actively in political life. And he added: 'We believe it necessary to increase the settlement of our Africa by European Portuguese, who will make their homes there and find in Africa a true continuation of their country.' Those with experience of Salazar's Estado Novo and its strong arm, the state security police (Policia Internacional e de Defese do Estado – P.I.D.E.) might regard this as a threat rather than as a promise.

The *New Statesman* of 1 September 1961 commented:

> The real test of whether the decree leads to any genuine reform will be seen in the future attitude to African labour. Can Africans who are full citizens of Portugal still be subject to forced labour? If so, what is the value of citizenship? If not, the present system of labour in Angola will collapse. It is significant that this new decree has been accomplished by a call to Portuguese soldiers to settle in Angola and by the threat that South African forces may be called on to help to restore order in the colony. The Portuguese are being virtually invited to seize land and pacify the country on similar lines to Cromwell's settlement of Ireland. They are promised South African help if they do not succeed. Yet the fact is that Africans in Angola and Moçambique will not consent to become Portuguese, whatever Salazar may tell them. Even if they wished to do so, and there is no evidence that they do, the rest of Africa would not allow any European power to establish itself permanently in their continent. The pressure of African politics now constantly stimulates nationalism, and will continue to do so until the last vestige of European rule is removed.

The leader of the U.P.A., HOLDEN ROBERTO, was born in 1925 in the town of San Salvador in the Northern Province of Angola. To a correspondent of *Le Monde*, he recently said:

> I have three names, but it is for reasons of the war. My name is actually Holden Roberto; my family name is Roberto, my first name Holden – something which always baffles Westerners. It would have been more simple certainly if my father had chosen Jean, Pierre, or Jacques, but my parents were peasants, rough people, and my father wished me to have the same name as one of the Protestant missionaries, Dr Holden, an American. . . .

Roberto received his secondary education in the Congo and worked in the Finance Department of the Belgian Administration at Leopoldville, Stanleyville, and Bukavu. Making four trips into Angola and much disturbed by the conditions he found there, in 1954 he formed, together with six others, the União das Populacões de Angola. Travelling widely in Africa and Europe, he attended the first and second All African Peoples Conferences (Accra 1958, Tunis 1960) and was elected to the Steering Committee at Tunis. In Accra he met and formed a close relationship with Kwame Nkrumah, and during the first All African Peoples Conference saw much of Patrice Lumumba. It was there that he first called himself José Gilmore, to escape the vigilance of the Portuguese political police.

He lobbied at the fourteenth United Nations General Assembly and attended the second Conference of Independent African States at Addis Ababa in June 1961. The U.P.A. openly claimed responsibility for the uprising of 15 March, and Roberto himself has been organizing it from a small office at 78 Rue du Dodoma in Leopoldville. The correspondent of *Le Monde* who interviewed him described him with admiration:

> Holden Roberto spoke in French more correctly than many of the important politicians in former French Africa or the once Belgian Congo. He is young, handsome, quiet, and elegant. He has the distinction of an Oxford student as well as the capacity. He does not raise his voice but speaks without hesitation; his phrases are well-constructed, well-balanced, without one word too many.

The U.P.A. is not the only movement active in Angola, though it has demonstrated more than any other its African support. More influential amongst the 'assimilated' and rather less of a grass-rooted nationalist party is the Movimento Popular de Libertacao de Angola (M.P.L.A.) led by Ilidio Machado, Dr Agostinho Neto, and Mario Pinto de Andrade. Founded in 1957 as an underground party, it merged a number of illegal groups, which had been active since 1953 in demanding independence and self-determination for Angola. Since its formation, its influence has rapidly spread outwards from Luanda; the territory has been divided into thirty zones, each organized by a secret committee, and a few Europeans have joined. Certainly seven Europeans were amongst those arrested in 1955 and tried in June 1960 for threatening the integrity of the State by advocating independence for Angola.

In January 1960, delegates from the M.P.L.A. attended the second All African Peoples Conference in Tunis, where they formed a united front (Fronte Revolucionaria Africana para a Independencia Nacional) with three other nationalist organizations. Nationalist movements from the Portuguese colonies in

Africa and Asia held a special conference at Casablanca from 17 to 20 April 1961, and resolved to establish a permanent coordinating organization, the Conferencia de Organizacoes Nacionalistas das Colonias Portuguesas (C.O.N.C.P.), with headquarters in Rabat. Convened by the M.P.L.A., the Goa League, and the Partido Africano da Independencia da Guine e Cabo Verde, the conference was attended by fourteen delegates from Angola, Portuguese Guinea, the Cape Verde and San Thomé islands, Goa, and Moçambique. The new coordinating movement is governed by a Conference, the supreme authority, composed of delegates from all the consistent organizations; by a Consultative Council, composed of two delegates from each colony; and by a Secretariat.

ILIDIO TOMÉ ALVES MACHADO was born in 1915 at Luanda, a member of the Kimbundu tribe, his father employed by the Portuguese administration and his mother a former slave. Educated locally to primary and junior secondary level, he worked in the Post and Telegraph office in Luanda until 1959, when he was arrested. One of the most influential leaders of the Liga Nacional Africana (African National League), an organization founded in 1929 with Portuguese permission – for the protection of the economic and social interests of the Africans – he left it to found in 1957 the M.P.L.A., of which he became first President. In May 1959 he was arrested while paying a brief visit to Lisbon and was returned to Luanda, where he has been imprisoned ever since. One of the fifty-six accused of high treason in 1959, he is now Honorary Vice-President of the M.P.L.A. and remains one of the most respected of the Angolan leaders, though he is a man of ideas rather than of mass appeal.

DR ANTONIO AGOSTINHO NETO was born in September 1922 at Icolo e Bengo in Angola, and educated to secondary level at Luanda. From 1944 to 1947 he worked in the Angola health services and played a considerable part in building up a cultural society in Luanda – political organizations were forbidden – which became increasingly nationalist in tone. Then in 1947 he went to study medicine at the famous University of Coimbra in Portugal and while he was there published a series of poems in which he gave voice to the sufferings of his people. He became active in the Portuguese youth movement and was imprisoned in 1952 for taking part in demonstrations. Freed, he was imprisoned again – from February 1955 to June 1957 – for subversive activities. In 1958 he qualified as a doctor and in the same year helped to found the Anti-Colonial Movement (M.A.C.) which, centred in Lisbon, grouped the representatives of resistance movements in all the Portuguese colonies.

In 1959 he at last returned to Angola, where he worked as a doctor until he was arrested in June 1960. The people of his own village staged a demonstration of protest at his arrest, but this was ruthlessly suppressed by Portuguese troops and the village itself was burnt. Dr Neto was secretly transferred to Lisbon and then in September 1960 deported to the island of Santa Antao. In October 1961 a number of distinguished British authors including Professor C. Day Lewis, Doris Lessing, Iris Murdoch, John Osborne, and Angus Wilson wrote a letter to *The Times* in which they claimed that Dr Neto's life might be in serious danger.

> It is not too much to say that the importance of Agostinho Neto in Portuguese speaking Africa is comparable with that of Léopold Senghor in French speaking Africa. We believe that every effort must now be made to save this distinguished poet of Portuguese Africa's nationalist awakening.

A representative of the Portuguese Embassy in London replied tartly that Dr Neto was in good health.

Dr Neto is an honorary member of the M.P.L.A. The movement's President is MARIO PINTO DE ANDRADE, who was born in August 1928 at Golungo Alto in Angola. Educated to secondary level at Luanda, he went to Lisbon University in 1948, where he studied Philosophy, and in 1954 proceeded to Paris, where he took a course in Social Science at the Sorbonne. At the same time he became active in the group of intellectuals around the magazine *Présence Africaine* in Paris and was one of the organizers of the Conference of Negro Writers which met at Rome in 1958. Since then he has travelled widely and, with his headquarters in Guinea, has vigorously canvassed the cause of Angolan emancipation.

The Progressive, an American monthly, published a report on the Angolan rebellion by Russell Warren Howe in its issue of October 1961. In it, the story of another Angolan rebel is told.

> One distinguished mulatto, who comes from a long line of mulattoes, is Monsignor Manuel J. Mendes das Neves, Vicar-General of Angola, heir-apparent to the archbishopric, and a favourite for elevation to membership in the College of Cardinals. Mendes das Neves is five feet tall and about seventy years of age, a slightly Orientally-featured prince of the Catholic Church who occasionally drops his clerical demeanour to flay from the pulpit Portugal's African policy and her contempt for human rights. 'Dropped', in the past tense, would be more accurate: the Monsignor was saying mass one morning last March when the P.I.D.E. showed up at Luanda Cathedral and bustled the little divine off to headquarters. Where is he now? Possibly still at P.I.D.E. headquarters. Perhaps in São Paulo jail. Possibly on his way to Sao Tomé slave-labour island. If he is lucky he will be deported to Portugal – if luckier still (on Vatican insistence) to the Gregorian University, Rome.

On 9 June 1961 the United Nations Security Council, by nine votes to nil, with Britain and France abstaining, called on Portugal to end repressive measures against the African population in Angola. Dr Salazar was not long in giving his reply, and in a speech to the National Assembly on 30 June he announced:

> The invitation to the Portuguese authorities to cease at once the measures of repression in Angola is an attitude we might call theatrical on the part of the Security Council . . . so seriously does it offend the duties of a sovereign state. . . . I hope that we who are sure that we are right and are convinced that we can prove it, will not be intimidated. International life is not all lived in the United Nations Organization. . . . At present the Afro-Asian powers seem to be in the right. But with a little courage on our part, they will finally come to understand that there are limits that cannot be outstripped.

On 11 February 1962, the *Observer* reported that the war in Angola was still being waged,

not on a scale that makes front-page headlines, but with inexorable momentum which can have only one end: the collapse of the Portuguese economy.

The rebels, after suffering thousands of casualties through foolhardy mass-attacks on military columns, have learned new tactics and taken to the bush. The multi-racial revolutionary movement M.P.L.A. claim to have 1,400 soldiers in columns and platoons. Their rival, the more exclusively African Union of Angolan Populations (U.P.A.), claim 25,000. . . .

Their success is considerable. They are pinning down a Portuguese army and air force of 20,000 men. And by mustering support at the United Nations they have enfiladed Portugal's Western alliance, dependent on the diminishing value of the Azores naval base.

*

The Salazar government is going to need rather more than what it measures as courage. With the Angolan rebels far from 'pacified', any uprising in Moçambique is likely to strain the resources of Portugal beyond its limits, and there are already organizations busy planning for national resistance in Portugal's second great African colony. Founded in Moçambique in October 1960, the União Democratica Nacional de Moçambique (UDENAMO) has members throughout the territory and amongst migrant workers from Moçambique in Nyasaland, the Rhodesias, and Tanganyika. Under the Presidency of Adelino Gwambe, it aims at immediate self-determination and independence for the people of Moçambique; the immediate abolition of the forced labour system; the removal of all discrimination by establishing the principle of equal pay for equal work, and by an intensified programme of popular education; and cooperation with other territories and organizations in Africa to promote peace and freedom throughout the continent.

In February 1961 the leaders moved to Dar-es-Salaam, though Gwambe himself was ordered to leave Tanganyika before 1 August and is now in Morocco. The officials still in Dar-es-Salaam maintain an office, though their supporters in Moçambique get short shrift when their sympathies are discovered. Chief Zintambira of Vila Continho was shot dead for addressing a group of people about the organization.

The Moçambique African National Union (M.A.N.U.) was formed in November 1960 to unite the Moçambique Makonde Union (operating illegally in the north of the territory) with other nationalist groups, several of which have been active in Moçambique since 1955. An illegal organization, M.A.N.U. cooperates with UDENAMO and has offices in Nairobi, Zanzibar, and Dar-es-Salaam. Dissatisfaction in Moçambique is not exclusively African, however, and a number of white settlers have been arrested and imprisoned for their opposition to the Salazar régime.

Certainly the most influential of the dissidents – if not the most militant – is MONSEIGNEUR SEBASTIÃO SOARES DE RESENDE, Bishop of Beira. Born on 14 June 1906 at Milheirós de Pioares in the Diocese of Porto, Portugal, de Resende studied at the Diocesan Seminary of Porto and was received into the priesthood on 21 October 1928. Going to Rome in the same year to further his studies, he gained Doctorates in Philisophy and Theology after five years, and in 1933 returned to Portugal as a teacher in the major Diocesan Seminary of Porto.

On 21 April 1943 he was elected Bishop of Beira in Portuguese East Africa and was consecrated on 15 August of the same year. He has published a large number of pastoral letters on religious, social, and educational matters, and he enjoys the reputation of having attempted – with little success and some risk – to liberalize the Portuguese administration in the territory.

Portugal encourages tourists; with the rising cost of defending its empire, foreign currency is more than ever required. It is naturally reluctant to reveal that the capital of its empire is only a little less squalid than some of its outposts. Rich tourists may encounter on their trips through the city such signs as 'E PROIBIDO MENDIGAR' – 'BEGGING IS FORBIDDEN'. It has for long been an order to the poor of Lisbon to keep their claims beyond the notice of foreign tourists. It might just as well serve as a signpost for the whole empire. Begging in Portugal's African 'provinces' has long been forbidden. It need not therefore surprise that the almost twelve million Africans in the African 'provinces' should find it necessary to further their demands in different ways.

The North Atlantic Treaty Organization, of which Portugal has been a member since the Treaty itself was signed on 4 April 1949, claims to be more than a mere defensive alliance against Soviet attack. The preamble to the Treaty states:

> The parties to this treaty reaffirm their faith in the purposes and principles of the Charter of the United Nations and their desire to live in peace with all peoples and all governments. They are determined to safeguard the freedom, common heritage, and civilization of their peoples, founded on the principles of democracy, individual liberty, and the rule of law.

Article 2 of the Treaty commits the signatories even further.

> The parties will contribute towards the further development of peaceful and friendly international relations by strengthening their free institutions, by bringing about a better understanding of the principles upon which these institutions are founded, and by promoting conditions of stability and well-being.

The Protestant missionaries arrested in Angola for protesting against the cruelties of Salazar oppression – let alone the African guerrilla fighters themselves – would be justified in asking to what degree the Portuguese empire 'safeguards the freedom, common heritage, and civilization of its peoples, founded on the principles of democracy, individual liberty, and the rule of law'. The more than 150,000 African refugees who have fled across the frontier into the Congo to escape the napalm bombs and machine guns of the Portuguese forces might be forgiven for asking whether at least one of the parties to the North Atlantic Treaty is contributing towards the further development of peaceful and friendly international relations by strengthening its free institutions, by bringing about a better understanding of the principles upon which those institutions are founded, and by promoting conditions of stability and well-being.

International diplomacy has seldom been a field for the practice of moral principles. There can be few Africans any longer who do not regard the posturings of East and West alike with distrust of their motives and disgust at their displays of casual cynicism. Yet there is a peculiar insult to the human intelligence in institutions which can assimilate the savageries of the Angolan war to the safeguarding of freedom and the 'principles of democracy, individual liberty, and the rule of law'. If the 'free world' has indeed any meaning, its protagonists would seem to be doing their utmost to conceal it from the many millions of Portuguese Africa.

5 A Limited Company: The Federation of Rhodesia and Nyasaland

In 1953 the three territories of Southern Rhodesia, Northern Rhodesia, and Nyasaland were associated, by choice of the Southern Rhodesian white electorate and by decision of the British government on behalf of the two northern Protectorates, into the Federation of Rhodesia and Nyasaland. Founded on the principles of racial partnership, it was planned – or proclaimed – as the first great experiment in establishing a shared society, where white and black could contribute to a common advancement.

Nine years later, the Federation – with its population of 8,080,000 Africans, 312,000 Europeans, and 41,000 Asians and Coloured, living in an area of 485,000 square miles – seems on the point of disintegration. To its north lie the independent States of Tanganyika and the Congo; to the west, Angola is in flames, while Moçambique, in the east, needs only a passing spark to set it alight; immediately to the south stretches the Republic of South Africa, defiant in its doctrine of white supremacy. The Federation is being pulled apart by the very forces embodied in its neighbours and partly reflected by each of its own three constituents – a Southern Rhodesia, dominated by its white population, which demands white rule for many years to come, a Nyasaland already enjoying territorial black majority government and straining to escape the white-controlled Federal Assembly in Salisbury, a Northern Rhodesia wavering between rebellion and repression. Here, perhaps more patently than anywhere else on the continent, the main political personalities embody the clash of power, the collision between administration and aspiration.

Born in 1907, the thirteenth son of a Lithuanian Jew and his Afrikaner wife, who trekked by ox-wagon from South Africa, SIR ROY WELENSKY, present Prime Minister of the Federation, grew up in the poor-white atmosphere of the rough boarding house which his father kept in Salisbury. Educated in primary schools to Standard 4 – too low an educational level automatically to qualify an African today for an ordinary vote in the Federation – he left school at the age of fourteen and worked, amongst other jobs, as a store-keeper and railway fireman. It was at this period that he took up amateur boxing, an interest that he has maintained all his life, and in 1925 he became heavyweight champion of Rhodesia.

Finding employment as an engine driver, he began increasingly to involve himself in trade union activities. During the thirties he moved up to Broken Hill in Northern Rhodesia and was caught up in the great economic depression that then lay over the mining areas of the territory. He endured all the insecurities and deprivations of poverty, and his experience convinced him of two principles which he has passionately pursued throughout his political career – the danger to whites from the competition of Africans in employment, and the importance of the 'economic man'. It is this last principle, indeed, which has led him consistently to maintain that if Africans are fed they will not concern themselves with politics.

While at Broken Hill, he encountered considerable anti-Semitism, but he pulled his way upward nonetheless, resuscitating the Broken Hill branch of the Railway Union and building it into a powerful political unit. In 1938, while still an engine driver, he was elected a member of the Northern Rhodesia Legislative Council and became one of the most vociferous and significant political figures in the territory, forming the Labour Party in 1941 together with six other members of the Council, and fighting against employers and African economic competition alike.

In 1946, Sir Stewart Gore-Brown, a leading settler politician, delivered a strong speech in which he claimed that Africans had lost confidence in the intentions of the white settler community. The outcry that resulted forced him to resign, and it was Welensky who took his place as Chairman of the Unofficial Members in the Legislative Council. Becoming a close associate of Sir Godfrey Huggins, the Prime Minister of Southern Rhodesia, he campaigned for Rhodesian amalgamation under a single government free of the British Colonial Office.

In 1948 while visiting Britain, however, he found not only the Labour government but also the Tory opposition solidly against this scheme. A federal structure was proposed instead, and Welensky returned to persuade Huggins into supporting the idea. Together they campaigned for Federation, stressing that it was the only way to defeat the right-wing Dominion Party in Southern Rhodesia and prevent the territory from joining the Union – now the Republic – of South Africa. The following year he participated in a Conference at the Victoria Falls Hotel, called to consider – though no single African was present – the future of Central Africa.

Southern Rhodesia approved its membership of the Federation in a special referendum by 25,570 votes to 14,729 – hardly any Africans at all having been qualified to vote – and when Federation was established in the same year, Sir Godfrey Huggins became first Federal Prime Minister, with Welensky clearly recognized as his heir. In 1955 Sir Godfrey was created Lord Malvern of Rhodesia and resigned the Federal Premiership to Welensky.

Strong as African nationalist opinion had been against Federation at the time of its imposition – Africans in Nyasaland and Northern Rhodesia were passionately hostile to any advance in the political power of Southern Rhodesia's white community – this feeling grew even stronger under what African leaders attacked as Welensky's 'white supremacy' policies and practices. And as African resentment and antagonism increased – reflected by doubts and criticisms of Federation within Britain as well – Welensky himself began to campaign for complete independence of the Federation from British control. In 1957 he visited London for constitutional talks, and at their conclusion a press statement was issued which announced that 'the British government would not initiate any legislation to amend or repeal any Federal Act, except at the request of the Federal government.' This was the beginning of Welensky's campaign to achieve dominion status for the Federation, and throughout 1957 and 1958 he spoke ever more frequently of the need for reaching this goal as quickly as possible.

In 1958 he personally opposed the new constitution for Northern Rhodesia, which he felt was giving Africans in the territory too large a voice in politics, and in November of that year he stated, during the course of the Federal election: 'Adult suffrage is a myth, and as long as I am head of the Federal government, it will never be given any consideration whatever.' He might have suspected that such remarks would be regarded by Africans as the embodiment of what they feared Federation to be, an attempt to entrench white settler rule throughout the three territories, and African hostility, especially in Nyasaland, increased. The following year widespread demonstrations by Africans against Federation led to the declaration of a State of Emergency in both Southern Rhodesia and Nyasaland, and Welensky backed to the full all emergency measures taken by the territorial governments concerned. Indeed, he showed himself bitterly resentful of all the criticism against white strong-arm rule made at the time by sections of the British press and subsequently by the Devlin Commission of Inquiry. Unconditionally opposing any discussion of secession by individual territories, he said in an interview with the *Daily Express* in April 1959:

> If the British Socialist Party is returned to power at the next general election and carries out its implied threats of tearing up agreements between the British government and the Federal government, we will go it alone.

In the same month, he stated in the *Central African Examiner:*

> There are some who feel it difficult to believe that men who pay so much lip-service to non-violence can have planned the violence they have in fact planned. These are people who have not realized that

primitive Africans – as has been shown in Kenya and elsewhere – easily turn to violence to settle matters which elsewhere are more naturally dealt with in the framework of law and order.

Continually stressing the importance of the economic aid which Federation had given to an undeveloped territory like Nyasaland, he claimed over and over again that the opposition of Africans to Federation was the result of professional agitators, pure ignorance, or communist conspiracy.

In October 1960 the Advisory Commission on the Review of the Constitution of Rhodesia and Nyasaland, popularly known as the Monckton Commission, issued its report, with the recommendation that the right to secession should be given to individual territories as a last resort after a fixed period of time. Welensky rejected these proposals 'out of hand', and his United Federal Party boycotted the Constitutional Conference on Northern Rhodesia in February 1961. Reports that the British government was considering African parity and even an African majority in the Northern Rhodesia Legislative Council, however, led to a series of attacks by Welensky on any constitutional change that would take government in the territory out of 'responsible hands', and he hinted that it might become necessary for the Federation to declare itself independent and 'go it alone'. Support for Welensky's stand and against the position apparently adopted by the British government led to disputes within the British Conservative Party and an attack in the House of Lords on the Colonial Secretary by the influential Marquis of Salisbury.

On 21 February Iain Macleod, the British Colonial Secretary, announced a plan for two voters' rolls, each to elect fifteen members of the Northern Rhodesia Legislative Council, and an additional fifteen 'national' members to be elected by both voters' rolls together.

African nationalists gave the new proposals grudging acceptance, but Welensky attacked them passionately, and substantial if minority back-bench Conservative support for his objections led to a change of front by the British government, which laid down electoral conditions for the fifteen 'national' seats, making it likely that Welensky's United Federal Party would capture most of them. T. R. M. Creighton of Reading University observed in the *Spectator* of 18 August:

> While the Africans in Nyasaland are to be free to control their own futures, the Africans in Northern Rhodesia are condemned, by a constitutional artifice which is a travesty of democracy, to a continuation of white minority rule – a rule they have made it perfectly clear they will in no circumstances accept. The reason is that they are necessary to a continuation of the Federation which Sir Roy Welensky and the United Federal Party wish to go on ruling, whereas the Nyasalanders are not; and the British government has chosen to abdicate responsibilities and break its solemn promises to its Northern Rhodesian subjects in order to appease Welensky and the British Conservative Party's right wing.

Violence broke out in Northern Rhodesia, and by September the British government appeared to be reconsidering its reconsiderations, while Welensky fulminated against British interference and irresponsibility. In the same month United Nations forces in Katanga clashed with the Tshombe régime, and Sir Roy extended his assaults to the United Nations, with its 'schemes cooked up in New York', and the Indian government, which had 'special fish to fry in that part of the world'. The *Guardian* of 25 September remarked, 'Sir Roy Welensky's excursions into foreign policy have been unhappy.'

On 5 December 1961 fighting between Katanga forces and United Nations troops broke out again, more fiercely than before, and the United Nations Acting Secretary-General, U Thant, officially asked Britain to supply bombs for use by the United Nations Congo Command. Welensky not only refused permission for such bombs to cross Federal territory, but even, a few weeks later, rejected a request from U Thant to allow the stationing of U.N. observers on the Northern Rhodesia-Katanga border, in order to prevent the crossing of men and supplies for the Katanga forces from the Federation. On 11 December 1961, the *Guardian* commented bitterly:

> Sir Roy Welensky says that the British bombs for the United Nations forces in the Congo will not be allowed to cross 'one inch of

Federal soil'. He also says that the United Nations is engaged on 'an operation of wanton and naked aggression against a simple people' . . .

Sir Roy's statement is in keeping with his past revilement of the United Nations. Once again he comes to the verge of declaring an independent foreign policy, although that is not a matter constitutionally for the Federal Government. More serious, however, is his own responsibility for the bloodshed in Katanga. If the U.N. action of August 28 and of mid-September had been carried through, instead of being stopped short by pressure from outside and by lack of air support, the foreign military and para-military personnel would have been removed or neutralised then. The present operation would not have been needed. What is more, the supply of arms and equipment across the Rhodesia-Katanga border, if it has taken place, is a direct breach of the Security Council's resolution of November 24.

The British Government, although it abstained from voting on that resolution, is bound under the Charter to assist in seeing that it is carried out. Its direct responsibility extends to Northern Rhodesia. Is it too frightened of Sir Roy to act there?

On 28 February 1962, the British government announced its finally revised constitution for Northern Rhodesia, changing the minimum qualifications required for election to the 'national' seats in such a way as to make it easier for Africans to win them. The concession was a small one and opened up the possibility of an electoral stalemate. It was apparently large enough, however, to incite Sir Roy Welensky. Flying to London on the same day, he stated at a press conference on his arrival that he would go 'the whole hog' to protect the Federation. Asked to explain his phrase, he replied: 'It is a well-known British description. It means I would take every step necessary to carry out the policy I wish to carry out. To use force if necessary.' His threats embarrassed a number of his supporters, and the substantial backbench rebellion within the Conservative Party predicted by some British newspapers did not materialize. Leaving London on 2 March, Sir Roy complained that he had failed to get a satisfactory reply from British Ministers over their support for the continued existence of the Federation. 'Worse than this,' he said, 'it is becoming more and more apparent that the British government is content that the Northern Rhodesian election should be won by an anti-Federal party or a combination of such parties. If they do not actually wish this result, they seem prepared to let it happen.' On his return to Salisbury, Sir Roy recalled the Federal Assembly and, at its specially summoned session on 6 March, outlined what he described as the 'sordid history' of the relations between the Federation and Britain. On 8 March he announced that he would dissolve the Federal Assembly and call a general election 'for a mandate to prevent the break-up of the Federation'.

In an editorial headlined 'Shadow Boxing', *The Times* of 10 March commented:

> Sir Roy Welensky is not asking – cannot in fact ask – the six million people of the Federation for a mandate 'to remain firm in refusing to accept the break-up of the Federation'. He is merely asking the 100,000 white voters and the few thousand black voters who put him in power some three years ago. There is nothing sibylline about their answer. He may lose votes to his opponents on the right, who are less concerned with the Federation as it is than with preserving white supremacy in the most succulent parts of it. He may lose some of the African members who get in more on white votes than black, yet may turn their coats under the gale of black protest. As, however, there is no real alternative to the United Federal Party for even the unhappiest follower of Sir Roy to vote for (and Sir Edgar Whitehead is only one of many who are unhappy these days) the predictable result is a 'victory for federation' late in April. Does Sir Roy think this has any real meaning?

A powerful beetle-browed personality, determined to maintain at any cost what he calls 'civilized standards' and African nationalist leaders call 'white rule', Welensky is unquestionably the dominant white figure in Central Africa today. His admirers claim that it is only his shrewd and vigorous policy that has kept the whites in Southern Rhodesia from demanding amalgamation with South Africa, and that he has influenced the lifting or lightening of the racial load in many Federal spheres. His critics, who are increasingly drawn from liberal white as well as almost every shade of African opinion, hold that he is personally power-hungry, and that the many years of Federal government in which he has played so crucial a rôle have only removed 'pin-pricks' of discrimination and not by any means most of these, and that for all his stated dedication to ultimate racial 'partnership', his basic allegiance is to perpetual white domination.

In this his most important ally, though one with whom he is reported to be on the uneasiest personal terms, is SIR EDGAR CUTHBERT FREMANTLE WHITEHEAD, Prime Minister of Southern Rhodesia. Born in 1905 at Berlin, where his father was Chancellor at the British Embassy, he was educated at Shrewsbury School and then at University College, Oxford, where he read history. Weak health took him to Southern Rhodesia in 1928, where he entered government service, and from 1930 to 1939 he farmed in the Vamba district, becoming a prominent member of the Umtali District Farmers Association and the Eastern Farmers Federation.

He unsuccessfully contested a parliamentary by-election, but was eventually elected the Member for Umtali North in 1939. After the declaration of war he went to England and joined the Royal Army Service Corps, serving in West Africa and attaining the rank of Lieutenant-Colonel. In 1945 he was appointed High Commissioner for Southern Rhodesia in London, but soon afterwards returned home to become Minister of Finance. A figure of considerable controversy, he stood for a degree of government participation in the economy which disturbed a large number of businessmen in the territory, who were unaccustomed to any form of interference by the State in their activities. He also urged constantly the closer association of the three Central African territories, in order to create a larger internal market. His health failed, however, and his sight became so poor that he had to resign in 1953 and return to his farm. In June 1954 he was knighted.

In 1957 he had recovered his health sufficiently to accept appointment as the first representative of the Federation in Washington, but he did not remain abroad for long. In February 1958 he was recalled to become its leader and so Prime Minister by a special congress of the governing United Federal Party, which wanted a compromise figure – between the liberal former Prime Minister, Garfield Todd, and the right-wing Sir Patrick Fletcher – likely to win the imminent election.

As Prime Minister, Whitehead soon revealed his deep distrust of African demands for political advancement, believing it the job of the European to lead the African in the right direction, whether or not the Africans were willing to be led, and on 26 February 1959, using the Nyasaland disorders as an excuse, he declared a State of Emergency in Southern Rhodesia, though there had been no political disturbances whatsoever in the territory. Proscribing the African National Congress and detaining 495 people, he proposed six draconian laws 'to tighten up security legislation', and though he was subsequently compelled to modify them in response to protests by liberals, academics, and prominent members of the legal profession, he made clear his intention to preserve at all costs the rule of the 2,870,000 Africans in the territory by the 225,000 white settlers.

In 1960 he ordered a police swoop on the offices of the National Democratic Party, the African political organization founded after the banning of the African National Congress, and the arrest of three senior leaders of the movement. Rioting broke out immediately in Salisbury and spread to Bulawayo and other parts of the territory. Property was destroyed and twelve Africans were shot dead – the first killed for more than fifty years in any police action – by security forces and white residents. More than 500 Africans were arrested, including the Vice-President of the multi-racial Central Africa Party, and further legislation was introduced by his government to control African political activities.

In February 1961 the Constitutional Conference on Southern Rhodesia was resumed in Salisbury – it had opened at London in December 1960 and quickly adjourned – to conclude with proposals for a bill of rights, the removal of the 'reserve clauses' which permitted the British government to withhold consent from bills passed by the Southern Rhodesian Legislative Assembly, and the extension of the Assembly's membership from thirty members to sixty-five. Fifty of these, it was proposed, would be elected on the old upper – predominantly white – voters' roll, and fifteen on the lower – predominantly black – roll, so providing for a minimum two-thirds white majority but the presence of African members in the Legislative Assembly for the first time. The opposition Dominion Party vigorously denounced the proposals, while Joshua Nkomo, President of the National Democratic Party, at first seemed to accept them and then flew to London to announce on 17 February his party's complete repudiation of any such constitutional agreement.

The proposals were accordingly put before a referendum of the overwhelmingly white electorate, and the Southern Rhodesian government achieved a sweeping victory in a 76·8 per cent poll, recording 41,949 votes in favour of the proposals to 21,846 against. *The Times*, however, echoed most political observers in reporting, in its issue of 28 July:

> It has been a squalid campaign, from which it will take Southern Rhodesia some time to recover. Posters on every tree have vied with each other in their appeal to every kind of fear and distrust. Perhaps the breach between Europeans can be repaired fairly quickly, but the breach with African political leaders, which was in part artificially created as a reassurance for right-wing Europeans, is potentially more dangerous.

On 9 December 1961, within 48 hours of receiving the Royal Assent to Southern Rhodesia's new constitution, Whitehead permanently banned the National Democratic Party. Then, on 30 January 1962, he announced that the Land Apportionment Act – the basic segregation law which divides the territory's land between Africans and whites, and excludes Africans from ownership of urban property – would be totally repealed in November, provided that his party congress and the electorate approved. As a first step against social and even economic race discrimination, Whitehead's gesture was not without significance. It did not, however, erase the consequences of his ban upon the National Democratic Party. His two moves, within seven weeks of each other, emphasized his individual approach to continued white rule in the territory. He clearly intended to maintain the political power of the white minority by suppressing as far as he could the activities of the African nationalists. The edge of resentment, he appeared to believe, would be blunted by measures of social and economic alleviation. It was no new experiment in modern African history, and it had nowhere succeeded.

Meanwhile the outside world was taking an interest in Southern Rhodesia's affairs. On 23 February, against British objections, the Trusteeship Committee of the U.N. General Assembly decided, by a vote of 56 to 20 with 22 abstentions, that Southern Rhodesia was in effect the concern of the United Nations. It requested the special committee of seventeen, recently established by the Assembly to speed the abolition of colonialism, to 'consider whether the territory of Southern Rhodesia has attained a full measure of self-government'. The General Assembly endorsed the resolution on the same day by 57 votes to 21 with 24 abstentions.

Two days later, Sir Edgar himself arrived in London for consultations with the British government, and it soon became apparent that he was canvassing his own solution to the Federal crisis, certainly distinct from Welensky's effort to retain the Federation in its current shape. On 28 February he addressed the Conservative Members' Commonwealth Affairs Committee at the House of Commons, and was reported to have claimed that the Federation could not continue much longer as it was and that it was accordingly imperative for an alternative structure to be considered. He favoured the creation of a single State which would consist of Southern Rhodesia and a large part of Northern Rhodesia, so echoing the original proposals of the right-wing Dominion Party for an independent Central African State composed of Southern Rhodesia and the Northern Rhodesian 'line of rail'. On 7 March the Commonwealth Correspondent of the *Guardian* reported that Sir Edgar was also considering the possibility of separate independence for Southern Rhodesia, the policy of 'go it alone'. This would secure the territory, in his view, from United Nations intervention and the effects of black dominated governments in Northern Rhodesia and Nyasaland.

The *Economist* of 10 March commented:

> The old concept of a central African alliance has also been revived. This is essentially a white plan under which the 'line of rail', which includes the Copperbelt and most of the European population, would amalgamate with Southern Rhodesia to form an independent, self-governing dominion. The remainder of the federation would be divided into a number of wholly African states linked in a loose alliance with the dominion and sharing common services like railways, posts, and telegraphs. The Monckton commission looked closely at this scheme and rejected it. In the commission's view, to detach the Copperbelt would be a breach of the British government's pledges regarding the protected status of the people of Northern Rhodesia, who would in any case fight the proposal tooth and nail.

A bachelor and a recluse, Sir Edgar has a cold and isolated personality with a quiet decisiveness in stark contrast to the flamboyance of Welensky. Determined to protect white rule in Southern Rhodesia, if necessary through an ever-increasing exercise of force, he has refused to compromise with the demands of African nationalism for majority rule. His rigorous repression of African political dissent inspired for the first time, in 1960, substantial white criticism, both in the large circulation local press and amongst public figures of influence. The most important of these critics, Sir Robert Tredgold, resigned as Chief Justice of the Federation on 1 November 1960 in protest against Southern Rhodesia's Law and Order (Maintenance) Bill, maintaining that it 'outrages almost every basic human right and is an unwarranted invasion by the Executive of the sphere of the Courts'.

While the 225,000 whites in Southern Rhodesia enjoy all legal forms of political power, the almost three million Africans demand with ever greater impatience and bitterness the right to share in the government of their own affairs. The President-General of their major nationalist organization, the new Zimbabwe African Peoples Union (Z.A.P.U.), JOSHUA NKOMO is at the moment the voice and symbol of African political striving in the territory. Born in June 1917 in the Matopa district, to peasant parents of the Matabele people, he was educated at Tjolotjo Government School, at Adams College in Natal, and at the Jan Hofmeyer School of Social Work in Johannesburg, South Africa.

In 1947 he returned to Southern Rhodesia and obtained employment as a social welfare worker on Rhodesia Railways, studying in his spare time and obtaining an external degree in Social Science from the University of South Africa. Then, in 1951, he became General Secretary of the Rhodesia Railways African Employees' Association – which had gradually been built up since the strikes of 1945 into one of the most powerful African organizations in the territory – and by 1952 he had organized twenty-two branches, with 2,600 members.

In the months before the imposition of Federation, he became leader of the African National Congress, and he attempted to bring all African organizations together into an All-African Peoples Convention, though he experienced no success. At this period he was strongly influenced by M.R.A., the Moral Re-Armament movement, and in April 1952 he was taken by Sir Godfrey Huggins, then Prime Minister of the territory, to represent African opinion at the London Conference on Federation. He was, however, bitterly opposed to all the proposals discussed, and he returned to Southern Rhodesia later in the year to protest against any imposition of the Federation of Rhodesia and Nyasaland.

His protests were ignored by the white settlers, however, and when in 1953, in the first Federal elections, he stood against Mike Hove for the African seat of Matabeleland, he was rejected by the predominantly white electorate. With Federation apparently inevitable, he gave up his posts on the railways and became manager of an insurance and auctioneering business in Bulawayo, continuing as President of Congress though the whole movement had clearly lost momentum, and only his own Bulawayo branch really remained active. In September 1957, however, mainly owing to the efforts of George Nyandoro and Robert Chikerema, Congress revived, and Nkomo himself was elected President-General, as an older man, greatly respected, with the reputation of possessing a moderating influence over the more radical of his associates. Congress grew rapidly and soon became the spearhead of African opposition to the Native Land Husbandry Act – a law supposedly aimed at improving African agricultural cultivation by substituting freehold for communal ownership, but which succeeded in forcing thousands of Africans into urban areas, where their employment and occupation rights were stringently restricted.

In December 1958 Nkomo left Southern Rhodesia to represent Congress at the first All-African Peoples Conference in Accra. On 26 February 1959 a State of Emergency was declared in Southern Rhodesia, under which the leaders of Congress were arrested and detained, and on 15 May the Southern Rhodesia Legislature passed the Unlawful Organizations Act, under which Congress itself was banned. Hearing the news while still on his travels, Nkomo became an exile, organizing the London office of Congress and touring round the world in an attempt to rouse public opinion against conditions in the Federation. When the National Democratic Party (N.D.P.) was founded at the beginning of 1960, he became Director of International and External Affairs for the movement and head of its London office. Then, elected President-General in October 1960, he returned to Southern Rhodesia, despite the warrant for his arrest that was still in force, calling just before his departure upon the British government to suspend the colony's constitution and develop democratic rule by force if necessary.

In December 1960 he went to London as N.D.P. delegate to the Federal Review and the Southern Rhodesia Constitutional Conferences, and he led the N.D.P. delegation to the resumed Southern Rhodesia Constitutional Conference at Salisbury in February 1961, which proposed constitutional changes for the territory. Though the N.D.P. delegation did not vote against the proposals at the time – since they seemed to offer some political advance, however slight, to the Africans – Nkomo immediately came under pressure within his party to repudiate any constitutional agreement, and on 17 February he did so. 'A leader', he stated at the time, 'is he who expresses the wishes of his followers. No sane leader can disregard the voice of his people and his supporters.' During the July referendum on the proposals, the N.D.P. called for a general strike, which met with little response, and organized an unofficial referendum in the African areas to coincide with the official one, since the latter was limited almost entirely to the territory's white voters.

The *Economist* commented on 29 July:

> The struggle between Sir Edgar and the N.D.P. President, Mr Joshua Nkomo, seems temporarily to have been won by the Prime Minister. A three-day general strike largely failed because the N.D.P. leaders decided only on the last day to defy the laws openly, and by then their supporters had been dispirited by two disorganized days during which clandestine orders caused only confusion. . . . Less convincing was Sir Edgar's mockery of the N.D.P.'s own referendum for not being made foolproof against multiple voting or incomplete secrecy. More than 300,000 Africans walked miles last Sunday to express their deep discontent with the government by means of their first ballot tin. . . . Sir Edgar proved himself a clever tactician in reaching referendum day without having to arrest the N.D.P. leaders. But any praise for his political strategy should be reserved for a few months. He forced the N.D.P. leaders into open defiance of the law, and both sides have now to face the unpleasant consequences of that collision. The toll of four Africans killed and hundreds arrested is hardly a good advertisement, and the deploying of 24,000 troops and police around the townships and country suggests that the government doubted its own claim to be opposed only by a 'small band of agitators'. The United Nations has fewer troops in the Congo.

Nkomo flew to London bearing the final results of his referendum, in which 467,000 votes were polled against the new constitution, and only 584 in its favour. He told Britain's Commonwealth Secretary: 'We have negotiated passionately. Now we are putting negotiations aside. We shall do everything in our power to break the new constitution.' Moderate at the start of his political career, so that many of the African radicals in the Federation distrusted him, Nkomo had been compelled by white intransigence and the logic of his own dedication into increasing militancy. His leadership, however, still came under challenge for mildness – though not with much effect – when Patrick Matimba and Michael Mawema left the N.D.P. in 1961 to form a rival organization, the Zimbabwe National Party. The new movement then issued a manifesto calling for all the reforms in the book, from universal adult suffrage to repeal of the Land Husbandry Act. The N.D.P., however, had all these demands on its platform already.

On 9 December 1961, while Nkomo was in Dar-es-Salaam for the Tanganyika independence celebrations, Sir Edgar Whitehead permanently banned the N.D.P. under the Unlawful Organizations Act of 1959. Nkomo immediately called on Britain to suspend the constitution of Southern Rhodesia and, denying Southern Rhodesia government allegations of a widespread resort to violence and intimidation by the movement, announced: 'If Whitehead has been intimidated at all, he has been intimidated by the knowledge that we are powerful.'

The *Observer* of 17 December 1961, under the headline – 'Asking For Trouble' – commented shortly: 'Last week's decision to place a permanent ban on the National Democratic Party – Southern Rhodesia's strongest African political party – is a confession of failure to get genuine European-African cooperation. Yet the Monckton Commission insisted that the only hope of saving the federation lay in the achieving of such cooperation.'

On 17 December 1961, eight days after the banning of the N.D.P., Nkomo publicly launched the Zimbabwe African Peoples Union and announced that he had been elected its interim President. On 2 March 1962, in London, on his way to New York in order to give evidence to the United Nations special committee of seventeen investigating the status of Southern Rhodesia, he warned the British government that

> any future decisions made without us and without our consent will not be considered binding upon the African people of my country ... We are demanding our full independence by the end of 1962. The whole of world opinion is now on our side. The pressure of our friends cannot be resisted for long by any government or combination of governments in Rhodesia ... When all three territories are free, with

majority governments elected by full adult franchise as in any normal country, then – and only then – will we consider negotiating about a federation. That is something that we will decide for ourselves. It may have advantages; we are not against federation as a principle; but we are the ones who must decide.

★

One African nationalist leader in the Federation at least has finally accomplished real political power – DR HASTINGS KAMUZU BANDA of Nyasaland. Born in 1902 of peasant parents, in the Kasungu district, he began his education at the Livingstonia Mission. In 1915 he set out to walk from Nyasaland to Lovedale College in the Eastern Cape of South Africa, and on his way he stopped at Hartley near Salisbury, where he worked as an orderly in an African hospital and was appalled by the conditions there.

Helped by an uncle to get to Johannesburg, he found work as a clerk in the gold mines and saved from his wages sufficient for his fare to the United States, where he attended the Wilberforce Academy in Ohio, graduating in 1928. He was offered a place at Chicago University by a professor who was studying Bantu languages, and he took courses in history and political science there, to graduate in 1931. Remembering his experiences at the hospital in Hartley, he decided to study medicine and entered medical college in Nashville, Tennessee, from which he graduated in 1937 as a Doctor of Medicine. Since he could not practise in British territories as a doctor with an American degree, however, he proceeded to Britain and obtained a diploma from Glasgow and from Edinburgh, becoming an Elder of the Church of Scotland during his stay in the second city. He then took a course in tropical medicine at Liverpool, and though qualified to return to Nyasaland and practise as a doctor there, he was unable to do so because his money had run out and the Second World War was at its height.

In 1944 he worked on Tyneside in the Mission for Coloured Seamen, and in the same year he wrote the preface to three prize essays by Nyasa authors, revealing his great interest in tribal traditions. Then from 1945 to 1953 he practised in

London, where he met Nkrumah and other political leaders concerned with the struggle of Africans for self-determination. But he was largely unaffected by the left-wing ideas with which he came into contact. Profoundly conservative, he acquired a great respect for the British monarchy and traditions, a respect that he has retained ever since.

In 1949 representatives of the white settlers in Central Africa met at the Victoria Falls to produce a plan for Federation, and Banda wrote a memorandum in protest – which he published at his own expense in 1951 – together with Harry Nkumbula, President of the Northern Rhodesian African National Congress, who was then studying at the London School of Economics. Attacking conditions in Southern Rhodesia, Banda asked for the continuation of British protection in Nyasaland and became increasingly active in the fight against Federation from his London base. When Federation was nevertheless imposed by the British government in 1953, Banda left London to set up medical practice in Accra. Angered by the action of Wellington Chirwa, a member of the Nyasaland African Congress, in becoming a Federal Member of Parliament, he decided to withdraw himself from the struggle against Federation until the people of Nyasaland showed themselves as militantly opposed to the rule of Salisbury as he was. He took no part in Ghanaian politics and set up medical practice among the poverty stricken Zongo people in Kumasi.

In 1956, Henry Chipembere was elected to the Nyasaland Legislative Council and began corresponding with Banda, requesting him to use his influence to get Congress in Nyasaland to demand the immediate withdrawal of Chirwa and his colleague Kumbikano from the Federal Assembly. Banda wrote a memorandum demanding that Chirwa and Kumbikano immediately resign their Assembly seats, and both were expelled from Congress when they refused. Chipembere was eager that Banda should return to Nyasaland and become the focal point of the Congress struggle against Federation, and early in 1958 Banda at last agreed.

On 13 June he led a delegation to Alan Lennox-Boyd, the

then British Colonial Secretary, to press for a new Nyasaland constitution, and on 6 July he arrived in the territory itself, where he was greeted by a vast crowd and gave an interview to the press in which he said that his mission was 'to work towards self-government by negotiation'. At first welcomed by members of the administration, who considered him a moderate, he soon aroused official hostility by the determination of his stand against Federation. On 1 August, at the Annual General Meeting of Congress, he was elected President-General, and he appointed to assist him young leaders like Chipembere and Kanyama Chiume who had the reputation of extremists. He toured Nyasaland to increase the influence of Congress and drew huge crowds everywhere, finding himself hailed as the political messiah who had come to deliver the people of the territory from Federation.

Meanwhile the British government still delayed constitutional proposals. On 26 October Banda spoke in the Blantyre market place, and when stones were thrown at the cars of Europeans and Asians, much was made of the incident in the local press. Banda had a meeting with various government officials but he achieved no concrete results, and a gradual increase in tension became noticeable all over Nyasaland. In December he attended the first All-African Peoples Conference in Accra, addressing an African audience in Salisbury on his way home. In January 1959, Congress held an emergency meeting in the open air to discuss methods of non-cooperation, and though Banda himself was not present, he was regarded by the administration as having promoted it. Resentment at the continuation of Federation was increasing rapidly throughout the territory, and incidents were reported from all parts of Nyasaland. At last, on 3 March 1959, the Governor declared a State of Emergency. Many Africans, including all the main leaders of Congress, were arrested, while Banda himself was imprisoned in Southern Rhodesia.

On 1 April 1960, after considerable negotiations and mainly owing to the resolution of the new British Colonial Secretary, Iain Macleod, Banda was released and flown to Zomba, where he appealed for calm. He immediately took over the leadership of the Malawi Congress Party – formed as the successor to Congress while he had been in prison – from Orton Chirwa, and then left for Britain and the United States, stating that a constitutional conference was to be held in June and that he would ask for self-government and secession. He also visited Tanganyika and discussed with Julius Nyerere the possibility of an East African Federation which would be extended to include Nyasaland and Northern Rhodesia.

In May he returned to Nyasaland, and in the following month he accepted new constitutional proposals by the British government which provided for an African majority in the Legislative Council. Nyasaland prepared for the elections, with 106,095 voters registered on the lower roll and 4,337 on the upper one. On 28 May 1961 Dr Banda addressed 15,000 people in Zomba and announced the party's candidates for the elections. He vigorously denied recent rumours that he would change his mind about Federation once he took power, and stated:

> If the British government or anyone else still wants this Federation intact here, they must declare another State of Emergency and send me back to Gwelo and then come to kill you all here. We want a government that will represent people of all races. Every European or Asian who is prepared to stay under African government is welcome, but any European or Asian who thinks that he is better than us . . . must pack up and go straight away.

Statements by United Federal Party representatives, given credit by Sir Roy Welensky, that there was widespread intimidation in Nyasaland failed to move the British government, and the general election took place on 16 August without incident. The Malawi victory was overwhelming, sweeping all twenty seats on the lower roll and gaining two of the eight on the upper one, while one independent European, supported by Malawi, also gained election. Only five seats were won by the United Federal Party on the upper roll, and five more were filled by civil servant ministers. Malawi and its supporters accordingly controlled twenty-three seats in a house of thirty-three, and were justified in treating the results as a virtual referendum on secession from the Federation. The *Economist* commented:

> The election campaign in Nyasaland has finally exploded the pretension of the United Federal Party to represent the best interests of all with a formula of 'partnership' which has never been applied, or even believed in. The party's local leaders, who harped on the virtues of federation, have shown themselves not only inept, but hopelessly out of touch with the electorate. They were beaten before they began; and they knew it. Their despairing call for Sir Roy Welensky's personal appearance was ill-advised. It is doubtful if the half-dozen speeches he made, mostly to private audiences, swayed a single vote. He was preaching to the converted few, and his abortive intervention has damaged his prestige.... The Malawi Congress Party has made good its claim to represent the hopes and the clamour of African nationalism in the territory.

The United Federal Party refused to accept one of the five elected seats in the Nyasaland Executive Council and decided to sit in opposition. At the beginning of September it was accordingly announced that the Malawi Congress would occupy all five elected seats, out of a total Executive Council of ten members, with Dr Banda himself as Minister of Natural Resources and Local Government and with his old colleague, Kanyama Chiume, as Minister of Education. The first black government in the Federation had been formed, and one unlikely to accept for long the survival of the Federation itself in anything like its present shape. Sporadic reports in the British press suggested that Dr Banda might be reconsidering his attitude to Federation with his own accession to power and his encounter with the responsibilities of government. But on 13 February 1962, after discussions with Duncan Sandys, British Secretary of State for Commonwealth Relations, in Blantyre, Dr Banda gave a press conference at which he announced that he was determined on secession as soon as possible, and that there were no circumstances in which he would support continued association, 'not even an economic association'. He said that he would meet Sir Roy Welensky provided that there was only one item on the agenda – the secession of Nyasaland from the Federation – and he maintained that, as an independent country, Nyasaland could and would succeed with assistance from abroad.

★

Salisbury, of course, has almost reconciled itself to the loss of Nyasaland. It is Northern Rhodesia, with its rich copper deposits, that must be retained at any cost. For with both Nyasaland and Northern Rhodesia controlled by black governments, the Federation would inevitably disintegrate, or so alter its character as to force the whites of Southern Rhodesia into a choice between political surrender and ultimate domination by the Republic of South Africa.

The key to the climax of African resistance in the Federation is accordingly Northern Rhodesia, while the key to Northern Rhodesia itself is KENNETH KAUNDA, President of the United National Independence Party, to which most of the 2,370,000 Africans and even a few of the 77,000 Europeans in the territory belong. Born in 1924 at a Church of Scotland Mission near Chinsali in the Northern Province – his Nyasa father an ordained priest who had become a teacher, and his mother one of the first African women teachers in the territory – Kaunda was brought up amongst the Bemba people. Educated locally and then at Munali Secondary School, he qualified as a teacher and in 1943 returned to teach at the Chinsali Mission, where he showed a natural aptitude that impressed his associates.

For two years he taught in Tanganyika and then took employment at the Welfare Office in Salisbury. In 1949 he returned to Northern Rhodesia, in order to act as interpreter for Sir Stewart Gore-Brown, a settler leader, and himself joined the African National Congress (A.N.C.) which had been founded the year before. Establishing a Congress branch in Chinsali, he rapidly became the most politically powerful African in the Northern Province, and in 1952 he was made Organizing Secretary of the A.N.C. in the area. Exhibiting a tireless energy, he was soon elected Secretary-General of the whole movement, second only to the President, Harry Nkumbula. He edited the Congress news circular with passion, sharpening opposition to the proposed Federation of Rhodesia and Nyasaland and everywhere spreading the spirit of resistance to white dominion.

When the Federation was imposed none the less, Congress attacks lost their momentum, and the organization turned its attention to assaulting the colour bar by means of demonstrations and boycotts. Kaunda himself spent two months in prison for having been found in possession of banned literature, and he emerged with a determination so to order his life that imprisonment would be no hardship to him; he gave up smoking, and alcohol in any form, and grew more resolutely ascetic. In 1957 he visited England and then undertook a long tour of India, where he was very ill for a time with tuberculosis.

Increasingly dissatisfied with the Congress leadership of Nkumbula, which he considered muddled and ineffectual, he began to consider an open breach. In February 1958, however, he made joint proposals with Nkumbula for a new Northern Rhodesian constitution, demanding universal adult suffrage for the election of Africans to twenty-one or half the seats in the Legislative Council and leaving the other half to seven government officials and fourteen white elected members. He was to write afterwards in *Africa South* (Vol. 3, No. 4, July–Sept. 1959): 'I must confess that I thought our proposals so moderate, it seemed to me difficult for the government to dismiss them. It did not take me long to discover how wrong I was.'

The complex constitution finally adopted, which employed a form of franchise similar to the newly evolved Federal one, cut right across Congress proposals, but Nkumbula refused to make any clear statement on how Congress should react, and criticism of his Presidency flared up throughout the movement. A split was now inevitable, and the Zambia African National Congress was formed by those who were determined to boycott any elections under the new constitution and to pursue a far more dynamic policy than the A.N.C. itself had done in the past. Kaunda was elected leader of the breakaway movement, which included Munukayumbwa Sipalo, Nkumbula's former private secretary, and virtually the whole intellectual wing of the A.N.C.

In December 1958 Kaunda attended the first All-African Peoples Conference in Accra and returned to continue his resistance to the new constitution. In the months before the elections, while the A.N.C. urged its members to register as voters, Zambia organized a boycott.. At last in March 1959 Zambia was banned and its leaders were rusticated. Kaunda himself nearly died from a recurrence of his old complaint during his detention in a remote part of the North West Province, but, convicted on a charge of having held an illegal meeting, he was sent to prison for nine months and there gradually recovered.

Released in January 1960, he immediately became President of the new United National Independence Party, which had been formed to replace the banned Zambia African National Congress, and vigorously canvassed the U.N.I.P. objective of independence by the end of the year. U.N.I.P., however, soon clashed with the administration and, after a series of incidents during which some violence took place, was banned on the Copperbelt. In May Kaunda visited London on his way from the United States, and though he condemned all forms of violence he stressed the growing tension and dangers of the situation in Northern Rhodesia. He saw the British Colonial Secretary, Iain Macleod, but no constitutional changes were proclaimed until October 1960, when the British government announced that Northern Rhodesian constitutional talks would take place concurrently with the Federal Review Conference.

Kaunda visited London in December to represent U.N.I.P. at both the Federal Review Conference and the Northern Rhodesia Constitutional Conference, and on 21 February 1961 Iain Macleod announced in the House of Commons the outlines of a new constitution which seemed likely to provide African parity – or a possible African majority – in the Legislative Council of the territory. Under a three-tier system, by which an upper and lower roll would each elect fifteen members and both rolls together elect a further fifteen 'national' ones, it seemed that U.N.I.P. and its sympathizers would win the fifteen lower-roll seats and most of the 'national' ones. The Colonial Secretary, however, permitted further discussion of detail, Sir Roy Welensky visited London to lobby within the Conservative Party, and in June 1961 the constitution was altered in two significant respects. The Asian community was taken off the upper and lower rolls and provided with a roll of its own to elect one member. Further, a qualifying minimum of support was required from each race for those elected to the 'national' seats, with each candidate required to secure 12½ per cent or 400 votes, whichever was the fewer, of the votes actually cast by each race. Since in any one national constituency there were likely to be some 2,000 European voters and 10,000 African ones, a U.N.I.P. candidate had accordingly to secure 250 European votes out of 2,000, whereas a candidate of Sir Roy Welensky's United Federal Party was required to secure only 400 votes out of 10,000. The changes were severely criticized in British newspapers like the *Guardian*, the *Observer*, and the *Economist*, the last of which claimed: 'There can be no doubt that if the new constitution for Northern Rhodesia weighs against the Africans, it does so because of the drama in Salisbury and the hidden persuasion in London which were put into production before Christmas.' Sir Roy Welensky's bluster, supported by elements within the Conservative Party and a very efficient public relations firm, appeared to have succeeded.

Northern Rhodesian Africans erupted into violence in the Northern and Luapula Provinces, where U.N.I.P. was soon afterwards banned, and Kaunda himself flew to London to appeal for a return to the February principle. On 13 September the British government finally announced that it would consider 'reasonable representations' against its revisions when the Governor of the territory was satisfied that violence had stopped. Then on 9 October Iain Macleod was moved from the Colonial Office to become Leader of the House of Commons and Chairman of the Conservative Party, and the new Colonial Secretary, Mr Reginald Maudling, prepared for a tug of war between white and black forces in the Federation over the Northern Rhodesian constitution.

The *Guardian* of 6 November commented:

This time Sir Roy must not be allowed to impose his veto on the advancement of Africans in the protectorate. One can sympathize with him in the double-dealing he has experienced at the British Government's hands, but not in his ambition to withhold from Africans the dominant voice in the government of their country. U.N.I.P. has asked for the Asians to be restored to the common roll and for the percentage qualification to be reduced. These are reasonable requests. Mr Kaunda is trying to negotiate a fair settlement.

The constitutional revision announced on 28 February 1962 met Kaunda's demands only in part. The numerical alternative to the necessary minimum voting percentage for the 'national' seats was dropped altogether, and the percentage itself reduced from 12½ per cent to 10 per cent. The Asian voters were not, however, restored to the common roll, but left on a separate roll to elect one of the 15 'national' members. On 1 March Kaunda commented that the British government had 'dodged the issue'. The new constitution, he said, 'could only result in a political stalemate because neither the United Federal Party nor ourselves can get the required number of votes. This will not give us the stable government which we need very badly'. Sir John Moffat, leader of the Northern Rhodesia Liberal Party, said that he was astonished that 'such a tremendous constitutional fuss could have produced such a mediocre result', while V. Mistry, an Indian member of the Northern Rhodesia Legislative Council, maintained that the revision would not satisfy the Asian community. The *Guardian* commented on the same day: 'The third draft Constitution for Northern Rhodesia is an exquisite compromise between the first two, and it is likely to produce either a series of invalid elections or another government like the present one – sound, respectable, and representing no one at all.'

On 5 March, after a day-long private session in Lusaka of his party's forty-eight-strong National Council, Kaunda announced that U.N.I.P. rejected the new constitution for Northern Rhodesia as unworkable, but that it would participate in elections, subject to certain conditions. Bans on political parties would have to be lifted, political prisoners would have to be released, and no further political arrests were to be made. To Sir Roy Welensky's dissolution of the Federal Assembly and announcement that he would 'seek a mandate to prevent the break-up of the Federation', Kaunda replied on 8 March: 'Whatever mandate Sir Roy may get, we shall not be bound by it. We shall boycott the election.' On 11 March, before some 20,000 Africans at Kitwe, he said that his party would fight the Northern Rhodesian election on two major issues, secession from the Federation and national self-government. He remained clearly determined to achieve democratic self-rule for the territory.

On his ability to do so soon and escape a show-down of terror, Kaunda's whole political future rests. Possessing enormous prestige far beyond the borders of Northern Rhodesia, he was elected Chairman of the Pan-African Freedom Movement of East, Central, and South Africa (PAFMECSA) at its meeting in Addis Ababa early in February 1962. He accordingly presides over an anti-colonial front which stretches all the way from northern Ethiopia through the African nationalist movements of Southern Africa to the Cape. Recognized as a man of the greatest personal integrity, Kaunda has an unwavering belief in non-violence. Not physically strong, his mild and almost benign manner gives no indication of his considerable intellect and determination. But, like Chief Albert Lutuli in South Africa, with whose personality his own has so much in common, Kaunda is vulnerable to attack by those who believe that only violent resistance can accomplish change against an intransigent white minority. A British government that refuses to give Kaunda what he demands might well find itself forced instead to negotiate with a successor far less likely to follow the road of persistent but peaceful change.

It seems improbable that the Federation can much longer survive the hostility and bitterness it has already engendered among its African peoples. The very word 'Federation' has become an incantation of fear and of fury. But if some slight chance still remains of resurrecting the Central African federal ideal in an entirely new shape, a society of white and black governed in racial peace by the majority of its inhabitants, it is a chance dwindling with every week that the Africans of

Northern Rhodesia are kept from enjoying the major say in the control of their own affairs.

Since its inception in 1953, the Federation has been a limited political company, in which the voting control has in the final analysis been held by its white inhabitants alone. In the Federal Economic Report for 1961, the average annual income of wage-earning Europeans was estimated at £1,209, the average annual income of wage-earning Africans at £87. Eight years after the great experiment in 'partnership' was initiated, in the key-note territory of Southern Rhodesia, 220,000 whites possess forty-one million acres of land, while two and a half million Africans possess forty-four million acres. Yet, even had the Federal government expanded its efforts beyond occasional 'pin-pricks of discrimination', to a dramatic attempt at closing the economic gulf between white and black, it would still have failed. For the rule that it chose to practise – however ornately excused – was the rule of race, the entrenchment of political privilege.

When Britain's colonial record comes, in the coolness that follows the years of conflict, to be assessed, it will be assessed in large measure by the way that British policy has treated the eight million blacks of Central Africa. Britain still has it in her power to rewrite the racial drama that she commissioned when in 1953 she imposed her will upon a hostile and sullen people. If she does not do so, the tragedy that will be staged must be as much her own as that of the many millions whose peaceful advance to self-government she sacrificed to the pressures of settler prejudice.

6 An Association of Nationalisms: East Africa

Within the 224,960 square miles that comprise contemporary Kenya, economically the most advanced and politically the most sophisticated territory in East Africa, 6,264,000 Africans live alongside 174,300 Asians, 67,700 Europeans, and 38,600 Arabs. African nationalism has a longer history there than in Tanganyika, Uganda, or Zanzibar, and has been inescapably dominated by the career of one man – JOMO KENYATTA.

Born of Kikuyu parents at Ichaweri, Kenyatta's early life is unknown, except that under the name of Kamau wa Ngengi he received medical attention and some education from the Church of Scotland Mission in Kikuyu. The year of his birth is uncertain, and he himself, giving evidence at his trial in 1952, stated: 'I do not know when I was born – what date, what month, or what year – I think I am over fifty.' The Deputy Public Prosecutor was a little less imprecise, and in opening the Crown case, stated: 'As far as the Crown knows, and subject to correction as the birth dates of Africans are always rather misty, his date of birth was 1893.' Employed in Nairobi as an inspector of water supplies, he is stated to have been given the nick-name of 'Kenyatta' from the beaded belt (in Kikuyu – *mucibi wa kinyata*) which he then wore.

Active in Nairobi politics from 1920, first as a member of the East African Association and then as General Secretary of the Kikuyu Central Association – the first nationalist movement in the territory, formed by the Kikuyu to win back the land appropriated by Europeans during the first years of white settlement – he published a Kikuyu-language newspaper, *Muigwithania*, and was responsible for formulating the African case against exclusive European occupation of the Kenya Highlands. In 1929 he gave evidence on the land question to the Hilton Young Commission and was a member of the Kikuyu delegation which travelled to Britain in order to petition the government there, above all for permission – which the delegation obtained – for the Kikuyu to found and run their own independent schools.

In 1931 he went to Britain again, and on this occasion stayed for fifteen years. At the beginning he lived at the Quaker College in Woodbrooke, Selly Oak, where he studied English. He then moved to London – where he shared a flat with Paul Robeson, the American Negro singer, and Peter Abrahams, the Coloured South African writer – and from 1933 worked at the School of African and Oriental Studies as an Assistant in Phonetics. In 1936 he took a post-graduate diploma in Anthropology at the London School of Economics under Professor Malinowski, where his fees were paid by the organization now known as the International African Institute, and published *Facing Mount Kenya*, a detailed study of Kikuyu customs, written to show how tribal life had been disrupted by the invasion of the European.

He travelled extensively in Europe and studied for a time in the Soviet Union, where he attended Moscow University. During the Second World War he worked as an agricultural labourer and as a Workers Educational Association lecturer, and in 1943 he married an Englishwoman, Edna Clarke. During this period he campaigned ceaselessly for African rights, and in 1945, with George Padmore, Kwame Nkrumah, and others, he formed the Pan-African Federation and organized in Manchester the fifth Pan-African Congress.

In 1945 he published a pamphlet, *Kenya – Land of Conflict*, warning that if the settlers did not agree to radical reforms in the territory, revolution might be necessary there. On his return to Kenya in 1946, where the Kikuyu Central Association had been proscribed during the war, he found that he himself was regarded as suspect by the administration. In June 1947 he became President of the Kenya African Union (K.A.U.), a new African political movement centred amongst the Kikuyu, and his passionate agitation for African rights, with his powerful oratory and his respect for tribal tradition, enabled him to unite both the Kikuyu elders and the younger élite in the struggle against European domination. At the same time he was careful to associate other tribes with the Kikuyu in the Executive of K.A.U. – Oginga Odinga was able in the late forties to organize considerable support for the movement among the Luo in Nyanza – and K.A.U. membership grew quickly, until it claimed 150,000 adherents in 1951 and attendances of 30,000 or more at meetings which Kenyatta himself addressed.

Appointed Principal of the independent Teachers' Training College soon after his return, Kenyatta had become so powerful by 1948 that influential settlers began to demand his deportation. In 1950 sporadic outbursts of violence were attributed by the administration to a secret society called Mau Mau, which was then proscribed. Kenyatta strongly denied assertions that Mau Mau was acting through the Kenya African Union, and time and again claimed that all he wanted was a programme of justice for the African community. At a meeting in Nyeri in the middle of 1952, he said:

> I want you to know the purpose of K.A.U. It is the biggest purpose the African has. It involves every African in Kenya, and it is their mouthpiece which asks for freedom. K.A.U. is you and you are the K.A.U. If we unite now, each and every one of us, and each tribe to another, we will cause the implementation in this country of that which the European calls democracy. True democracy has no colour distinction. It does not choose between black and white. . . . We are not worried that other races are here with us in our country, but we insist that we are the leaders here, and what we want we insist we get. . . . He who calls us the Mau Mau is not truthful. We do not know this thing Mau Mau . . . K.A.U. is not a fighting union that uses fists and weapons. . . . Remember the old saying that he who is hit with a *rungu* returns, but he who is hit with justice never comes back.

On 22 October 1952 Kenyatta and five other leaders of K.A.U. were detained, to be charged on 18 November with managing Mau Mau. Widespread terrorism swept the country after the arrests, and when the security forces composed of troops from the United Kingdom and loyalist Kikuyu retaliated, the terrorists formed guerrilla bands, and a collision amounting to civil war took place. Kenyatta was tried in the territory and defended by the English counsel, D. N. Pritt, assisted by lawyers from India, Nigeria, and the West Indies. Finally, on 8 April 1953, he was convicted and sentenced to seven years' imprisonment.

Walter Odede, a Luo, took over the Presidency of K.A.U.; but the organization was banned soon afterwards, and Odede, together with several hundred K.A.U. supporters, detained. Open political activity was resumed by the Africans only in 1956 – with the formation of the Nairobi District African National Congress – in preparation for elections to the Legislative Council under the Lyttelton constitution, which gave eight seats to the African community. Under the emergency regulations, African parties could be organized on a district level alone, and after his election for the Nairobi seat, Tom Mboya, then the twenty-six-year-old General Secretary of the Kenya Federation of Labour, formed the People's Convention Party as a Nairobi organization, which rapidly overtook the Nairobi District African National Congress and became a training ground for the younger leadership. In 1958, six more Africans were elected to the Legislative Council under the Lennox-Boyd constitution, and a Constituency Elected Members' Organization was formed – with the support of one European elected member – to express the views of the African and Asian elected members.

In 1958, six months before his sentence was due to end, the African elected members of the Kenya Legislative Council started a campaign for Kenyatta's release, proclaiming that he was still the real leader of the African people. At last, in April 1959, Kenyatta was freed from prison, but indefinitely restricted to Lodwar in the remote Northern Frontier Province. The campaign for his unconditional release mounted, and by the time that the Kenya Constitutional Conference was held at London in January 1960 his continued detention had become a major issue in Kenya politics. In March the Kenya African National Union (K.A.N.U.) was formed, with Kenyatta elected as

President. The Governor of Kenya responded by refusing either to release Kenyatta or to register K.A.N.U. as a legal organization. In the end, K.A.N.U. was registered under the Presidency of James Gichuru, a former President of K.A.U., who proclaimed, however, his personal allegiance to Kenyatta and his pledge to resign the position as soon as Kenyatta was released.

In February 1961, general elections in Kenya gave Africans a majority in the Legislative Council. K.A.N.U. emerged as the strongest party, winning eighteen seats in the Legislative Council to eleven for the opposition Kenya African Democratic Union (K.A.D.U.) and registering 467,472 votes to K.A.D.U.'s 142,580. K.A.N.U. refused to form a government while Kenyatta was detained, and on 2 March 1961 the administration announced that Kenyatta was being removed from Lodwar to Maralal near Nairobi. On 18 March K.A.D.U. agreed to help form a government, but K.A.N.U. continued to make participation conditional upon Kenyatta's release. Then, on 11 April, at Maralal, Kenyatta gave his first press conference since his imprisonment. In the words of *The Times*:

> For three hours he faced questions from more than fifty journalists with a sharpness and agility that many western politicians might envy, dispelling once and for all the illusion that he is an old man who wants nothing better than to spend his last years in peace. . . . He said that Europeans would find a place in the future Kenya provided that they took their places as ordinary citizens, and that farmers would be secure provided that they were farming well. . . . He condemned violence and the oath-taking ceremonies of Mau Mau and implicitly denied his own connexion with the worst aspects of that movement when he said that the Corfield Report, which sought to establish such a connexion, was a 'pack of lies and a one-sided document aimed at one purpose – to crush Kenyatta'.

At the beginning of August the British Colonial Secretary announced in the House of Commons that Kenyatta was to be moved to Kiambu just outside Nairobi and released from restriction in the middle of the month, though he would be disqualified from membership of the Legislative Council, since he had served a prison term of more than two years.

The Kenya African Democratic Union took the credit for the announcement, on the grounds that Kenyatta's release was due to its agreement to form a government, while K.A.N.U. claimed that only its own persistent agitation and refusal to cooperate with the administration had forced the British government's hand. This, however, represented the least of the disputes dividing Kenya's African politicians. K.A.N.U., with its support from the African urban masses and the territory's two largest tribes, the Kikuyu and Luo, was opposed by K.A.D.U. as the proclaimed representative of the smaller pastoral tribes, with their fear of Kikuyu and Luo domination. Though K.A.D.U. itself seemed united, it was manifestly a minority movement, while K.A.N.U. was riven by leadership disputes. Even the February 1961 general elections had failed to unite the party, and Oginga Odinga, with his overwhelming following in Central Nyanza, had openly clashed with Tom Mboya, whose hold over Nairobi proved to be unshakeable.

'Peace talks' started between the K.A.N.U. and K.A.D.U. parliamentary groups at Kenyatta's insistence, and, some weeks after he had begun addressing meetings again, it was clear that Kenyatta's hold over majority African opinion was as strong as ever. By October, however, the gulf separating the two parties seemed unbridgeable; K.A.D.U. demanded a federal constitution for Kenya, based on tribal regionalism, while K.A.N.U. insisted upon a strongly centralized government. On 28 October Kenyatta announced that he had accepted the Presidency of K.A.N.U., and on 6 November he flew to London, at the head of a K.A.N.U. delegation, to demand independence for Kenya at the beginning of February 1962. In an interview with *The Times* on 7 November he claimed that K.A.D.U.'s fear of domination by the Kikuyu and Luo tribes was unfounded. 'We do not think in tribal terms. . . . Our aim is not to select a man because he is black or white or brown but on his capability. . . . We have no room for dictatorship in Kenya. We believe in democratic government.'

Referring in London to attempts made by K.A.D.U. and the Governor of Kenya to keep him out of politics, Kenyatta commented that only a monarch could stand above politics. No leader could enjoy 100 per cent support. 'Does Mr Macmillan hold even fifty per cent of the English people? I am not a demi-god that I should do what other people cannot do.' Certainly Kenyatta seemed to have made a substantial impact on British public opinion, and the African Correspondent of *The Times* cabled from Nairobi on 14 November:

> The Kenya African Democratic Union, the main government party in the Kenya Legislative Council, has a growing fear that it is about to be abandoned by the Colonial Office in favour of the Kenya African National Union.... The good impression made by the rival Kenya African National Union in London, under the leadership of Mr Kenyatta, seems to nullify the value of K.A.D.U.'s public image as the only moderate African party in Kenya. K.A.D.U.'s policy of regionalism has found no favour outside its own ranks, and even within the party has caused dissatisfaction. Several K.A.D.U. members who hold government positions have already had to be warned that they will be dismissed unless they stop inciting their tribal supporters with inflammatory statements.
>
> The K.A.D.U. leaders fear that the British government may become convinced that K.A.N.U. is capable of running an independent Kenya on its own, and may rush Kenya to independence under a K.A.N.U. government, without the sort of regional guarantees that K.A.D.U. wants. To avoid this, they are prepared to hold up Kenya's independence with the threat of civil war and a second Congo. Officials are convinced that much of the K.A.D.U. talk of civil war is bluff, but there remains a worry that the bluff may artificially stir up a violence that the leaders can no longer control.

On 23 November 1961 the British Colonial Secretary, Reginald Maudling, announced in the House of Commons that the constitution of Kenya would be amended to permit those who had served a prison sentence of two years or more to stand for election to the Legislative Council. And on 28 November he announced in Nairobi that a constitutional conference on Kenya's future would open in London on 14 February 1962. Britain's *Financial Times* suggested on 30 November that the Colonial Secretary was considering a date in the middle of 1963 for the independence of the territory.

On 27 December the way was formally cleared for Kenyatta's entry into the Legislative Council when the Governor accepted the resignation of Kariuki Njiri, member for the Fort Hall constituency. The leaders of K.A.D.U. decided not to contest Kenyatta's candidature, and he was returned unopposed for the vacant seat on 12 January 1962. On the following day he entered the Legislative Council for the first time, as Leader of the Opposition.

On 14 February the Kenya Constitutional Conference opened in London, and it early became clear that the K.A.N.U. and K.A.D.U. delegations were dangerously far apart in their ideas of how an independent Kenya should be governed. A fundamental deadlock ensued, which had not been resolved by the middle of March. The *New Statesman* of 2 March commented:

> The K.A.D.U. demand is for a regional system of government which differs little from a form of cantonal federalism. K.A.N.U. wants a unitary government, but is prepared to make concessions in the form of a bill of rights and strong local government.
>
> The situation would be less serious if the internal condition of Kenya were not deteriorating so fast. The original and classic British error was to obstruct the formation of national political parties in Kenya, thereby encouraging tribal and regional loyalties. Now the divisions have become so deep and so charged with fear that compromise is barely possible.

A solution of some sort, however, seemed every day more urgent as strikes and disturbances further shook the stability of Kenya. Compromise suggested a two-chamber parliament for the territory, with an upper house possessing limited powers of revision, but no veto over money bills, and a degree of decentralization somewhere between the demands of K.A.D.U. and those of K.A.N.U. The *Spectator* of 16 February, while recognizing the enormous difficulties in any constitutional settlement for Kenya, had none the less maintained:

> One mistake must not be repeated. The thesis is often put forward that the advance towards independence in Kenya or Central Africa must be slowed down because the Africans are not yet fit for it. But what people can claim to be fit for self-government? The record of

few European countries would stand scrutiny by this test. Self-government must come when the people support nationalist leaders who are ready to grasp it: and if they are not allowed to, there can be only futile bloodshed and anarchy on the Cyprus pattern. To try to slow down constitutional progress in Kenya or the Rhodesias at this stage will be far more dangerous for the Europeans in those countries than to grant independence, or concede African majorities in their legislatures, this year.

*

There are many who believe that an East African Federation of Kenya, Tanganyika, Uganda, and Zanzibar is essential for the economic development and political stability of the individual territories, and to such a federation the British government appears to be giving its increasing encouragement. Were this to be achieved it seems probable that Kenyatta, as the senior nationalist leader in the whole area, would become President. The man most widely considered the potential Prime Minister is Julius Nyerere of Tanganyika, with its 362,000 square miles of territory, 9,099,000 Africans, 87,000 Asians, 25,400 Arabs, and 22,300 Europeans.

Born in 1921 in the Northern Province, son of Chief Burito Nyerere of the small Zanaki tribe, JULIUS NYERERE began his formal education at the age of twelve at Tabora Government School, and then studied from 1943 to 1945 at Makerere, the University College of East Africa in Uganda, where he gained his teacher's diploma. In 1929 the Tanganyika African Association had been founded by a group of British Colonial Officers as a discussion forum for African opinion, but growing African political consciousness gave rise to the demand for an overt nationalist organization, and the Tanganyika African Association became increasingly involved in political activity. Nyerere interested himself in the movement, and while at Makerere he organized a branch of it at the College. A convinced Catholic, he returned from his studies in Uganda to teach at St Mary's Mission School in Tabora.

In 1949 he became the first Tanganyikan student to go to a British University and took his Arts degree at Edinburgh, where he grew interested in the whole problem of colonialism. Though he returned in 1952 to Tanganyika in order to teach, he was already resolved upon a political career and found the Africans in the territory restless but lacking a leader to spearhead their demands. In 1953 he became President of the Tanganyika African Association and deciding that the time had come to form a new political movement, openly committed to the cause of Tanganyika independence, he founded on 7 July 1954 the Tanganyika African National Union (T.A.N.U.), of which he became President.

He set out to organize branches up and down the country and – since Tanganyika was a United Nations Trust Territory under British administration – took the movement's demands to the U.N. itself in 1955. Increasingly opposed by the Tanganyikan government, he became the popular hero of African nationalism throughout the territory. Nominated a member of the Legislative Council, he resigned in December 1957 in protest at 'lack of progress' and stated: 'During the last four months I have made a series of compromises to demonstrate my understanding of the spirit of give and take. . . . I would feel that I am cheating the people, cheating my own organization, if I remain on the Council.'

After much debate, Nyerere decided to accept the 'tripartite' election proposals of September 1958, by which special Asian, European, and African seats were allotted in the Legislative Council but all voting was to be by common electorate. Since the immigrant community in Tanganyika was never large enough safely to challenge the forces of African nationalism, T.A.N.U. was able and anxious to collaborate with those Europeans and Asians of good-will. Supporting and supported by several Europeans and Asian candidates, T.A.N.U. campaigned for independence and the building of a united non-racial democracy in Tanganyika, to emerge from the elections as by far the largest party. Nyerere himself stated constantly that he regarded any immigrant who had made his home in Tanganyika to be as much a Tanganyikan as any Tanganyikan-born African, and his approach unquestionably stilled much of the racial fear that Asians and European settlers might otherwise have had at the prospect of approaching African rule. The thirty newly elected members of the Legislative Council, ten from each race, formed together a single Tanganyika Elected Members' Organization, with Nyerere himself as Chairman, Derek Bryceson, a European, as its Vice-Chairman, and Amir Jamal, an Asian, as Treasurer.

After the elections, Nyerere promoted the slogan '*Uhuru na Kazi*' – 'Freedom and Work', and though he refused to accept a ministry himself, he allowed members of T.A.N.U. to take up posts in the administration. In June 1960 he advocated the establishment of an East African Federation at the Conference of Independent African States in Addis Ababa, and he then announced that he was prepared to postpone complete independence for Tanganyika if by doing so he could further the independence of the other East African territories. In the new Legislative Council elections of August 1960, T.A.N.U. sponsored candidates were returned unopposed to fifty-eight of the seventy-one seats – ten European, eleven Asian, and fifty 'open' – and won election in all but one of the remainder, where a T.A.N.U. member objected to the official Candidate and stood successfully against him. In October the territory gained responsible self-government, and Julius Nyerere became Chief Minister. Derek Bryceson was made Minister of Health and Labour, and Amir Jamal, Minister of Communications, Power, and Works. The non-racialism of the Cabinet was further confirmed by the retention of Sir Ernest Vasey, another European, as Minister of Finance.

Nyerere has always been a determined Pan-Africanist, believing in the need for all African States to assist in emancipating those territories still under white settler or colonial rule, and he was amongst the first African leaders to support the economic boycott of South African goods. On 5 March 1961 he cabled to the London *Observer* an article on the Commonwealth in which he stated: 'We believe that the principles of the Commonwealth would be betrayed by an affirmative answer to South Africa's readmission as a Republic. Inevitably, therefore, we are forced to say that to vote South Africa in is to vote us out.' There can be little doubt that his intervention was material in the proceedings at the Conference of Commonwealth Prime Ministers which began on 7 March and which led to South Africa's withdrawal of her application to remain a member of the Commonwealth after she became a Republic at the end of May.

The constitutional conference on Tanganyika's future opened on Monday, 21 March 1961, in Dar-es-Salaam, under the Chairmanship of Britain's Colonial Secretary, Iain Macleod. Two days later the Colonial Secretary announced that Tanganyika would have full self-government from 1 May, with Nyerere assuming the office of Prime Minister and presiding over cabinet meetings instead of the Governor, while on 28 December the Governor's remaining powers over defence and external affairs would be relinquished, and Tanganyika would become a fully independent state. Broadcasting to the nation at the beginning of April, Nyerere carefully outlined the difficulties of independence and stated: 'Self-government is an expensive business, and there is no one to pay the cost but ourselves.'

The *Guardian*, commenting on the constitutional change, emphasized the poverty of Tanganyika, with its average annual income of less than £20 a head. 'She has escaped the problems which large-scale European settlement has brought to her neighbours, but she has missed the corresponding economic benefits too.' Tanganyika's poverty, however, did not prevent Nyerere's government from stopping the supply of labour for the Rand gold mines as a protest against South Africa's racial policy, even though this decision also put a stop to an annual income of nearly £500,000 which the labour scheme had been bringing into the country. The decision had only been taken, as the Minister of Labour stated, 'after considerable heart-searching'.

Tanganyika on the path to independence presented to observers a picture of inner calm, its politics controlled by an undisputed national leader whose standing with Africans, Asians, and whites was alike high. All the while, however, tensions were developing within T.A.N.U. itself, as was inevitable in the absence of any significant outside opposition.

The *African Mail* of 10 October 1961 reported a clash between the T.A.N.U. leadership and Ksanga Tumbo, General Secretary of the Tanganyika African Railway Union. 'If the government will not see to it that Africans get better posts, then I will collide with the government,' Tumbo had said. He had angrily accused the railway administration of reserving the best jobs for Asians and Europeans, and had claimed: 'If you visit the railway head offices in Dar-es-Salaam, you can think you are in Bombay or London.' Rumours persisted that Tumbo planned to form an opposition party to T.A.N.U., but this he himself denied, and there seemed little support in the country for any such move.

Tumbo had support, however, within T.A.N.U. itself, on whose ticket he sat in the National Assembly.

In the same month, the Nyerere Cabinet clashed with many of the T.A.N.U. back benchers in the Assembly over the Citizenship Bill, which would enable a large number of non-Africans in Tanganyika to become citizens, either – for persons from other Commonwealth countries – by registration, or – for those from countries outside the Commonwealth – by naturalization. A growing section of T.A.N.U., disturbed by the slowness with which Africans were acquiring senior posts in the civil service, and embittered by the degree of control which the Asian and European community still possessed over the country's commercial life, wanted the leadership to place less emphasis on non-racialism and more on African advance.

Rashidi Mfaume Kawawa, then President of the Tanganyika Federation of Labour, soon to be Minister without Portfolio and suddenly successor to Julius Nyerere as Prime Minister, had written in *Africa South* (Volume 5, No. 1, October–December 1960):

> The demand for Africanization is made by the black people and means a replacement by them of those of different origin. Despite the wider meaning that the term African has acquired today, the blacks are still at the bottom of every ladder and identify themselves completely and practically with the struggle for change. To ask the indigenous Africans to forget the agony of their past is to ask them to ignore the lesson that their experience has taught them. Asians and Europeans

are crying in Tanganyika today for non-racial parties, but just how practical is this? Those non-racial political parties which have been formed in Tanganyika have never succeeded, for they never aimed at emancipating the African, but only at deluding him into satisfaction with the lowest rung. It is the experience of the present that will constitute African reaction in the future; and the place that the Asian and the European will build for themselves in Africa will be governed by the degree of sacrifice they are prepared to make in the cause of a life in joint advancement and dedication with and amongst the Africans.

The clash – it was widely rumoured – was more than one between wings of the Tanganyika African National Union. It was also one over where ultimate authority for government policy should lie – with the T.A.N.U. National Executive or with the Cabinet. Julius Nyerere upheld the ultimate authority of Cabinet decisions, while a powerful group within the National Executive claimed that the party itself should be the final arbiter of government policy. It was the party on which the task would fall of harnessing popular energy for economic advance, the party itself which represented the aspirations of the Tanganyika masses.

On 11 December 1961 Prince Philip opened the first parliament of an independent Tanganyika and outlined, in the Speech from the Throne, the three principles on which the Nyerere government intended to base its foreign policy. They were to be: regard for the United Nations Charter, the promotion of movements towards African unity, and the development of Commonwealth links – in that order. Internally, a three-year development plan would be promoted 'with energy and with flexibility'; 'old fashioned Native Authority Councils' would be converted into 'modern and effective local authorities'; educational facilities would be improved, with the particular expansion of secondary and university education; and Africanization of the civil service would be pursued 'at the greatest rate compatible with the maintenance of a sound standard in all fields'.

Relations between the T.A.N.U. leadership and several strong trade unions continued to deteriorate, and with the independence celebrations over, rumours circulated that Ksanga Tumbo had openly threatened to start a new party. On 16 December the 120-strong T.A.N.U. National Executive was summoned into session and suddenly, on 22 January, Julius Nyerere resigned as Prime Minister. In a statement, he announced:

> I have taken this action and have won the support of my colleagues after a long debate which has gone on for days because of our firm belief that this is the best way for achieving our new objective – the creation of a country in which the people take a full and active part in the fight against poverty, ignorance and disease.
>
> To achieve this it is necessary to have an able elected government which has the full support and cooperation of the people. This we have had and will have. It is also necessary to have a strong political organization, active in every village, which acts like a two-way all-weather road along which the purposes, plans, and problems of the government can travel to the people and at the same time the ideas, desires, and misunderstandings of the people can travel direct to the government. This is the job of the new T.A.N.U.
>
> These two needs can best be served by the government being carried on by a very able set of Ministers in whom I have full confidence, while I myself devote my full time to the work of T.A.N.U.
>
> Through these means cooperation between the government and the political organization can for the present best be secured, and their common plans and desires more quickly and more effectively carried out.

Sir Ernest Vasey, Minister of Finance, resigned at the same time, and Nyerere explained that Sir Ernest did not qualify to become a Tanganyika citizen under the Citizenship Act. 'Though I have full confidence in his loyalty and devotion to this country, it is not appropriate that any non-citizen should be a member of the Cabinet.

'I have therefore asked him to make his knowledge and experience available to the new government by becoming the government adviser on finance and economic development. He has agreed to do this.'

Nyerere affirmed: 'In conclusion I want to say definitely and categorically that the policy of the government has not changed either internally or externally. The changes I have announced are a reflection of our unity and of our determination to give every Tanganyika citizen a full opportunity to take part in the struggle which confronts us.'

Comment on the resignation reflected general British shock, and the first leader in *The Times* was typical. 'What may happen to Tanganyika if Mr Nyerere does not keep control can only occasion the gravest misgivings. African talent is desperately thin on the ground; few African countries can less afford to bully or frighten expatriates and capital away. Extremism in foreign policy, furthermore, besides injuring a very weak economy, would worsen an already difficult outlook for East Africa as a whole.'

RASHIDI MFAUME KAWAWA was born in 1928 in the Songea District of Tanganyika, his father a Mngoni game-ranger, and he was educated first at Dar-es-Salaam Junior Secondary School and then at the Government Secondary School in Tabora.

Joining the Tanganyikan Government Social Development Department as a film assistant, he became President of the Tanganyika African Civil Servants Association. In 1955 he resigned his job, and he began to build up the trade union movement, forming the Tanganyika Federation of Labour and becoming first its General Secretary and then its President, as well as a member of the Central Committee of the Tanganyika African National Union. In 1956 he attended a trade union course in London and in the 1958–9 elections won a seat in the Tanganyika Legislative Council for Dar-es-Salaam.

In August 1960 he was re-elected to the Tanganyika Legislative Council for the Southern Province constituency and became Minister of Local Government. Able and efficient, he ran the Tanganyika Federation of Labour in close association with T.A.N.U., and at the end of April 1961 he was appointed Minister without Portfolio to assist the Prime Minister, a promotion which led to his general recognition as Nyerere's deputy.

There seems little doubt that Nyerere's decision to resign the

Premiership was his own and not one forced upon him by the T.A.N.U. National Executive. Courageous and determined in the pursuit of non-racialism, he is amongst the wisest political leaders in Africa, able to see a situation from the outside and take a decisive stand after calm consideration. An electric personality with an infectiously warm manner, he has already spread his influence far beyond the borders of Tanganyika, and in Tanganyika itself he is without question the dominant political figure. Had the break with the T.A.N.U. National Executive been anything like complete, he would certainly have resigned the Presidency of T.A.N.U. as well as the Premiership – to take his future over the heads of the National Executive to the country itself – and he would probably have won. Kawawa, too, is a long-time friend of his and firmly in his confidence; it is unlikely that he would have agreed to accept the Premiership had it meant the driving of Nyerere into the political wilderness.

Nyerere's decision, indeed, was the only one possible for him in the circumstances. The independence of Tanganyika constitutes no more than a prelude to a vast and prolonged struggle for economic advance. For such advance, unity of aspiration must be forged, and this can only be done within the Tanganyika African National Union itself. Nyerere clearly believed that it was impossible to permit any growth in the breach between the government and party, and that he would be better advised to carry his policy to the country through the party itself than through government directives. Whatever observers abroad may think, Tanganyika is not controlled by a man as much as by a movement. And it is the future shape of the movement that will dictate the future shape of Tanganyika.

Concluding his own comments on Nyerere's resignation, Clyde Sanger wrote in the *Guardian* of 23 January:

> Throughout the press conference Mr Nyerere behaved as national leader with the new Prime Minister sitting quietly beside him. The truth (without any offence intended to Mr Kawawa, who is a steadfast lieutenant and a most capable administrator) is that Mr Nyerere will in the eyes of nearly everyone continue to be the leader of Tanganyika whatever political title he chooses to hold.

On 9 February, Kawawa strongly condemned the threats of strike action made by African railway workers, and accused the Tanganyika African Railway Union of 'endeavouring to disrupt the country's racial harmony'. He appeared to be taking precisely the same line against demands for over-rapid Africanization and agitation for a rise in industrial wages as Nyerere had done. On 13 February the Tanganyika government announced that it would introduce measures to convert all land titles in Tanganyika from freehold to leasehold, so that it might demand the development of land before permitting any transfer to new ownership. The government envisaged the granting of 99-year leases, with development conditions attached, at nominal rents. For land already developed, the conditions would merely require that such development be maintained. Current owners of undeveloped freehold could dispose of their land, when converted to leasehold, if they wished, but subsequent owners would not be permitted to sell their holdings until the development conditions had been fulfilled. 'Freehold is an alien conception to Africans, associated in their minds with exploitation and privilege,' Mr T. S. Tewa, Minister for Lands, Forests, and Wild Life, maintained. On 15 February the Tanganyika parliament passed a resolution requesting the government to 'draft such amendments to the constitution as may be necessary to provide that Tanganyika becomes a Republic within the Commonwealth as soon as possible'.

*

Where the problems of Tanganyika are those of economic backwardness, and Kenya's political future is shadowed both by tribal rivalry and the status of a large white community, Uganda – with its 6,590,000 Africans, 76,200 Asians, and 11,700 Europeans living in an area of 93,981 square miles – faces the clash between traditionalist rule and modern nationalism. This clash is embodied in the career of EDWARD FREDERICK MUTESA II, KABAKA OF BUGANDA.

Ever since Dr Nkrumah suppressed the power of the Ashanti Confederacy in the name of national unity, African Kings and

Chiefs have feared for their thrones. The Baganda, though possessing only twenty-eight per cent of Uganda's African population, retain perhaps the richest lands. Buganda itself produces some ninety per cent of the colony's coffee, accounting for almost half of Uganda's revenue from foreign trade, and its loyalty to the Kabaka, re-enforced by his battle with British authority, threatens the whole existence of an independent Uganda, capable of associating itself with its neighbours, in an East African Federation.

Born in November 1924, son of the reigning Kabaka and Lady Irene Drusila Namaganda, Mutesa II was sent to King's College, Budo, for his early education. In 1939, on the death of his father, he was chosen to be Kabaka by the principal political leaders of Buganda – reportedly on the grounds that he was believed to be the only son born in Christian wedlock – with three regents appointed to run the country until he was eighteen. In 1943 he came of age, was formally installed as Kabaka, and went to study at Makerere, the University College of East Africa.

In 1945 he went to Magdalene College, Cambridge, for two years in order to read History, Law, and Economics, and in 1947 became an Honorary Captain in the Grenadier Guards. In 1948 he married – in the face of strong opposition, since the alliance cut across all tribal tradition – Damale Kissosonkole, and in 1949 serious disturbances broke out in Buganda, partly against the Kabaka himself and partly against the Protectorate government, with demonstrating groups surrounding the Kabaka's palace. The hostility soon died down, however, and in 1952 Sir Andrew Cohen, the new Governor of Uganda, agreed with the Kabaka upon a series of constitutional reforms for Buganda, proclaimed in a joint memorandum early in 1953. But the new accord between the representative of Britain and the ruler of Buganda was not to last for long.

On 30 June 1953, Oliver Lyttelton, Britain's Secretary of State for the Colonies, hinted in a speech to the East African Association that he was thinking in terms of an East African federation. This was immediately reported in the local press of East Africa, and the Kabaka returned to Buganda from a holiday in Europe to find widespread consternation among his Ministers. The imposition of the Federation of Rhodesia and Nyasaland, despite the almost unanimous hostility of the African population in the three territories involved, had made a profound impression upon African opinion in East Africa. The Kabaka therefore immediately demanded that Buganda be transferred to Foreign Office control and granted independence within a stated period. He refused to cooperate with British government policy in developing Uganda as a unitary state and refused also to nominate Baganda Ministers to the Legislative Council. Remaining resolute throughout all negotiations, he was exiled on 30 October to London.

The whole of Buganda, including those nationalist leaders who had been opposing him, rallied to his support, while the Nalinya, his sister, fell dead at the moment she heard the news of his banishment. The Governor established a Regency and twice declared a state of emergency, but disturbances continued. Meanwhile the Kabaka himself lived in London, on a grant of £8,000 a year tax free from the British government. After prolonged negotiations he was finally permitted to return, on condition that he accepted reforms which would make him more of a constitutional monarch, and on 17 October 1955 he entered Buganda in triumph, with his position among his people incalculably strengthened.

With his influence much greater than it had been in 1949, it became increasingly difficult for any nationalist leader to oppose him within Buganda itself. Much disturbed by the example of what had happened in Ghana to traditionalist rulers once the nationalists had taken control of the country, he ceaselessly and strenuously opposed all democratization, demanding the withdrawal of Buganda from the commitments he had made on his return and pressing for the establishment of the territory as a separate state. In June 1960 his government called for the end of British protection and announced that Buganda would not participate in Uganda-wide elections unless acceptable constitutional arrangements were agreed beforehand. In August he visited London for constitutional talks with the Colonial Secretary and in October the Lukiko, the Parliament of Buganda, resolved upon secession.

The Baganda widely boycotted the general elections of March 1961, and the victorious Democratic Party of Benedicto Kiwanuka, himself a Buganda, won fifteen contested seats in the area with only 11,880 votes, as well as collecting five uncontested constituencies. The Democratic Party was therefore able to emerge with forty-four out of eighty-two seats, to thirty-five for its rival, the Uganda People's Congress, though receiving only 407,416 out of 983,718 votes, or 80,918 less than the U.P.C. The Buganda Lukiko acted vigorously to show its antagonism towards the new Legislative Council and claimed that the British had no right to impose any constitution on the Baganda, since they were 'neither British subjects or British citizens, and owe allegiance to the Queen only through the Kabaka'.

A special Relationships Commission, appointed by the British government, recommended in 1961 that Uganda should be a single democratic state with a strong government at the centre, but that Buganda should enjoy a federal relationship with it, retaining its Kabaka, his government and civil service, and his authority over traditional matters. In September a Constitutional Conference of Uganda leaders met in London, while the Colonial Secretary had concurrent talks with the Kabaka and other hereditary rulers in the territory. At one stage the conference seemed certain to fail, but eventually it concluded in accord between the Buganda delegates and the British government, with acquiescence from the representatives of the territory's political parties.

The draft agreement provided a federal relationship for Buganda, which was to be represented by twenty-one of the eighty-two elected members in the Uganda National Assembly. The Buganda Lukiko was itself to have sixty-eight members directly elected, by secret ballot and universal adult suffrage, six nominees of the Kabaka, twenty Saza chiefs, and six Ministers elected by the Lukiko, and was itself to decide whether Buganda's representatives in the National Assembly were to be directly elected or chosen by the Lukiko sitting as an electoral college.

The draft agreement further reflected the recommendations of the Relationships Commission by establishing a Buganda High Court, possessing concurrent jurisdiction with the Uganda High Court 'save in constitutional matters', by giving control over urban local government for the smaller towns of Buganda to the Lukiko, and by permitting a Buganda police force under the overall command of the Inspector-General of Police. On 26 October the Buganda Lukiko decided by seventy-seven votes to nil, with two abstentions, to accept the London agreement, and on 31 October the Kabaka at last put his signature to the accord. *The Times* reported:

> The text of the agreement now available shows it to be a skilful balance of concessions to Buganda on matters of detail, with firm safeguards for the powers of the central government in essentials. Buganda Ministers will no longer require to be approved by the central government before taking office and some important services hitherto controlled by the central government, such as senior secondary schools and urban medical services, are transferred to Buganda. But the Buganda Legislature will have limited scope, nearly all important matters in home affairs being on the concurrent list where the national Legislature will have overriding powers.
>
> In finance, provision is made to increase Buganda's revenue, but this will come mainly from central government grants which can be revoked in case of maladministration.

BENEDICTO KAGIMU MUGUMBA KIWANUKA, present Prime Minister of Uganda, was born in May 1922 at Kisabwa in the Masaka District of Buganda, the son of a minor but wealthy Chief. Educated at Roman Catholic missions to junior secondary standard, he served from 1942 to 1946 in the African Pioneer Corps, spending one year in Kenya, three years in Egypt and Palestine, and reaching the rank of sergeant-major.

In April 1946 he returned to Uganda and in November joined the Judicial Department as a clerk and interpreter. Wishing, however, to take Law, he left in 1950 for a school in Basutoland, where he studied Latin and matriculated in the following year. From 1952 to 1956 he studied Law at London University, and, called to the Bar, returned to Buganda to set up practice.

In September 1958 he became President of the Catholic-supported Democratic Party, which had been formed in 1956 by a group dissatisfied with the policy of the then powerful Uganda National Congress. Under his leadership the party became extremely active and won a reputation for good organization. His own policy, which he frequently stated, was to win independence first and then decide, together with the properly representative African authorities, the system under which the country should be governed. At last, in September 1959, he gave up his practice altogether, in order to devote himself full-time to politics.

In 1960 he openly clashed with the Kabaka of Buganda who, in an attempt to force the British government to accept a federal system for Uganda, ordered his people not to register for the March 1961 elections. The Democratic Party, however, emerged from the national elections as the strongest force, largely as a result of the Baganda boycott, and Kiwanuka himself was elected for North East Masaka in Buganda, to become Minister without Portfolio, Leader of the Legislative Council, and then Chief Minister. With the constitutional accord in London, the British government agreed to full internal self-government for the colony on 1 March 1962 and full independence on 8 October of the same year. Kiwanuka himself withdrew from the conference briefly in protest against what he called the 'undemocratic' option given to the Buganda Lukiko, by which it could, if it wished, choose the twenty-one Buganda members of the National Assembly itself by sitting as an electoral college. He was eventually reassured, however, by a provision for nine specially elected members – chosen by the eighty-two other elected members – in the National Assembly, so allowing his own co-option were he to lose his seat in Buganda. Able and efficient, Kiwanuka is now faced by a dynamic Uganda People's Congress opposition, led by Milton Obote, and the hostility of the Kabaka himself. He will need all his talents to survive in power.

The Buganda elections of 22 February 1962, to the sixty-eight elected seats in the Lukiko, resulted in a sweeping victory for the Kabaka Yekka (Kabaka Only) party, formed in November 1961 and allied with the Uganda People's Congress. The Democratic Party succeeded in winning only three seats and so seemed unlikely to receive any of the twenty-one Buganda seats in the National Assembly, should the Lukiko – as the Kabaka Yekka demanded – decide to fill them as an electoral college. On the other hand, the close alliance between the traditionalist Kabaka Yekka and the Uganda People's Congress could be expected to erode the influence of the U.P.C. as a radical party in the rest of Uganda.

On 1 March Uganda received internal self-government, and an enthusiastic crowd watched Kiwanuka sworn in as the first Prime Minister of the territory – with a Cabinet of twelve Africans, one European, and one Indian – at a ceremony on the steps of the National Assembly building in Kampala. The public holiday was not observed by the Buganda government, however, which celebrated instead the opening on the same day of the new Buganda High Court by the Kabaka. The kingdoms of Toro, Ankole, and Bunyoro, and the Paramount Chieftaincy of Busoga also boycotted the ceremony in protest at their failure to achieve a federal status similar to Buganda's. On 8 March the Uganda National Assembly called upon the British Colonial Secretary to open negotiations with Toro, Ankole, Bunyoro, and Busoga over the grant of full federal status to them before the general elections in April.

★

Layer upon layer, new peoples have for centuries been borne across the seas and put down upon the islands of Zanzibar. The latest eruption is partly due to fossilized hatreds built up when Arab masters imported African slaves. Intermarriage has created a small population of Zanzibaris among whom it is impossible to tell Arab from Shirazi, or Comorian from central African. For the rest, it is easy enough to distinguish between the 40,000 Arabs who own the land, the few thousand Asians who run the businesses, and the 300,000 Africans who do the work and most of the politics. This would leave room enough for antagonisms even without the new topsoil of African nationalism which the mid-century has laid down.

So the *Economist* wrote at the time of the June 1961 race riots in Zanzibar, the smallest of the four East African territories under British administration, a mere 1,020 square miles in area. SHEIKH ALI MUHSIN, leader of the dominant Zanzibar Nationalist Party (Z.N.P.), was born in 1919 on the island, his family of Arab origin but resident for three generations there. His father a religious leader, he himself went to Makerere, the University College of East Africa in Uganda, where he studied agriculture.

Becoming active in politics, he adopted an extreme anti-colonial position and returned to Zanzibar, joining the staff of the Teacher Training College and continuing with political work. In 1951 he was nominated a member of the Legislative Council and headed the opposition to the administration with widespread backing. In 1955 he led the Arab representatives in boycotting the Legislative Council altogether as a protest against proposals for communal elections, advocating instead a common electoral roll and himself visiting Britain in order to make vigorous representations to the Colonial Secretary.

In 1956 he formed the Zanzibar Nationalist Party as a radical movement – mainly among the youth and the intellectuals – against colonialism, and he became, together with his following, increasingly unpopular with the administration. In July 1957 elections were held, on a basis of qualified adult male suffrage, to six out of the twelve unofficial seats in the Legislative Council. The contests were all fought on distinct racial lines and the Z.N.P. was heavily defeated, while the Afro-Shirazi Party (A.S.P.) under Abeid Karume, supported by the island's African majority, won five seats. Ali Muhsin himself was overwhelmingly defeated by Karume, but was again nominated by the Governor to the Legislative Council.

In 1958, however, he resigned from both the Legislative Council and the island's Executive Council to devote himself full-time to the Z.N.P. and began energetically to build what soon became the most efficient party organization in Zanzibar. Travelling widely throughout Africa, he solicited support at various Pan-African conferences and persistently demanded full and immediate independence for the island. In July 1960, Sir Hilary Blood, appointed by the British government as Constitutional Adviser, recommended that twenty-one out of the twenty-nine members in a new Zanzibar Legislative Council should be elected on the basis of universal adult suffrage, and that a ministerial system under a local Chief Minister should be established immediately after such elections. In the elections of January 1961 that accordingly followed, to an increased number of twenty-two elected seats, the Z.N.P. won nine, the A.S.P. ten, and the Zanzibar and Pemba People's Party (Z.P.P.P.) three, while Ali Muhsin himself was comfortably elected. Since the Z.P.P.P. elected members, however, divided into two for the Z.N.P. and one in support of an A.S.P. administration, no majority government could be formed and new elections were called for June that year, to a total of twenty-three seats instead of twenty-two.

Nationalist and left-wing in outlook, on the friendliest terms with President Nasser of the United Arab Republic and rumoured to have established contact with the government of the People's Republic of China, Ali Muhsin and the Z.N.P. were increasingly accused of seeking Arab domination, though it was clear that the party was projecting its appeal – with increasing success – to the total electorate, some four-fifths African. Leaders of the Tanganyika African National Union gave open support to the Afro-Shirazi Party – although Julius Nyerere himself at no time intervened – and T.A.N.U.'s woman leader, Bibi Titi Mohammed, spoke on its platforms. Despite interference from the mainland, however, the Z.N.P. emerged from the elections of 1 June with ten seats, the Zanzibar and Pemba People's Party with three, and the Afro-Shirazi Party with ten. The results were followed by several days of severe rioting, during which scores of islanders were killed and hundreds injured, and five Companies of the King's African Rifles were sent into Zanzibar to keep the peace. The Z.N.P. joined with the Z.P.P.P. to form the government, Muhammad Shamte Hamadi, the leader of the Z.P.P.P., became Chief Minister, and the Z.N.P. received the remaining four of the five unofficial Executive

Council seats. Ali Muhsin himself became Minister of Education and Welfare.

*

The race rioting and the intervention of the Tanganyika African National Union on behalf of the unsuccessful Afro-Shirazi Party have undoubtedly increased tensions within Zanzibar itself. At the same time the tensions have made it more than ever necessary for Zanzibar to enter an East African federation, in order to sink local differences in a common democratic and fast developing society of almost twenty-three million people.

An East African federation seems, indeed, imperative, not only for rapid economic advance, but to avoid clashes amongst the territories themselves. Most urgent of the potential collisions is that between Zanzibar and Kenya over the latter's coastal strip.

Since 1895 Britain has leased a strip of Indian Ocean coast land, ten miles deep and 300 miles long, from the Sultan of Zanzibar, for an annual rental of £11,000. It stretches all the way from Vanga on the Tanganyika border to Chiamboni on the frontier of the Somali Republic, and includes the only sea port that either Kenya or Uganda possesses – Mombasa. Kenya African leaders insist that the coastal strip is an integral part of Kenya, 'like the hem of a dress', and Kenyatta himself has said that there can be no question of ceding it. A number of Arabs in the strip, however, have been demanding coastal autonomy, though they claim that they would welcome an East African federation with the coastal strip as a constituent and Mombasa itself as the federal capital.

There is certainly a desire for unity amongst the elected political leaders of Kenya, Tanganyika, and Uganda. They agreed at their London Conference in the middle of 1961 to build, on the foundations of the old East African High Commission, a new structure, the Common Services Organization, which would effectively transfer power from the British Colonial Office to representative ministers from the three territories. The new organization would be run by a triumvirate of the three 'principal elected ministers', Tanganyika's Prime Minister,

Uganda's Chief Minister, and Kenya's Leader of Government Business. Services formerly provided by the High Commission would be run by four committees of three ministers apiece, one from each territory, while it was decided to establish a Central Legislative Assembly, composed of the twelve ministers running the Common Services together with nine members from each territory, elected by the territorial legislatures, and two officials. Zanzibar, it was resolved, would receive services on an Agency basis, but there seems little doubt that Zanzibar too would inevitably be drawn into a firmly established and profitable East African federation.

A more spectacular and not unlikely possibility is the association of an independent Nyasaland – and even, should the Federation of Rhodesia and Nyasaland break up, an independent Northern Rhodesia – with the four territories of East Africa in one vast East and Central African federation, covering an enormous area and comprising a population of twenty-eight million people.

Nationalist leaders in the area have since September 1958 met annually as members of PAFMECA, the Pan-African Freedom Movement of East and Central Africa, while there have been the closest contacts between East African leaders and both Dr Banda from Nyasaland and Kenneth Kaunda from Northern Rhodesia. It is a cliché of Pan-Africanism that the continent's modern national boundaries are imperial creations, often gratuitously drawn. But the passion for African unity is often belittled even by those who admit that territorial frontiers are almost entirely artificial. Pan-Africanists reply that they have had little time in which to test the validity of their thesis. East Africa, if not the whole of East and Central Africa, is likely to provide the first really massive popular experiment, and may well lay the foundations for a federation that will stretch from Ethiopia and the Somali Republic to the Victoria Falls.

7 Africa's Islamic Horn

Of all the problems created or left unsolved by colonial rule in Africa, none is as potentially dangerous as that of Somali division in the east of the continent. From the Horn of Africa itself to the west stretch the Somali people, most of them today in the Somali Republic, some of them in French Somaliland, some in Kenya's Northern Frontier Province, some in the eastern regions of Ethiopia, and nearly all of them passionately loyal to a reunited Somali nation. Militantly Moslem, the Somali Republic, with its 265,936 square miles of territory and its two million people – formed in July 1960 by uniting the formerly British Somaliland Protectorate with the formerly Italian Trust Territory of Somalia – is in a virtual state of undeclared war with Ethiopia over the frontier between the two countries and has given its official sanction to the Somali secessionist movement in Kenya.

HAJI MOHAMED HUSSEIN, opposition leader and President of the Greater Somalia League in the Republic, was born in 1913 at Mogadishu, son of a poor trader whose family had lived in the town for several generations. Educated at Koranic school, he was forced to leave before completing his studies, and became increasingly determined to liberate his country from Italian rule. When the British occupied Somalia during the Second World War, he became active in nationalist politics and in 1943 was one of the thirteen men who founded the Somali Youth League (S.Y.L.), a radical reformist movement aimed at the reunification of all Somalis and the liquidation of both colonial rule and traditional tribalism.

At the end of the Second World War, the three Somali areas became United Nations Trust Territories under Italian, British, and French administration respectively. Elected President of the S.Y.L. as a neutral figure who belonged to no particular tribe, Haji Mohamed refused to cooperate with the administration in Italian Somalia, and serious riots against trusteeship took place during his period of office. In 1953 he left for Cairo to pursue Arabic studies at Al Azhar University and later joined the staff of the Arts Faculty there. After his departure, the S.Y.L. cooperated with the Italian administration, and he broadcast over Cairo radio a series of speeches in which he urged all Somalis to revolt against British, French, and Italian rule. In 1956 the S.Y.L. won forty-three of the seventy seats in the territorial elections to form a government, and Abdullahi Issa, its new President, became Prime Minister. The League, however, soon lost popular support over accusations of rigged elections, tribalism, and administrative corruption, and it accordingly re-elected Haji Mohamed as its President. Already widely known through his broadcasts, Haji Mohamed returned to Somalia and advocated violent resistance to Italian rule. Proclaiming that the promise of independence was all a trick, he stated 'no trees can grow without water, no freedom can be won without blood'. In 1958 he was suspended by the S.Y.L. Executive under right-wing pressure and, leaving the movement altogether, he founded the Greater Somalia League, accusing Abdullahi of failing to support Somali unification.

In March 1959, just before new elections, serious rioting took place against the government, Haji Mohamed was arrested, and the Greater Somalia League was itself banned. He was soon released, however, and continued his campaign against the government. Independence at last, the unification of Somalia with the formerly British administered Somaliland, and attempts by the S.Y.L. itself to conciliate him, led him at last to drop some of his passionate hostility to the government and concentrate instead on demanding the return of the Haud and 'Reserved' areas in Ethiopia to Somali rule. Though he is still outside the administration, Haji Mohamed remains a political figure of importance in the Republic and one ready to marshal militant sentiment for Somali reunification the moment that the energy of the government shows any signs of flagging.

The Minister of Foreign Affairs in the Somali Republic is ABDULLAHI ISSA, who was born in 1922 at Afgoi in the central agricultural district of Somalia. Moving as a child to Mogadishu, the capital, he was educated at Koranic school there and then at the Italian Government School. In 1937 he entered the Italian government service as a clerk but, dismissed in 1942 when the British military administration took over, he went into business at Belet Uen, an important road junction inland. Joining the Somali Youth League in 1944, he established a branch at Belet Uen during the following year and was made Secretary-General of the League in 1947. In 1948 he went to the United Nations, then meeting in Paris, as the League's representative, to ask for four-power trusteeship of Somalia, but he failed in his mission, and in 1950 the Italians returned. Under the leadership of Haji Mohamed Hussein, the League bitterly opposed any cooperation with the new administration, and several branches of the movement were accordingly banned. In 1953, however, when Hussein left for Cairo, Abdullahi himself took over the leadership and agreed to cooperate with the Italian administration. In 1956, when the S.Y.L. won a clear majority in the territorial elections, he became Prime Minister and Minister of Justice, proving to be an enlightened moderate, anxious to modernize the Somalis as soon as possible and prepared to cooperate closely with the Italian government. In 1959 he was re-elected Prime Minister, but was bitterly attacked by Hussein, who had returned from Cairo, for doing so little to promote Somali unification. When the new government was formed with independence in July 1960, he was therefore replaced as Prime Minister by a less controversial figure, Dr Abdiraschid, in an attempt to unite the country and conciliate Hussein, and became Minister of Foreign Affairs instead. Fluent in English and Italian, a cultured, quiet, and determined man, Abdullahi is not a mass leader or orator and is attacked by the militants for being too friendly to the West and too attached to Italy. Attacked also for too modern an outlook towards Somali traditionalism, he has antagonized the more extreme Moslems, especially for having proposed that the Somali language should be written in the Latin script.

Still a dominant force within the Somali government, Abdullahi Issa has spearheaded the demand to part of Kenya's Northern Frontier Province, a largely desert area where a Somali secessionist movement is gathering strength. On 9 November 1961, he wrote in the *East African Standard* that unification remained part of Somalia's national policy, and he rejected as 'showing ignorance of history' claims made by Kenya African politicians that the 'movement for unification' was of recent origin. He continued:

> All that we ask for is that the Somali homeland, which has been unjustly partitioned, must now be reunited. To the achievement of unification by peaceful and legal means we are committed by our constitution. In the circumstances the least we can do is to uphold the right of the Somali people in the Northern Frontier Province and other neighbouring African countries to free self-determination.

Aware, however, that a mere demand for extra territory would only inflame nationalist allegiances, perhaps to the point of war, Abdullahi Issa, on behalf of his government, expressed support for the creation of an East African federation. 'We will welcome and favourably consider any proposals inviting us to join,' he announced.

Active too in the struggle for Somali reunification is the President of the Republic, ADEN ABDULLAH OSMAN. Born in 1908 at Beledwein, Aden Abdullah endured a childhood of considerable poverty, but in 1922 an Italian befriended him, gave him some education, and taught him to type. In 1929 he entered the Italian administration and served until 1941, when he left to establish his own business in Beledwein. In 1944 he became an active member of the Somali Youth League, but he was one of those most strongly in favour of cooperation with the Italian administration, in the belief that it would advance independence, and he showed himself unequivocally opposed to the policy of Haji Mohamed Hussein. When Hussein left for Cairo in 1953, he took over the leadership of the S.Y.L. with Abdullahi Issa, and became President of the League from 1954 to 1956. He himself pursued a policy of moderation towards the Italian government and, after the 1956 elections, was made President of the Somali Legislative Assembly. In 1958, when Hussein had left the League altogether in order to form his own party, Aden Abdullah once more became its President.

Events were meanwhile furthering Somali nationalism in the British Protectorate. The Somali National League, which had existed under various titles in the territory since 1935, boycotted the 1959 elections because they did not provide for an unofficial majority. Largely as a consequence of the movement's pressure, fresh elections were called for February 1960, and from these the Somali National League emerged with twenty of the thirty-three seats. When British Somaliland became independent on 26 June 1960, therefore, the S.N.L. leader, Mohammed Haji Ibrahim Egal, served as Prime Minister of the territory for the few days till union with Italian Somalia on 1 July. The two Territorial Assemblies then merged, and Aden Abdullah Osman was elected President of the new Somali Republic.

Quiet, moderate, efficient at compromise, Aden Abdullah is widely respected, especially amongst the older and less radical political elements. The popular passion for Somali unification, however, has not permitted him to enjoy his office in tranquillity. Nor does the tone of his speeches suggest that it is with any reluctance that he has devoted himself to the cause of Somali nationalism. On 15 April 1961 he spoke at Hargeisa.

> It is appropriate today, being African Solidarity Day, that I as your Head of State make clear to the world that this Republic reaffirms its adherence to the cause and aspirations of the African nations as a fellow African State.... Furthermore our constitution from the very beginning makes it clear that we are an Islamic people, with Islam as the only recognized State religion, and that any law enacted by parliament must be based on the general principles of Islam.

The President went on to proclaim that only two of the five Somali territories had so far been reunited in the Republic, and that there was to be no relaxing of efforts to achieve the freedom of the remaining three – French Somaliland, with its 8,376 square miles of territory and 55,000 people, the Haud and 'Reserved' areas in Ethiopia, claimed by the Somali government to contain well over a million Somalis, and the eastern section of Kenya's Northern Frontier Province.

He reaffirmed the Republic's dedication to neutralism.

> There are fifteen countries, of which nine are from the East, who have either diplomatic representation in this country already or who have established friendly relations with us. We have clearly told them that our policy is one of strict neutrality and that we wish to maintain friendly relations with all who are prepared to reciprocate. I must emphasize, however, that as an African State and as an Islamic people, we feel that we have special ties with fellow African and Islamic countries.

He concluded by referring to what he called the Dagahbour massacres, which had taken place at the end of 1960 and in which Somalis in Eastern Ethiopia were reported to have been killed by Ethiopian troops.

> This tragedy, following so soon after other similar tragedies, is a matter of the gravest importance, and the government must carefully consider what action is appropriate. While we as an African State stand by our pledge to reject violence as a means to an end, or even the advocation of violence, it is simply not possible for us to stand aside and remain silent while innocent men, women, and children are being mercilessly slaughtered, simply because they refuse to surrender their national heritage of race, their religion and their land.
>
> In 1957, Abdullahi Issa and myself saw the Emperor of Ethiopia in Addis Ababa. We emphasized that the Somalis were determined to achieve independence and unity, that as an Emperor of an African State it was incumbent upon him to give the lead by giving the Somalis under his control their independence. . . . I take this opportunity to tell the Ethiopian people and their Emperor, Haile Selassie, that the Somalis under their control should be given the right to determine their future.

With the independence of Kenya fast approaching and border incidents between Ethiopia and the Somali Republic increasingly embittering relations between the two States, little is required to set a vast area of East Africa alight. Nowhere indeed are the claims of African unity more pressing than along the East Coast of the continent, where only federation on a massive scale can prevent the devastation of conflicting nationalisms. An East African federation is already being posed as the only effective settlement of tribal dissensions and economic problems in the four territories of Uganda, Kenya, Tanganyika, and Zanzibar. Nyasaland and Northern Rhodesia are already looking towards such a federation in their hostility to any control from white-dominated Salisbury. It is not inconceivable that the projected federation would take in as well Ethiopia and the Somali Republic, creating a State powerful in the number of its people and rich in its combined resources. It would be well if the experiment were tried. For if it is not, the artificial frontiers of colonial rule may yet blaze into open war.

8 The Palace Politics of Ethiopia

On 30 March 1961 General Mengistu Neway was publicly hanged in Addis Ababa for having led a revolt of the Imperial Bodyguard against the rule of Haile Selassie I, King of Kings, Elect of God, the Emperor of Ethiopia. The General had replied shortly to the judges who had sentenced him to death:

> I will not appeal your decision. You have already denied me justice by not letting me have proper defence in this trial. I have done what you say, but I am not guilty. Ethiopia has been standing still, while our African brothers are moving ahead in the struggle to overcome poverty. What I did was in the best interests of my country.

It was a rather different commentary on modern Ethiopia from that usually projected in the world press.

A country of 400,000 square miles, with an estimated population of twenty-one million, Ethiopia enjoys the distinction of having retained its independence throughout the European scramble for Africa. Only for some five years, with its conquest by fascist Italy, did it endure foreign dominion. For centuries, as today, its people have enjoyed an indigenous government, though one always absolute, hardly dented by pressures for reform.

HIS IMPERIAL MAJESTY HAILE SELASSIE I, the present Emperor of Ethiopia, was born at Harar in July 1892 as Lij Tafari Makonnen, son of His Highness Ras Makonnen, councillor, statesman, soldier, and relative of the Emperor Menelik II. Beginning his education in Amharic and the Coptic Christian faith, he was later taught by French Roman Catholic missionaries in Harar and learnt to speak fluent French. News of his scholastic ability then reached the ears of the Emperor, who ordered him to be brought to Addis Ababa so that he might pursue his education there.

At the age of fourteen, he was appointed Governor of Gara Huleta in Harar Province, and in 1906, when his father died, he was summoned to the Imperial Court, where he continued his studies. In 1908 he was made Governor of Sidamo Province and proved himself an able administrator, so that when, in 1910, he became Governor of his home Harar Province, he used his experience to overhaul the whole administrative system there. All the while he continued to read widely in French and was deeply influenced by French culture.

In 1913 Menelik II died, and the crown passed to his grandson, Lij Yasu. The new Emperor revealed a growing attraction towards Islam, though this was regarded as something like national betrayal in a country which had clung for centuries to Christianity, despite the Moslem forces surrounding it. In 1916, therefore, a *coup d'état* deposed him, and Princess Zauditu, the daughter of Menelik II, was crowned as Empress in his place.

Tafari Makonnen, because of his generally acknowledged administrative ability and relationship to the Imperial family, became chief adviser to the new Empress, as well as Regent and Heir Apparent. He used his great power to reorganize the country, building more schools and hospitals, and sending young Ethiopians overseas to study, while he seized every opportunity to travel in Europe himself. In 1923 he succeeded in getting Ethiopia accepted into membership of the League of Nations, and in 1924 he abolished the slave trade. In October 1928 he became King and in April 1930, after the death of the Empress, was crowned Emperor as Haile Selassie I. Announcing that it was his aim to modernize the country, he introduced in 1931 a written constitution which established a parliament, though this – as today – was given only advisory powers.

Suddenly, in 1935, Italy attacked Ethiopia, using a border dispute as its pretext, and the great powers stood aside for fear of becoming involved in war. Ethiopia fought on alone for a year, the Emperor himself directing the army in the north;

then, in May 1936, he appointed Commanders to continue the war and left the country in order to carry his struggle before the League of Nations. Ethiopians continued the fighting until they were overwhelmed, and the Emperor himself was forced to find exile in London.

It was not until the outbreak of the Second World War that the liberation of Ethiopia seemed possible, and in 1940 the Emperor flew to Khartoum and began to prepare for the liberation of his country by rallying Ethiopian refugees in the Sudan and Kenya. At last, in January 1941, he crossed the frontier with troops under the command of Colonel Wingate, and in May re-entered Addis Ababa. 'It is with a deep sense of gratitude to the Allied Governments', he proclaimed, 'that I stand today in my palace from which fascist forces have fled. It is my firm purpose to merit the blessing I have received; first by showing gratitude to my allies for my return and for the benefit I have received, by the release of Imperial troops for warfare on every front and by my supplying them with armed forces wherever they may need them, and second by establishing in Ethiopia Christian ethics in government, liberty of conscience, and democratic institutions.'

Nine months of military administration followed, and in January 1942 an Anglo-Ethiopian agreement was signed. In November parliament was recalled and a new Cabinet formed, and in the period that followed, the Emperor made efforts to extend educational facilities while reorganizing and reforming social and judicial administration. In 1955 the constitution was revised to make the Emperor Head of Government and Head of State with power to appoint a Cabinet. Two chambers were established, a Senate appointed by the Emperor and a Chamber of Deputies, which was in 1957 for the first time directly elected by the people, though remaining in fact no more than an advisory council.

Taking an increasing interest in Pan-African affairs, the Emperor invited the leaders of independent African States to hold their second conference at Addis Ababa in June 1960. 'Those who seek independence must be prepared to struggle for it rather than accept it,' he stated in opening the conference, 'and having won it, to stand on their own feet without dependence and without favours.' In December 1960 he visited Ghana and issued a joint communiqué with Dr Nkrumah, stressing the need for a joint African High Command.

Then, while he was paying a state visit to Brazil later in the month, a section of the Imperial Guard under the leadership of General Mengistu Neway revolted and installed the Crown Prince on the throne. Broadcasting from Addis Ababa, an announcer quoted the Crown Prince as having issued a statement condemning the Emperor's rule:

> The laws and regulations of the country have been abused to deprive the common people of their rights and privileges in order to boost the riches of the favoured few. The people of Ethiopia have waited for a long time with patience in the hope that they will be free some day of oppression, poverty, and ignorance. In doing this they have amply demonstrated their abundant patience. But empty promises can no longer satisfy the people, who now want concrete action, aimed at improving the standard of their living.

The army and the air force, however, remained loyal to the Emperor, who flew home to lead his troops and enter Addis Ababa in triumph on 17 December, the fourth day following the announcement of the revolt. Though the popular acclaim which greeted him was undoubtedly impressive, he was deeply disturbed by the widespread hostility to his rule revealed among the young intelligentsia of the country. During their few days of power the rebels had shot several of the 'old guard' of Ministers, and it was noticeable that the Emperor chose somewhat younger and more progressive men to replace them. He also showed unexpected mercy to the rebellious elements, and only the rebel leader himself was executed. It was as though the motives of the revolt had at last forced their way into the Emperor's presence. Yet the fundamental structure of rule remained unchanged.

The Emperor announced that the Crown Prince had acted 'under duress' and would continue to be associated with the government of the country. Born in July 1916, the eldest son of the Emperor, Asfa-Wossen Haile Selassie, the CROWN PRINCE, was educated at court and in November 1930, soon after his father became Emperor, was himself declared Heir Apparent and Crown Prince. In 1932 he visited Europe and Egypt, and when in 1935 the Italians invaded Ethiopia, he fought with the army against them. In 1936, however, he was forced into exile with his father and settled in Britain, where he studied at Liverpool University.

On his return to Ethiopia in 1941, he was made Governor of Wollo Province and Lieutenant-General in the Imperial Army. A member of the Crown Council which advised the Emperor, he worked very closely with his father in government and was never – until the revolt of 17 December 1960 – rumoured to have opposed his father's rule. It seems improbable that he played any part in the revolt other than submitting to what he believed was its success.

Despite the appointment of several younger Ministers by the Emperor after the revolt, most of the senior administrative posts remain in the hands of his old friends. The Prime Minister, HAPTE-WOLDE AKLILOU, was born at Addis Ababa in 1912 into a humble Amhara family, the son of a priest in the Coptic Church. Educated in France, where he took an Arts Degree at the University of Paris, he was appointed Secretary and Chargé d'Affaires to the Ethiopian Delegation in Paris, and remained there after the Italian invasion as the Emperor's personal representative. In 1941, when Ethiopia was at last liberated, he was given a post in the Foreign Office and rose to be Minister of Foreign Affairs in 1949.

From 1945 to 1952 he was active in the negotiations which took place with the Italian government over the restoration of Eritrea to Ethiopia, and in 1958 he became Deputy Prime Minister and Minister of the Pen, the department which acted as the mouthpiece of the Emperor. In 1960 he became Minister of Foreign Affairs again in addition to his other portfolios, and he accompanied the Emperor to Brazil in December, when the revolt of the Imperial Guard took place. In March

1961, the Cabinet was reconstituted, and Aklilou became Prime Minister.

The public hanging of General Mengistu Neway may seem to have ended a sudden interruption in the normal play of Ethiopian politics. It would be better to see it as a prelude to events that must sooner or later change the shape of Ethiopia. Though the Emperor has consistently announced plans for national development, his programmes appear to have fed only the court parasites, while increasing the frustration of the middle class and the educated youth. Millions are being spent on producing the appearance of progress, while large numbers of the workless and the diseased beg in the broad streets that decorate the capital. The provinces have been heavily taxed to develop Addis Ababa, but left relatively undeveloped themselves; thirty-seven per cent of the capital's children go to school, but only four per cent of the children in the provinces. Social services deteriorate the further from the capital they stretch. Land reform, the most pressing demand of the population, was initiated in September 1959 by permitting several hundred peasants to borrow money from the government, on condition that it was paid back with interest after five years. On 20 August 1961, the Ethiopian government announced that a second five-year plan would be launched in 1963. No report was made of the first five-year plan, which had been initiated with a flourish in 1957.

Dr Donald Levine, after three years in Ethiopia, wrote in *Africa Today*:

> Personal loyalty, to the Emperor or one of his Ministers, has been the basis of government appointments. The office-holder who ventures to do something more efficiently or imaginatively – in short, to carry out his responsibility to the people – finds himself 'promoted' to a lesser position. . . . The returned students tried many ways of adjusting to this state of things. Some got used to the pace and the intrigue of Ethiopian administration and worked as best they could; some withdrew to drink or orgies of chess-playing; some shed their school-day principles to become informers and apologists for the régime.

Undoubtedly those foreign-educated Ethiopians, who are the

pride of the Emperor's rule, soon after their return home acquire a passionate distaste for the widespread corruption and inefficiency of the régime. The government attempts to contain such discontent by a system of '*shum–shir*', or 'appoint-demote', by which officials are prevented from establishing any significant personal following and only an absolute loyalty to the régime assures any personal advancement. This system, however, has hindered any sustained development, since officials no sooner get acquainted with one post than they are transferred to another, while new programmes are developed in an atmosphere of distrust and envy.

The *Financial Times* of 4 July 1961 emphasized the dangers of an imperial rule which lacked progressive direction.

> Under the calm surface a great deal of resentment is building up. The situation is a familiar one in the Middle East, though perhaps rather less so in Africa. The Emperor and his feudal advisers rule, but the growing young middle class is increasingly discontented. Their demands are for land reform and the economic development of the country with the aid of foreign capital. The young men also, of course, want more jobs and more responsibilities.
>
> However, they are aware that the Emperor retains an enormous and semi-religious popularity with the people, and that he is the one factor which holds the various sections of the nation together. The Emperor and his family are not entirely unsympathetic to the middle class aspirations, but they are surrounded by the old feudal rulers and it is difficult to learn new tricks at the age of seventy. . . .
>
> The Emperor's position has in fact been weakened in recent months. He has had, unwillingly, to accept a demand from the army for a big rise in pay, and, though the rank and file are loyal, his dependence on army support has become more and more apparent. In Ethiopia, as in the Middle East, it is from the ranks of the younger officers that trouble is always liable to come. . . .

Perhaps in flight from his domestic problems, the Emperor increased his interest in continental politics. On 2 February 1962, fifty leaders from eighteen countries in East, Central, and Southern Africa gathered at Addis Ababa. Before their conference began, the Pan-African Freedom Movement of East and Central Africa (PAFMECA) had been a simple association of political parties coordinating the independence campaigns in Kenya, Uganda, Zanzibar, the Rhodesias, and Nyasaland, with Tanganyika the only constituent state to have achieved its independence already. By the time the conference broke up on 9 February, PAFMECA had been widened into the Pan-African Freedom Movement of East, Central, and South Africa, and had been joined not only by the Southern African nationalist movements, but by the governments of Ethiopia and the Somali Republic. Representatives from the six East African countries – Ethiopia, Kenya, the Somali Republic, Tanganyika, Uganda, and Zanzibar – agreed 'to work relentlessly' to establish a federation, and the Emperor himself told journalists that 'the problem of establishing such a federation would not be very difficult, even though Ethiopia is a constitutional monarchy'. Certainly, the new organization could no longer be dismissed as a group of powerless agitators. By admitting Ethiopia, it had acquired a member with thousands of years of independence behind it, a four-division army, and an air force of American jets. The Emperor himself, in opening the conference, had deplored the 'untold oppression in South Africa', the 'colonial régime' in Northern Rhodesia, and the 'tragic suppression of defenceless Africans by Portugal'.

The Times of 8 February commented unhappily:

There is some incongruity in the spectacle of the dignified figure of the Emperor of Ethiopia haranguing an appreciative audience of young African nationalist politicians on the iniquities of the remaining colonial régimes in East and Southern Africa. Even the politicians in question feel this, while gladly availing themselves of the facilities in Addis Ababa which the Emperor has placed at the disposal of the 'Pan-African Movement of East and Central Africa' – a peripatetic body devoted to the overthrow of white rule from Kenya to the Cape. It is true that Haile Selassie has fought for the independence of Ethiopia as single-mindedly as any nationalist intellectual winning power elsewhere in Africa. He can claim to be their doyen. Yet he hardly seems the natural associate of men who see African rule and the 'African personality' very differently from the feudal institutions of his ancient dynasty. Their sympathies lie rather with the young Ethiopian intellectuals who are waiting for the Emperor to die to put impetus into the modern reforms that he has been cautiously introducing.

The Emperor, however, has the best of reasons for ingratiating himself with the rising generation. His own position may be secure, but he has plainly had to find a safety valve for the discontent which lay behind the abortive revolt of his household troops just over a year ago.

The Emperor himself may indeed be popular; the throne has a mystic grandeur which the established church does everything to maintain. But the government is an increasingly unpopular one, and the dependence of the government on the throne increasingly apparent. The December revolt was crushed, but its causes still fester, and the Emperor has done little to treat them. He alone has the power to sweep away the feudal dust that still lies thick upon contemporary Ethiopia. If he fails to do so, his removal – with the removal of the throne – may well be the sacrifice demanded by popular frustration.

9 Dark Conspiracies in the Sudan

Within an area of 967,500 square miles live the 11,615,000 people of the Sudan. Since November 1958 they have been governed by a Supreme Council of the Armed Forces, under the Presidency of General Ibrahim Abboud, while opponents, including two former Prime Ministers and the leader of one of the two major religious sects, have demanded and organized for a return to democratic elections. On 11 July 1961 the Supreme Council arrested twelve politicians, including the two former Prime Ministers, Abdullah Khalil and Ismail El Azhari, accusing them of 'spreading rumours and conspiring against the people's interests'. President Abboud said that they had put themselves above their country and placed their interests against those of the nation. For some time, he continued, these activities had been tolerated; when dark conspiracies persisted, however, the Supreme Council had at last decided to act.

ISMAIL EL AZHARI was born in 1902, of a distinguished religious family, at Omdurman and was educated at Gordon Memorial College. In 1921 he entered the Department of Education and was sent by it to take a degree at the American University in Beirut. Returning to work in the Department of Education, he became in 1939 Secretary, and in the following year, President of the Graduates Congress – the first attempt at a modern political organization in the Sudan – which grouped some 1,200 young men schooled beyond elementary level.

Increasingly insistent upon an end to British administration, he visited the United Nations in 1946 to give his views on the dispute between Britain and Egypt over the Sudan. One of the group of seven who formed the Ashigga Party out of the radical wing of the Graduates Congress, he played a leading part in the establishment during 1952 of the National Unionist Party (N.U.P.), which incorporated the Ashigga Party and other pro-Egyptian groups. Though he publicly advocated some form of union with Egypt, he made it clear in private that he valued the Egyptian connexion primarily as a way of ridding the Sudan of British control.

In 1951 the Egyptian government formally abrogated the Condominion Treaty of 1899 and the Anglo-Egyptian Agreement of 1936, whereby Egypt and Britain exercised joint sovereignty over the Sudan, to proclaim the King of Egypt as King also of the Sudan. Under nationalist pressure the British government prepared a draft Self-Government Statute in 1952; but in July the Egyptian revolution put in power General Neguib, who had himself been brought up in the Sudan, and the new Egyptian government proposed a series of amendments. These the N.U.P. under Azhari's leadership supported, and though the Statute had already been forced through the Sudanese Legislative Assembly, the British government bowed to nationalist demands and signed a final agreement with Egypt in February 1953. In terms of this, Egypt conceded sovereignty to the Sudanese, leaving them the choice between a link with Egypt and an independent Sudan, while self-determination was pledged before the end of three years. Given considerable financial aid by Egypt and strongly backed by the Khatmia religious sect, under Ali El Mirghani, Azhari won the 1953 elections and in January 1954 became Prime Minister.

Forming the first all-Sudanese Cabinet, he took the Ministry of the Interior for himself, and sensing the general desire of the Sudanese for their own state, broke the Egyptian connexion and led the country to complete independence in January 1956.

Fierce attacks upon him by Egypt nourished his rivals within the party, and his old ally Ali El Mirghani not only withdrew his support, but encouraged his Khatmia followers to form the People's Democratic Party and go into opposition. Faced by the combined assault of the country's two most powerful religious leaders – Sidik El Mahdi, head of the Mahdist sect, was President of the strong opposition Umma (Independence) Party – Azhari was forced to form a coalition government with all the other parties in parliament and in July finally lost the Premiership. Though his following was still strong in the towns, he had lost most of his support in the rural areas, and the N.U.P. emerged from the elections of February 1958 with only forty-five seats out of 173 in the House of Representatives.

Azhari negotiated with influential members of the Umma Party over the forming of a strong coalition government to ensure stability; but Abdullah Khalil, the Umma leader and the new Prime Minister, feared for his position and encouraged senior army officers to intervene. At last, in November 1958, a military coup banned all political parties and established the Supreme Council of the Armed Forces, with General Ibrahim Abboud as President and Prime Minister of the Sudan. Azhari continued to live as a private citizen, unmolested and granted a pension by the military régime. Then, in November 1960, together with Sidik El Mahdi, his former enemy Khalil, and seventeen other political leaders, he called upon the Supreme Council of the Armed Forces to end its military rule and restore 'public freedoms', after holding national elections. Declaring that 'government is not the function of the Army', the twenty politicians proposed that a permanent constitution be drawn up by a new parliament. Azhari's pension was stopped, and on 11 July 1961 he was arrested.

ABDULLAH KHALIL was born in 1888 in Egyptian Nubia, a member of the Kanuz tribe, and was commissioned in the Sudanese battalions of the Egyptian army in 1910. In 1925 he transferred to the Sudanese Defence Force, which had been formed in that year, and served until 1944, becoming the first Sudanese to reach the rank of Miralai (Brigadier).

In 1945 he was prominent in the founding of the Umma Party, hostile to union with Egypt and prepared to collaborate with the British in moving the Sudan by gradual steps to full and separate independence. Strongly supported by the Mahdists, the party grew rapidly, while Khalil, as its Secretary-General, showed himself an energetic administrator. In 1945 he was nominated a member of the Advisory Council, and in 1948 nominated to the Sudan Legislative Assembly, where he was elected its Leader, a member of the Executive Council, and made Minister of Agriculture. The elections of 1953, however, gave power to Azhari and the National Unionist Party, and Khalil went into opposition. In July 1956, however, after Ali El Mirghani and his followers in the Khatmia sect had deserted the N.U.P., Khalil became Prime Minister as head of a coalition government between his own Umma Party and the People's Democratic Party of El Mirghani.

Though he was a hard-working administrator Khalil never became popular in the towns, where Azhari remained unassailable, and he depended for his own support on the strongly Mahdist rural areas. His position was confirmed by the elections of February 1958, from which the Umma Party emerged as the strongest force, with sixty-eight seats out of 173; but soon afterwards – claiming that intrigue both inside and outside his coalition government was damaging the country and that there was growing likelihood of Egyptian intervention – he appealed to senior military officers, who had formerly been his colleagues, to take over power. The military coup of November 1958 left him a private citizen and even granted him a government pension, though he possessed considerable business interests of his own. But the solution that he himself had sought did not seem to satisfy him for long, and in November 1960 he joined with the Mahdi and his former enemy Azhari to call for an end to the military régime. As a result of his protests, his pension was stopped, and he was one of those arrested on 11 July 1961.

General Ibrahim Abboud was born of Shaigi origin in October 1900 at Mohamed-Gol on the Red Sea, the son of a junior official in the British administration. Educated locally to intermediate level, he joined the Engineering Section of Gordon Memorial College at Khartoum in 1914. In 1917 he graduated and joined the Military College as a cadet, receiving his commission in July 1918 as Second Lieutenant in the Sudanese battalions of the Egyptian Army. From 1918 to 1925 he served as a military engineer, and when the Sudan Defence Force was formed in 1925, he transferred to the Sudan Service Corps.

In 1948 he became Staff Officer in the Camel Corps, and in 1949 was appointed Officer Commanding the Sudan Service Corps, the first Sudanese ever to hold the post. Then in May 1952 he became Principal Staff Officer at the Sudan Defence Force headquarters and, with the Sudanization of the Force, was promoted in August 1954 to Lewa (Major-General) and Assistant to the Kaid (Commander-in-Chief).

In April 1956 he became Kaid of the Sudanese Army, and though he enjoyed a position of considerable influence he took no part in politics until late in 1958, when Khalil approached army leaders to form a military régime. The November coup gave him control of the government as Prime Minister and Supreme Commander of the military junta, and he has ruled the Sudan ever since.

Considerably respected within the army as some fifteen years older than any of the other officers, he has shown marked ability in keeping the military leaders together in spite of serious rivalries, revealed in the unsuccessful revolts of March, May, and November 1959. A quiet man who believes that firm government alone can secure the nation's resources from the ravages of democratic conflict, he has instituted a strict régime with little respect for personal liberty, and all the restrictions of a state of emergency – including a ban on all political parties – have been proclaimed.

Under his rule the country's economy has substantially improved, and a satisfactory sale of the cotton crop has made possible the advance of development plans. Taking aid from East as well as West, he signed an agreement for Soviet technical assistance on 21 November 1961, under which the Soviet Union will help to build grain elevators, milk processing and fish preserving factories, asbestos and cement works, a cotton experimental station, and scientific research laboratories in the Sudan. A compromise figure and able mediator within the army,

Abboud is himself a member of the Khatmia sect and has throughout been supported by Ali El Mirghani, its leader, who refused to sign the opposition demands at the end of November 1960. The military régime, however, clearly lacks the prop of nationalist fervour that sustains President Nasser's power in Egypt, and it is increasingly unpopular with the civil service and the urban population of the Sudan.

In June 1961, despite a resolution from the Supreme Council dissolving the Sudan Railway Workers Union, the largest trade union in the country, 27,000 railway workers demanded a wage increase of almost half their existing salaries and went on strike. The union declared afterwards that similar seven day strikes would be held every month until the union was made legal again and its demands met, and the army began to fear an alliance between the industrial workers and the urban population in a campaign of open resistance. Abboud clearly felt that he had to strike first at the opposition or wait to be struck down himself, and he admitted the growing difficulties of his position with his arrest of twelve politicians in the following month.

El Mahdi alone of all the opposition leaders escaped arrest, to die at the beginning of October. *The Times* commented:

> In Sudan, as in other Middle Eastern countries, there had been disillusionment at the working of parliamentary government, and widespread hope that military efficiency and honesty would be worth the temporary loss of liberty. Sayyid Siddik was, however, always insistent that this loss must be only temporary. A year ago he was one of twenty political leaders who urged a return to civilian government and the drawing up of a constitution. The appeal was not answered, and in July many of the signatories, including two former Prime Ministers, were arrested and sent to detention in the South.
>
> Sayyid Siddik was not among those removed, perhaps because to challenge him outright was judged too risky. Since the arrests he is understood to have been urging that the prisoners should be brought back to liberty if not to activity, and some compromise might have been reached, since the army leaders themselves are not altogether happy about the future. They may be conscious of the need for broadening the government, and this can be done only by bringing in civilians. Now, unfortunately, the death of Sayyid Siddik will bring

discreet negotiations to an end. It may be tempting for the army to feel that a rival is out of the way and that there is therefore less urgency to take action. That would be dangerous. Just because Sayyid Siddik was a focus of loyalty, his death makes the need for unity in Sudan greater than ever.

The two most formidable opponents of the generals who now rule the Sudan unquestionably remain Azhari himself, whose urban support has increased rather than declined with his political persecution, and the trade union movement, dominated by the now illegal but still active Anti-Imperialist Front. This last was formed under its present name in 1952 by left-wing reformists, and it continued its work underground after the military coup in November 1958. Fifty-six members were imprisoned without trial in May 1959 and detained until the end of the year, while the Secretary-General, Abdel-Khalig Mahgoub, was arrested in 1960 after a long police search and released only several months afterwards. The government of the generals may indeed have brought stability to the Sudan, but it is a stability ever more dependent upon the detention of influential opponents and the repression of industrial discontent.

In an article for *Africa South* (Vol. 5, No. 3, April–June 1961), Peter Kilner wrote:

> For two years now, the ordinary basic liberties have been suppressed in the Sudan. That political parties and demonstrations are not allowed under military rule is natural enough. Repression has, however, become all-pervading. The closing down of newspapers, which have avoided anything but the mildest criticism in any case, the careful watch by the police on opinions expressed in public places, the pressures brought on suspected opponents of the régime, the occasional arrests and trials by military courts, the virtual suspension of the rule of law through the operation of a new all-embracing Act which punishes critical words or actions with heavy sentences, the control of the trade unions, and now, the latest move, the end of Khartoum University's former independence from government control – all these limits on liberty have spread a growing dislike and discontent.

The new Mahdi, Sayed Elhadi, brother of his predecessor, is known to be agitating for the repeal of all emergency legislation and a speedy return to civilian rule. In November 1961 President Abboud announced the formation of a committee to advise on the appointment of a central national council, which would then in its turn appoint a committee to resolve a permanent constitution for the Sudan. And, doubtless as an offering to popular distrust, he at last released Azhari and Khalil, together with their ten associates, late in January 1962. The general clearly envisages a prolonged period of closely disciplined change. One may wonder if he will have all the time that he appears to want.

10 The Calamity of The Congo

At the end of June 1961 the Congo Republic, with its approximately 13,540,000 Africans and 113,000 Europeans together inhabiting an area of some 904,754 square miles, became independent. For long known as Belgium's silent empire, it erupted into the news at the beginning of 1959 with riots in Leopoldville; it has dominated the headlines ever since.

For eighty years, a ruthless Belgian rule had shut off the Congo from prying eyes. During the first thirty years, when the territory was under the personal control of King Leopold II, the native population was drastically reduced – some estimates claim, by more than a third – while royal agents drove Africans in search of ivory and rubber, and claimed limbs and lives as the penalty for unfulfilled quotas. In 1908 international agitation at last forced Leopold II to surrender his dominion to the Belgian government, and the curtains were at once drawn around the colony so close that only an occasional whisper escaped when some traveller or missionary moved them for a moment aside. Throughout the half century of rule by the Belgian government, forced labour was assiduously if silently practised, while political protests were stilled by imprisonment or death. Hardly a handful of years ago, there were over 4,000 political prisoners in Congo jails, and though the Belgian policy of paternalism protested economic rather than political advances, its sudden withdrawal revealed not one African doctor or lawyer or architect, and only one African engineer, in its wake. If, as so many political commentators have since had occasion to say, the independence of the Congo was a calamity, it was a calamity in the long run less for the Africans themselves than for a Western world that had decorated its colonial ambitions with claims to the advance of civilization.

Of all the political figures who have come and gone or managed to survive during the many months of crisis, the dominant remains JOSEPH KASAVUBU, President of the Republic. Born in 1910 at Tshela in Leopoldville Province, not far from the coast – his mother was a Mukongo and one of his grandfathers a Chinese labourer, who had come to the Congo as a worker on the railway – Kasavubu was educated to primary level at Kizu by the Roman Catholic Pères de Scheut.

From 1928 to 1936 he studied at a seminary in Mbata Keila, and then proceeded to the important Kabwe seminary in Kasai. After three years of studying theology and philosophy there, however, he decided against priesthood as a career and spent a year at school in Kangu, where he qualified as a teacher in 1940. He taught for two years and then in 1942 entered the Belgian administration in the Congo, receiving a job in the Treasury.

Belgian rule permitted the organization of 'old boy' societies by African *évolués*, and Kasavubu served as General Secretary of the Association des Anciens Élèves des Pères de Scheut, while becoming a key member of the Union des Intérêts Sociaux Congolais (UNISCO). Beginning early to have political ambitions, he aimed at the reunification of the Bakongo people – scattered through the French Congo, the Belgian Congo, and Portuguese Angola – into a resurrected form of the old Kingdom of the Congo, which had been rich and powerful during the fourteenth and fifteenth centuries. Indeed, in 1946 he delivered a paper to UNISCO entitled *The Right of the First Inhabitant*, in which he claimed that the Congolese and in particular the Bakongo should own and control the Congo by right of first possession.

In 1950 Edmond Nzeza-Landu had founded the Association des Bakongo pour l'Unification, l'Expansion et la Défense de la Langue Kikongo, soon called ABAKO, as a purely cultural society. Kasavubu took an increasingly active part in the activities of the movement and himself became President in

1955. The Association grew rapidly – partly owing to the fear of the Bakongo that they would be swamped by the influx of other tribes into industrially booming Leopoldville, but partly also to Kasavubu's own dynamic leadership – and by 1956 the movement had become a political party in all but name.

The political explosion in the Congo was sparked off by a Belgian, Professor A. A. J. van Bilsen, who in 1954 published *A Thirty Year Plan for the Political Emancipation of Belgian Africa.* This was immediately taken up by a group of *évolués,* who issued a manifesto in the Catholic-sponsored magazine *Consience Africaine,* and in August 1956 Kasavubu himself demanded on behalf of ABAKO the speedy independence of the Congolese and their immediate freedom to form political parties.

In an attempt to meet the increasing political pressures, the Belgians in December 1957 introduced democratic elections for the major urban councils, and the superior organization of the Bakongo, through ABAKO, enabled them to defeat all other tribes in Leopoldville. Kasavubu himself became Mayor of Dendale, one of the communes, and in April 1958, after his installation, he demanded full freedom of press and association, democratic elections, and self-government.

In August 1958 General de Gaulle paid a visit to Brazzaville just across the river from Leopoldville, and offered the French Congo the choice in a referendum between membership of the French Community as an autonomous republic and complete independence. This had an immediate impact upon Congolese opinion. Two days later a group of influential *évolués,* led by Patrice Lumumba, who had been President of the African Staff Association in Stanleyville and had rapidly acquired a reputation as a brilliant orator and pamphleteer, addressed a respectful but firm memorandum to the Governor-General of the Belgian Congo. This demanded eventual independence for the Congolese and the inclusion meanwhile of representative African leaders in the Study Group set up in Belgium to formulate a new policy for the Congo. The signatories themselves followed up their memorandum by establishing in October 1958 a political party – the Mouvement National Congolais (M.N.C.) – to prepare 'the masses and the élite to take control of public affairs', and to combat all forms of regional separatism by promoting unity in the country. This policy was in direct contrast to that followed by all the other major Congolese political groups – especially ABAKO – which were based on tribal loyalties.

In December Kasavubu made plans to attend the first All-African Peoples Conference in Accra, but was unable to go because his papers were not in order. Lumumba together with two other M.N.C. leaders went instead and, returning to Leopoldville, addressed a mass meeting there on 3 January 1959, at which the objective of immediate independence was announced. Unrest in the city was already high, and after an ABAKO meeting had been cancelled by the authorities, there was violent rioting in Leopoldville on 4 January, set off by a march of 30,000 unemployed workers through the city. Kasavubu was arrested together with most of the other leaders of ABAKO on 8 January, and on 12 January the association itself was disbanded. The administration, however, recognized that it could no longer contain the political discontent, and on 13 January it announced long term reforms, with territorial and communal elections promised for December.

Imprisoned without trial, Kasavubu was provisionally released at the personal intervention of the Minister for the Congo, Van Hemelrijck, and taken to Belgium with Daniel Kanza, the Vice-President of ABAKO, and Simon Nzeza, its Treasurer. In May the charges against him were finally dropped, and he returned to the Congo to take up his duties as Mayor of Dendale and to rebuild ABAKO under the new name of the Alliance des Bakongo.

The mood of ABAKO became increasingly separatist, and in June six leaders presented Van Hemelrijck with a detailed plan for the establishment of a separate state in the Lower Congo, announcing that they would boycott the December elections and would not recognize the Belgian administration after 1 January 1960. Violent incidents increased in the Lower

Congo and, with the situation speedily deteriorating, the Belgians agreed at the end of 1959 to hold a Round-Table Conference in Brussels during January 1960.

By this time it had become clear that the main forces in Congolese politics were Lumumba's M.N.C., which advocated a unitary state, and the separatist ABAKO. In December Kasavubu himself was instrumental in forming the ABAKO Cartel, comprising ABAKO itself, the Parti Solidaire Africain (P.S.A.) of Antoine Gizenga, the M.N.C.-Kalonji, a breakaway movement from the M.N.C. under Albert Kalonji of Kasai, and other groups supporting a federal form of government. Kasavubu was elected President of the group by forty-two votes out of sixty, and on 20 January he led the delegation of the ABAKO Cartel to the Round-Table Conference in Brussels. He pressed strongly for a federal constitution, but five days later withdrew from the talks altogether when he failed to persuade the Belgian government to set up a provisional constituent assembly at once.

ABAKO itself split over personality and policy differences between Kasavubu and Kanza, with Kanza forming his own much weaker wing, and Lumumba emerged as the dominant figure at the Conference. Kasavubu returned to Leopoldville, where he was overwhelmingly confirmed in the leadership of ABAKO by the party's central committee and became Finance Minister in the Executive College attached to the Governor-General.

In the national elections of May 1960 Lumumba's M.N.C. emerged as the strongest parliamentary party and the only one with support throughout the Congo, winning thirty-three seats in the National Assembly of 137, to ABAKO's twelve. ABAKO, however, won thirty-three out of the ninety seats in the Leopoldville Provincial Assembly and showed itself absolutely dominant in the Lower Congo. After a series of complicated manoeuvres – during which Kasavubu was asked by the Belgian Governor-General to form an administration and failed to secure a parliamentary majority – Lumumba succeeded in marshalling sufficient support to become Premier, with Kasavubu as President.

When the Congo became independent at the end of June, the *entente* between Kasavubu and Lumumba seemed to promise a period of relative calm; but five days later, the Force Publique mutinied against its Belgian officers, anti-white violence broke out, the Belgian government flew troops into the country, and the Central Government of the Congo called for United Nations assistance. On 11 July, less than two weeks after independence, the Provincial President of Katanga, Moise Tshombe, declared the province independent and was vigorously supported in his secessionist stand by the Belgians in Elisabethville. This cut off from the Central Government all the vast tax revenue from the Katanga copper mines and further deepened the crisis throughout the country.

Still faithful to his federal objectives, Kasavubu nonetheless seemed reconciled at first to working a unitary form of government and, though keeping carefully in the background, appealed for order and loyalty to the administration. During the ensuing weeks of chaos, however, he gradually and quietly dissociated himself from Lumumba, reverting to his federalist policy. In September the break with Lumumba at last became open and he attempted to dismiss him as Premier, appointing in his place Joseph Ileo, a key member of the M.N.C.-Kalonji. He himself was then suspended by Lumumba, but both moves were cancelled by the Congolese Senate.

On 15 September Colonel Joseph-Désiré Mobutu, Chief of Staff in the Congolese Army, seized supreme power and announced that he was suspending both Kasavubu and Lumumba from their constitutional functions. Stating that he would cooperate with the United Nations, he ordered all officials at the Communist embassies to leave the Congo within forty-eight hours, and gained considerable prestige when his order was obeyed. Stating that he would establish a College of Commissioners, an advisory body of graduates, to work in close cooperation with the United Nations, he gradually – during October and November, and with the connivance of the United Nations Congo Command – consolidated his position. By late November it appeared that he had come to an understanding with Kasavubu – there are many who believe that he acted throughout on Kasavubu's behalf – but remained bitterly opposed to Lumumba.

Lumumba then fled from Leopoldville, which was clearly under the control of Kasavubu's forces, and attempted to reach his own stronghold at Stanleyville in the province of Orientale. But on 2 December he was captured by Mobutu's troops on a warrant signed by Kasavubu and on 18 January 1961 removed from prison at Thysville to be flown to Elisabethville in Katanga. On 13 February 1961 he was reported killed while trying to escape, and Kasavubu himself came in for much of the bitter condemnation that swept the world at the news of his rival's murder.

The special U.N. Commission of Inquiry into the murder blamed 'Kasavubu and his aides' for having 'handed over Lumumba and his colleagues to the Katanga authorities, knowing full well, in doing so, that they were throwing them into the hands of their bitterest political enemies.' Antoine Gizenga, who had been Deputy Premier of the Central Government and had grown politically close to Lumumba, refused to recognize any administration appointed by Kasavubu and, having established a strongly pro-Lumumba Provincial Government in Stanleyville, assumed as Lumumba's deputy the constitutional leadership of the Congo.

In November 1960 Kasavubu himself flew to the United Nations to request the seating of his delegation as legally representative of the Congo's Central Government, and though he succeeded, he did so only after an open split in the Afro-Asian bloc and against the votes of twenty-five states, including Ghana, Guinea, Mali, India, and the Communist countries. His declared intention was to call a round-table conference of Congolese political leaders to find a federal solution to the Congo crisis, and early in March 1961 he attended talks at Tananarive in Madagascar at which representatives of all the main Congolese factions, except the Stanleyville régime of Antoine Gizenga, were present. The conference resolved to establish a loose confederation of Congolese states under the

Presidency of Kasavubu, and shortly afterwards attempts were made to negotiate with the Gizenga government in Stanleyville.

The crisis caused by Katangan secession remained, however, and no permanent solution seemed possible until the Tshombe régime in the breakaway province had been stripped of its mercenary forces and Belgian settler assistance. In pursuit of this objective, the United Nations Security Council carried a resolution on 21 February 1961 which authorized the use of force by the U.N. if necessary to prevent civil war and urged measures to remove all foreign military and political advisers not under U.N. command from the Congo. On 17 April Kasavubu formally announced that the Congolese Central Government would accept the resolution and was willing to cooperate with the United Nations in its implementation.

MOISE KAPENDA TSHOMBE was born in November 1919 at Musumba in the Province of Katanga, into a rich commercial family related to the royal house of the Lunda tribe. Educated at American Methodist missions, he took an accountancy course by correspondence and then went himself into commerce. He was, however, rather less successful than his relatives and was declared a bankrupt on three occasions.

From 1951 to 1953 he served as a member of the Katanga Provincial Council, and in July 1959 he helped to found the Rassemblement Katangais, later called the Confédération des Associations du Katanga (CONAKAT), with its principal strength among the Lunda tribe. Openly supported by the Belgian government and by Union Minière, the company controlling the rich copper mines of the province, he became President of CONAKAT and in December 1959 went in a delegation to Brussels to press for elections and a Round-Table Conference.

At the Round-Table Conference in January 1960, Tshombe demanded a loose federation for the Congo, with a considerable degree of provincial autonomy and close ties with Belgium, but he was denounced as 'big-business controlled' and ignored even by the Belgian government. After the Conference he drew close to ABAKO over their joint federalist position, but differed with Kasavubu over any future relationship between an independent Congo and Belgium. In May 1960, he was a member of the Round-Table Economic Conference and travelled to America on a United States government invitation.

In the May 1960 elections, CONAKAT won only eight of the 137 seats in the National Assembly, but it succeeded in gaining twenty-five of the sixty seats in the Katanga Provincial Assembly and was enabled with its allies to achieve an overall majority. Tshombe was accordingly elected Provincial President and formed a wholly CONAKAT administration. For a while he negotiated with Lumumba over membership in a coalition central government, but he demanded more seats in the Cabinet than his support in the National Assembly reasonably warranted and, when negotiations broke down, he began instead to talk of Katanga secession. His opportunity came when the Force Publique mutinied, and a few days afterwards he announced the province's secession with support from the mining interests and Belgian settlers in Katanga. It was at this stage that the right-wing *Daily Telegraph* in London published, on 27 July, a report from its correspondent in Elisabethville:

> The masquerade of Katanga 'independence' is becoming daily more pathetic. M. Tshombe, the self-styled President, is today far more under the domination of Belgian officials than he was as an obscure politician before Congo independence. His régime depends entirely on Belgian arms, men and money. Without this, his government would in all probability be quickly pulled down from within and without. The outline of Belgium's emergency policy for Katanga is now discernible. It is to protect the great Belgian financial stake here and hold a political bridgehead in the hope of a Congolese union amenable to Belgium and the West.

Tshombe consistently refused to permit Kasavubu or Lumumba to enter the province, or to accept the stationing of U.N. troops there, and on 5 August the U.N. decision to enter Katanga in force was postponed. Tshombe's position was enormously strengthened as a result, though Katanga was not recognized as an independent state by Belgium or any other country, and he gradually confirmed himself in power since no one appeared willing or able to challenge him. On 8 August he was elected Head of State by the Katanga Provincial Assembly, which the opposition party in the province, the Balubakat Cartel of Jason Sendwe, was boycotting, and on 5 September he associated himself with Kasavubu in demanding a confederal solution to the Congo crisis. The murder of Lumumba caused a wave of disgust and anger throughout the Afro-Asian world, and Tshombe was widely held to have been directly responsible for the killing. The reaction of his Minister of the Interior, Godefroid Munongo, certainly suggested that the Katanga régime had chosen to brazen out its responsibility rather than attempt to conceal it; in reply to questions from journalists on the responsibility of the Katanga government for Lumumba's death, Munongo had simply stated: 'Prove it!' On 14 November 1961 the special U.N. Commission, established to investigate the circumstances of Lumumba's death, reported that Lumumba and his two companions had probably been shot by a Belgian officer in the presence of Tshombe and senior Katanga leaders, on the very day that the three had arrived in Elisabethville. The Commission also held that Munongo had played an extensive rôle in the murder plot.

At the end of February 1961 Tshombe signed a defence agreement with Albert Kalonji of South Kasai and Joseph Ileo, Kasavubu's nominee as Premier of the Central Government. Then, on 5 March, he attended the conference of Congo politicians in Tananarive. It seemed as though all the Congolese leaders, except for Antoine Gizenga, were agreed on proposals for a Congo confederation, but when they met at Coquilhatville in Équateur Province during the following month, Tshombe walked out, reportedly because Kasavubu had agreed to the presence of more United Nations troops in the Congo. The following day he was arrested at the airport while attempting to leave for Elisabethville, and on 30 April the Central Government announced that he would be put on trial for various acts of treason, including 'Katanga secession and counterfeiting' (the Katanga régime had issued its own currency). The Central Government simultaneously asked for United Nations help in disarming Tshombe's gendarmerie and in ridding Katanga of all foreign soldiers and advisers. The *Guardian* of 8 May commented:

> Politically, Tshombe has done immense harm by bolstering up an anti-Congolese State by European army officers and advisers. Whether or not he is a Belgian puppet he has behaved like one, and relations between Black and White in Africa are so delicate that any suspicion of European domination in a new form serves only to prevent true cooperation between the races from coming about. Judicially it is now for a Congolese court to say whether he has committed any crime. Unlike Lumumba, he is not to be shot by unknown villagers.

In the event, however, Tshombe was released after he had signed an eleven-point agreement with representatives of the Congo Central Government in Leopoldville, by which the Congo and Katanga were to have the same monetary system and diplomatic representatives abroad, and which provided for a 'National Congolese Parliament to be convened in Leopoldville as soon as possible'. This agreement was rejected on 4 July 1961 by the Lower House of the Katanga Parliament, however, after the President of the Chamber told deputies at a special session that Tshombe had signed it 'to gain his liberty'.

Negotiations were meanwhile taking place between representatives of the Gizenga régime in Stanleyville and the Kasavubu régime in Leopoldville for a reconvening of the Congo's National Assembly. The *Economist* commented on 22 August:

> For a province that claims to be an independent African State, Katanga has odd friends – amongst them Sir Roy Welensky, Dr Verwoerd, and Dr Salazar. The source of inspiration for Katanga policy may not be directly traceable to these authorities, or to the Belgians who advise its ministers and run its army; nor is it certain that Union Minière has everything to do with it. On the other hand Mr Moise Tshombe, head of the administration, is either a more devious politician than even his worst enemies say he is, or he is being prevented from being as receptive as he would like to be to overtures from Leopoldville. . . . In spite of his friends, however, Mr Tshombe cannot hope to remain in his present apparently strong position for long. If the meeting of the rest of the Congolese parliamentarians at

Leopoldville proves a success Mr Tshombe, sitting on his pile of copper, will be arguing with a united opposition. Further patience and firmness from the United Nations could make his position as the black ant of Congo unity even more untenable.

The national Congo parliament eventually met, without representatives of the Tshombe régime in Katanga, at the beginning of August 1961. It was announced that a 'Government of National Unity' had been formed under Cyrille Adoula, with Antoine Gizenga, Jason Sendwe (President of the Balubakat Cartel in Katanga), and Jean Bolikango (a political leader from Équateur) as Vice-Premiers. Katanga now seemed to be on its own.

On 13 September United Nations troops attempted to seize control of the province. Dr Sture Linner, U.N. Chief Representative in the Congo, reported on the following day that 'security measures' had been taken to 'prevent inflammatory broadcasts or other threats to the maintenance of law and order, while the U.N. resumed its task of apprehending and evacuating foreign military and para-military personnel'. There was a 'dangerous menace' to U.N. personnel and property in the 'terroristic conspiracies and activities' of foreign officers in the Katanga armed forces who had escaped measures for the evacuation of foreign personnel. 'Most prominent among them were a group of officers of French nationality, some [of whom] were unable to return to their own country because of their implication in the recent revolt by French military elements in Algeria.' Sir Roy Welensky, Prime Minister of the Rhodesian Federation, strongly attacked the United Nations activities; and a British Foreign Office spokesman announced: 'The British Government have always accepted that Katanga should form part of the Congo, but that this should be achieved as a result of official negotiation and not by force'. The Katanga forces, officered by white mercenaries and assisted by Belgian settlers, clearly revealed stronger resistance than the United Nations Congo Command had expected, while one jet piloted by a white mercenary caused considerable embarrassment to United Nations ground troops. On 18 September the United Nations Secretary General, Dag

Hammarskjöld, was killed while flying to Ndola in Northern Rhodesia in order to arrange a cease-fire, and the Congo crisis had claimed another victim. Two days later, Katanga and United Nations officials signed a provisional cease-fire agreement providing for an exchange of prisoners and a complete standstill on the movement of troops, arms, and munitions. The crisis was still unresolved.

On 2 November Central Government forces under the command of Mobutu launched an offensive to 'end the secession of Katanga,' but within two days were forced to retreat with heavy losses. Under pressure from the U.N. Acting Secretary General, U Thant, and Afro-Asian States, the Security Council adopted a resolution on 24 November – Britain and France abstained from voting – which called for an end to all secessionist activities in Katanga and authorized the use of force if necessary to remove the foreign mercenaries in the province. *The Times* was disturbed. On 27 November, it complained that the resolution added a 'menacing note of urgency' to the existing mandate and pointed 'directly at President Tshombe'.

> Tension in Elisabethville has been undesirably raised. All this may precipitate a second attempt by the United Nations to lay hands on Mr Tshombe's white mercenaries and executives, and an equally determined resistance to their arrest, which would probably provoke a more violent clash than the one which occurred on September 13.

The Sunday Telegraph of 26 November was less restrained. Its correspondent in Elisabethville, Douglas Brown, had attacked U.N. action in Katanga as 'persistent sabotage' and reported on the mercenary 'survivors' – 'mostly Rhodesians, South Africans, Germans, and French, with a handful of Britons'.

> Unlikely, unshaven Galahads, they alone in this tortured continent are ready to shed their blood in the cause of non-racialism. . . . Could they have won, against all the odds, they might have created the nucleus of a Euro-Africa to counterbalance the hate-crazed Afro-Asia.

On 1 December Dr Conor Cruise O'Brien, U.N. representative in Katanga, announced in New York his resignation from the U.N. Secretariat. On the following day he publicly attacked the governments of Britain and France, claiming that they had deliberately obstructed U.N. work in the Congo and forced his own resignation because he had loyally implemented U.N. instructions.

On 5 December, after a number of provocations including an assault by Katanga gendarmerie on U.N. senior officers, the erection by Katangan 'para-commandos' of road blocks between Elisabethville airport and the city, and other signs that a Katanga attack, led by mercenaries, was imminent, the U.N. Command in Katanga launched an attack on Tshombe's forces. U Thant authorized the use of jets, and the United States provided transport planes to airlift U.N. troops to Elisabethville. Despite the British government's call for an immediate cease-fire and increasingly violent attacks on the U.N. by Sir Roy Welensky, Prime Minister of the Rhodesian Federation, the fierce fighting continued, with the United States government declaring that no cease-fire was feasible 'until the minimum objectives of the U.N.' had been attained.

On 14 December Tshombe asked President Kennedy to mediate in the Congo dispute. On 16 December three companies of U.N. Swedish troops captured Camp Massart, the stronghold of the Katanga gendarmerie in Elisabethville, and three days later, with the city completely sealed off by the U.N. and fighting suspended, Tshombe flew to Kitona for peace talks with the Central Congolese Premier.

CYRILLE ADOULA, Premier of the Congo, was born, a member of the Mongala tribe, at Leopoldville in 1923[1]. He attended primary school at a Catholic mission and then had five years of further schooling at the St Joseph Institute, where he graduated with distinction in 1941. He was employed in various commercial houses in Leopoldville and was the first Congolese to be engaged by the Banque Centrale. Becoming interested in trade unionism, he joined the Fédération Générale des Travailleurs Belges and was appointed permanent Secretary-General of its Congolese division. He was also one of the signatories to

1. *Congo* 1960, Centre de Recherche et d'Information, Brussels. Leopoldville's *Courrier d'Afrique* gives 1921.

the memorandum, demanding reforms, which leading *évolués* presented to the Governor-General in August 1958 after General de Gaulle's speech on the French Community at Brazzaville.

In 1958 he participated in the formation of Lumumba's Mouvement National Congolais and in April 1959 was a member of the M.N.C. delegation to the conference of Congo political parties at Luluabourg. In July, however, disputes arose within the M.N.C., particularly over Lumumba's leadership, and in consequence the more moderate members resigned and formed a new group under Albert Kalonji from Kasai. Adoula participated in the formation of the breakaway movement at Elisabethville and presided over its Economic and Social Commission. In December the ABAKO Cartel was formed as an alliance of ABAKO, the Parti Solidaire Africain, and the M.N.C.-Kalonji with other federalist groups, and Adoula was elected Vice-President. A member of the Cartel delegation which visited Brussels in December, he participated at the same time in the conference there of the International Confederation of Free Trade Unions (I.C.F.T.U.). At the Round-Table Conference in Brussels during the following January he was very active, and he attended as an observer the Economic Conference which followed.

Returning to the Congo, he resigned from the M.N.C.-Kalonji, claiming that it had acquired a tribal character incompatible with the objectives for which it had been founded. He gave himself up exclusively to trade unionism and concentrated in the weeks before independence on the creation of the Fédération Générale des Travailleurs du Kongo (F.G.T.K.), directly descended from the Congolese section of the Fédération Générale des Travailleurs Belges. The F.G.T.K. was allied to the I.C.F.T.U., and Adoula, who became its Secretary-General, was elected a member of the I.C.F.T.U.'s Executive Committee.

In the elections of May 1960, he stood for the Parti de l'Unité Nationale (P.U.N.A.) led by Jean Bolikango, and was elected as a Senator from Équateur Province. Though he held no office in the Lumumba government, he was nominated Minister of the

Interior in the Ileo administration which Kasavubu appointed in September, and he represented the Congo at the United Nations in November 1960, leading its delegation to the General Assembly in March 1961.

In March 1961 he also attended the conference of Congolese politicians at Tananarive and opened negotiations with the Stanleyville régime of Gizenga at Coquilhatville. He then participated in the negotiations of June 1961 which led at last to a meeting of the Congolese central parliament in Leopoldville after its many months of enforced recess, and the consequent establishment of a coalition government.

His nomination as Premier by Kasavubu received votes of confidence from both the National Assembly and the Senate at the beginning of August – though parliament revealed a Lumumbist majority – and the crisis that had begun with independence over a year before seemed to have been resolved for at least five of the country's six provinces. In early September Adoula led the Congo delegation to the conference of non-aligned nations at Belgrade, together with his Vice-Premier, Antoine Gizenga, and received support from many Afro-Asian States who had till then extended recognition only to the Gizenga régime in Stanleyville.

It seems clear that the United Nations action in Katanga later in the month was taken after consultation with the Central Government, and Adoula himself strongly attacked the cease-fire negotiated by the Tshombe régime and the U.N. Congo Command. The Central Government, after a secret session of the central parliament, announced on 22 September in Leopoldville that it would have to resort 'to its own measures to put an end to the secession of Katanga', and at the beginning of November Katanga forces clashed with troops of the National Congolese Army in a 'police action'.

The Central Government troops under the command of Mobutu were, however, forced to withdraw from Katanga within two days, and Tshombe's position appeared considerably strengthened. Then, on 5 December, the U.N. Command in Katanga clashed with Tshombe forces, and fighting only ceased when the U.N. troops had gained control of Elisabethville and Tshombe himself had flown, on 19 December, to Kitona for peace talks with Adoula.

Two days later, it was announced by the Central Government that Tshombe had signed a declaration in which he –

> Accepted the application of the *loi fondamentale*, the basic law of 19 May 1960 which had established the political shape of the Congo Republic;
>
> Recognized the indivisible unity of the Congo Republic;
>
> Recognized President Kasavubu as Head of State;
>
> Recognized the authority of the Central Government over all parts of the Republic;
>
> Agreed to the participation of Katanga provincial representatives in a government commission, which would meet in Leopoldville on 3 January 1962 to study the draft of the constitution;
>
> Promised to permit Katanga deputies and senators in the central parliament to take their proper seats and assist in the government of the Republic from 27 December 1961;
>
> Agreed to place the gendarmerie of Katanga under the authority of the President of the Republic;
>
> Committed himself to respect the resolutions of the U.N. General Assembly and Security Council, and to facilitate their execution.

Though, on his return to Elisabethville, Tshombe declared that the eight points of his agreement with Adoula had still to be endorsed by the Katanga 'Ministers and by the National Assembly', an official U.N. spokesman publicly claimed: 'As far as we are concerned, [the document] is signed, sealed, and delivered.' On 28 December Katanga deputies and senators took their seats in the central parliament, and on 8 January the Foreign Affairs Committee of the Katanga Assembly was reported to have accepted in principle the eight-point Kitona declaration. The secession of Katanga was not yet at an end, but Adoula – with United Nations and strong United States help – appeared to be winning the struggle for a reintegrated Congo under his own Premiership and the Presidency of Kasavubu.

On 3 January the Central Government placed Albert Kalonji, self-styled President of South Kasai, under detention at a military camp outside Leopoldville. Then on 13 January the

Central Government, having summoned Gizenga to leave his Stanleyville stronghold and return to Leopoldville in order to face charges of secessionist activity, sent troops to arrest him. After brief fighting, the Gizenga gendarmerie surrendered, and on 14 January Gizenga himself announced that he would return to Leopoldville. On the following day, he was censured by a vote of sixty-seven deputies in the National Assembly – only seventy-two of the total 137 were present – and on 16 January Adoula dismissed him as Deputy Premier. Those politicians and newspapers in the West which had bitterly condemned any armed action against the secessionists in Katanga, applauded with enthusiasm the armed action taken to bring the Stanleyville régime under the authority of Leopoldville.

Born in 1925 at Mushiko, ANTOINE GIZENGA attended the seminary in Kinzambi and served on the staff of a Catholic mission in Leopoldville. In April 1959 the Parti Solidaire Africain (P.S.A.) was formed by *évolués* as a movement of small rural workers and peasants from the twenty-five tribes who inhabit the Kwango-Kwilu region of Leopoldville Province, one of the most populous areas in the country, and Gizenga himself was elected President. At first advocating detribalization and a federal form of government for the Congo, he joined Kasavubu's ABAKO Cartel in December 1959 and led the P.S.A. delegation to the Round-Table Conference at Brussels in January of the following year. He attended, however, none of the sessions and visited Eastern Europe instead, stopping off in Conakry on his return to the Congo.

In the May 1960 elections, the P.S.A. won thirteen seats out of 137 in the central parliament, all from Leopoldville Province, and thirty-five to ABAKO's thirty-three seats of the ninety in the Provincial Assembly. Becoming Deputy Premier of the Republic, he increasingly supported Lumumba against Kasavubu in the conflict that followed independence, and considering himself in danger from the troops of Colonel Mobutu, who regarded him with obvious distrust, he fled from Leopoldville in the late summer, to establish a strong pro-Lumumba provincial government in Stanleyville.

Widely assailed as a Communist, Gizenga claimed to be a passionate African nationalist with socialist sympathies. Certainly the assertions of his Communist affiliation, scattered so liberally through many Western newspapers, were denied in an interview which he gave to *Le Monde* on 26 March 1961: 'Our foreign policy is based on positive neutralism. Because we are an African country and underdeveloped, we need to keep out of the Cold War and not ally ourselves with either of the two blocks.'

The *Economist* of 29 September 1961 had commented on the rivalry of the three régimes:

> In this three-cornered battle between Leopoldville, Stanleyville and Elisabethville there will be no swift victories and perhaps no victories at all. Past experience of the Congo has shown that chickens can scarcely be counted even after they seem to be hatched. But equally it has revealed that all hope is never lost. What is needed now is the same as before – cool heads and practical hands and a determination not to put hopes too high or let despair become overwhelming.

Cool heads and practical hands were certainly busy in the new year. Gizenga was handed over by the United Nations Command, which had given him protection since his arrival from Stanleyville, to the Central Government on 22 January 1962, and the next day was transferred from Leopoldville to the paratroop camp of Cent Maisons. Adoula himself assured U Thant that Gizenga would be fully protected and 'treated within the law of the Congo'. On 27 January Adoula arrived in Lagos for the conference of independent African States there and announced that Tshombe was putting into effect most of the points agreed upon at the Kitona conference of December, while in northern Katanga, and in the other five provinces, order was being restored. Speaking at the United Nations on 2 February, Adoula said that the Central Government was firmly determined to re-establish the unity of the Republic and safeguard its territorial integrity. Three days later, he met President Kennedy in Washington, and was reported to have been assured that his government would continue to receive all necessary assistance from the United States. On the same day, in Leopoldville, Edgar van der Straeten, Vice-Governor of the Belgian Société Générale, was reported to have taken the first steps towards a reconciliation between Union Minière, the Belgian mining concern, and the Central Government of the Congo. On 15 February the United States government announced that it had refused to grant Tshombe a visa to visit the United States in order to address a rally in New York. A spokesman for the State Department explained: 'We believe that a visit to the United States by Mr Tshombe at this time would interrupt and jeopardize progress towards common objectives. This is also the view of the Central Government of the Congo.' On the following day, the Katanga 'parliament' voted to accept the Kitona agreement as a basis for discussion. And on 13 March Tshombe himself announced that he would visit Leopoldville for talks with Adoula, bearing with him a mandate from his Assembly to discuss the end of Katangan secession on the basis of the Kitona declaration. The three-cornered battle between Leopoldville, Stanleyville, and Elisabethville seemed fast to be drawing to its close.

11 The Equatorial Quartet

For almost fifty years the territories of Moyen-Congo (now called the Republic of Congo), Gabon, Oubangui-Chari (now called the Central African Republic), and Tchad (or Chad), composed the administrative federation of Afrique Équatoriale Française or French Equatorial Africa. Governed for so long together, they all became independent in August 1960, and though Gabon, the richest territory of the four, refused to join the proposed federal Union des Républiques d'Afrique Centrale, the four States agreed in principle to adopt a common external customs tariff and harmonize their defence systems. All members of the Brazzaville bloc of pro-Western African States, they today all exhibit a degree of friendship for France that substantial budget subsidies, if not their political histories, have carefully nourished.

Portugal was the first European country to assault the Congo basin in the search for gold dust, ivory, palm oil, precious woods, and, above all, slaves. In the sixteenth century, rivals appeared in the shape of Dutch, British, and especially French merchants, whose ships traded along the Guinea and Angolan coasts, and by the seventeenth century chartered company monopolies had largely replaced adventurous individuals. By the French Revolution, indeed, some seventy French firms were trading with the coast of Gabon and had beaten their European rivals throughout the area in the race for slaves from the interior.[1]

With the end of the Napoleonic Wars, France set out upon an expansionist colonial policy, and in July 1830 decided to establish missionary, trade, and naval refuelling posts along the Gabon

1. *The Emerging States of French Equatorial Africa* by Virginia Thompson and Richard Adloff.

coast. Treaties were signed with various Chiefs to facilitate penetration into the interior, and the decision of the European powers to suppress the slave trade stimulated expeditions of discipline throughout the area. In 1849 captured slaves were settled on the right bank of the Gabon estuary at a place given the name of Libreville, and this became the centre of French administration and influence along the coast after Gabon itself was freed from the jurisdiction of Dakar in 1881. After the Franco-Prussian war, the scramble for control of Equatorial Africa began, and it was largely due to the work of a naturalized Frenchman, Savorgnan de Brazza, that France emerged triumphant. Brazza's explorations and treaties established France in a vast area and one which the government at Paris was led to believe would provide it with access to large ivory and wild rubber resources.

The Act of Berlin, signed on 26 February 1885, established general rules to govern European occupation and development of Central Africa, so providing for zones of influence and sustaining the colonial ethics of occupancy. An agreement with Portugal on 17 May 1885 settled the French Congo's south-eastern boundary, while two treaties with the Congo Free State, in 1887 and 1892, recognized the Oubangui river as the frontier between French territory and the personal possessions of Leopold II, King of the Belgians. French expeditions occupied the territory that is now the Central African Republic, to found the post of Bangui there in 1889, and by 1900 France had acquired the pastoral and desert area of Chad. With subsequent frontier alterations, France was thus in possession of a large strip of Equatorial Africa, one that joined, through what is now the Republic of Niger, its vast possessions in the West. In 1910 the four territories in the area were administratively welded after the federal model of French West Africa, and though each was theoretically to retain economic and administrative autonomy, the Governor-General at Brazzaville gave increasing coherence and centralization to the whole area.

Brazza himself opposed the turning of these new possessions into a field for economic exploitation and strongly attacked the various decrees which transferred ownership of the land and waterways from the Africans to France. The Third Republic, however, regarded with envy the profits of the Belgian concessionary companies in the Congo, and in 1898 gave to private companies the exclusive rights over all agricultural, forest, and industrial exploitation for thirty years, after which they might receive outright ownership of whatever land they had developed. In return, the companies were to pay a capital sum and fifteen per cent of their annual profits, to build roads and maintain order, to safeguard the legal rights of Africans, and respect their customary use of land and forest. In effect, between March and July 1899, monopolies were conferred over an area greater than that of France itself to more than forty concessionary companies, with a total registered capital of 59,500,000 francs. Though the so-called Colonial Party in France defended the commercial monopoly of the ivory and rubber trade, stories of the low wages paid to labourers, the forced collection of rubber to meet tax demands, and the establishment of hostage camps for women and children began at last to stir French public opinion. The area was not as rich as had at first been supposed, and consciences could not be soothed by an inflow of spectacular profits. Ivory virtually disappeared from the conceded areas, rubber trees decreased because the companies did not bother to replant, trade stagnated, and the African population itself was drastically reduced.

In 1925–6 André Gide visited French Equatorial Africa and, on his return, published in the *Revue de Paris* of 15 October 1927 a full-scale assault against concessionary rule. The prominent French daily, *Le Petit Parisien*, sent to Africa one of its chief reporters, Albert Londres, to investigate for himself, and the report that followed was even more violent a denunciation. Londres claimed that the lives of some 17,000 Africans had been sacrificed in order to lay 140 kilometres of railroad through very difficult jungle country without the aid of modern machinery, and he commented:

> We work in a tunnel without any general plan, clear idea, or funds. . . . We have only one real port, poor roads, and a poor railroad. French Black Africa does not simply slumber, it snores . . . because of France's indifference and the colonies being forced to live off their

own meagre resources. . . . What we practise is no longer thrift, it is stupidity.

On the eve of the Second World War, Marcel Sauvage, in *Sous le Feu de l'Équateur*, wrote of the colons in the area:

> Most of their principles seem to melt away under the tropical heat, and their courage goes no further than what is required for making money or satisfying their vanity. And the Africans naturally bear the consequences.

Although the number of large companies declined, those that survived became seemingly all-powerful. It was only with the Second World War that the landscape was to change. The area reacted quite unexpectedly to the collapse of France and its armistice with Germany in June 1940. French officials rejected Vichy, while Africans volunteered in large numbers to join de Gaulle's Free French. On 25 August 1940 Chad, under the leadership of its West Indian Negro Governor, Félix Éboué, re-entered the war, three days later the Free French took control of Brazzaville, and on 30 August Oubangui-Chari followed suit. Only Gabon remained loyal to the Vichy régime, but Libreville was besieged by Free French forces, and on 9 November the last of the four territories joined the side of de Gaulle.

The Free French in return promised so to develop the territories as to restore them to France after the liberation in better economic and political condition than ever before. De Gaulle toured the area in October 1940 and set up a High Commission of the Free French at Brazzaville, while African forces fought against the Italians in North Africa. The influence of the war stimulated the economy of the area, reviving rubber and cotton cultivation and encouraging gold mining. The presence of numerous troops and officials brought prosperity to the merchant class, though the living standards of rural Africans continued to decline with the frenzied cultivation of cotton and collection of rubber for the war effort.

On 8 November 1941 Félix Éboué became Governor-General of the whole federation. Distressed at the degree to which European economic enterprises had disrupted tribal traditions among the rural Africans, he increased the power of the Chiefs in the hope of creating an élite closer to the bulk of the population, and making clear his opposition to the recruiting of Africans for European plantations or industrial enterprises, he encouraged instead the development of an indigenous peasantry. Before he died in 1944, he was to play the paramount part in the Brazzaville Conference of that year, at which Free French politicians and colonial officers from all over French Black Africa promised Africans a share in drawing up a post-war constitution for France, with the ultimate effect of changing the colonial empire into the French Union and granting parliamentary representation in Paris to France's African territories.

★

With an area of 102,290 square miles and an estimated population of over 420,000, Gabon is the richest of the four territories. Covered in dense forests that contain substantial mineral resources – mainly manganese and iron – and a wealth of okoumé wood, it is very like the Ivory Coast of Félix Houphouet-Boigny in its desire to keep its riches to itself and not share them in any close federation with its neighbours. Its President, Leon M'ba, is indeed a close associate of Houphouet-Boigny's and has long looked to the Ivory Coast leader for political advice and support.

Born in February 1902, a member of the dominant Fang tribe, at Libreville, the capital of the territory, LEON M'BA was educated locally at Roman Catholic schools and worked successively as an accountant in the French Administration, as a journalist on *Échos Gabonais*, and then as a member of the Administrative Board of the Société d'Études pour l'Équipement Minier, Industriel et Agricole du Gabon.

For many years the headman of the Libreville district, he made an early entry into politics and became the leader of the Mouvement Mixte Gabonais, the local section of the inter-territorial Rassemblement Démocratique Africain (R.D.A.), as well as a member of the R.D.A. Working Committee, with special responsibility for the Press. In 1951 he stood for election to the French

National Assembly but was defeated, and in 1952 gained election to the Territorial Assembly. In the following year he reorganized the Mouvement Mixte Gabonais into the Bloc Démocratique Gabonais (B.D.G.), which remained the local section of the R.D.A., and in 1956 he became Mayor of Libreville after the municipal elections.

In the March 1957 elections the B.D.G. was successful in the face of strong opposition from the Union Démocratique et Sociale Gabonaise, and when a new constitution in terms of the 1956 *loi-cadre* was implemented, M'ba himself became Vice-President of the Gabon Executive Council under the French Governor as President. At the 1957 conference of the R.D.A. in Bamako he strongly supported Houphouet-Boigny and the Ivory Coast delegation in opposing the proposal that a federal executive should be established in the French-speaking territories of West Africa, preferring that each country should preserve its own separate political system and maintain its own links with France.

After new territorial elections in July 1958, he became President of the Executive Council, and after the de Gaulle referendum in September 1958 – when Gabon voted unanimously for autonomy within the French Community and against complete independence from France – he became President of the Republic of Gabon. On 27 February 1959 he was elected Prime Minister and in 1960, when Gabon at last declared its full independence, Head of State.

For a long time dominant in Gabon politics, he has recently encountered mounting opposition within his own party over his conservative and pro-French policies, and in November 1960 he imprisoned several leading members of the B.D.G. including Paul Gondjout, President of the Assembly. Shrewd, cautious, and considerably influenced by the French, he has consistently shown himself reluctant to sacrifice any degree of territorial sovereignty to the demands of federalism, and has discouraged all links among the independent states of equatorial Africa that go beyond loose forms of economic and military cooperation.

*

The Central African Republic, with its 238,000 square miles of territory and some 1,200,000 people, has more than twice the area and almost three times the population of Gabon. Its economy is mainly agricultural, with a few small-scale mining industries, and though it possesses relatively small forests and great stretches of savannah, it has an excellent system of internal communications, both by road and river. Unlike Gabon, it has no great natural resources, outside of its most important product, cotton, and it has only one real town, Bangui, which is both an administrative and trading centre.

The modern political development of the territory really began after the Second World War. In 1952 Barthélemy Boganda, who had been elected to the French National Assembly in 1946 and regularly elected thereafter with the backing of the French Mouvement Républicain Populaire (M.R.P.), formed his own party, the Mouvement pour l'Évolution Sociale de l'Afrique Noire (M.E.S.A.N.), which he dominated entirely until his death in an air crash on 29 March 1961. Boganda himself spent little time in Paris but devoted most of his energy to building up M.E.S.A.N., which speedily became the spearhead of popular advance and, after the application of the 1956 *loi-cadre* constitution, the government. He persistently approached the leaders of the other three territories in French Equatorial Africa with proposals for federation, and might well have succeeded in persuading even the reluctant Gabon had he lived longer. His death, however, threw politics in his own territory into turmoil, and it was only after considerable dispute that his cousin, David Dacko, was elected leader and so became his successor as Prime Minister.

Born in March 1930 at Bouchia in the M'Baiki district on the southern border of the Republic, DAVID DACKO was educated locally at secondary school in Bambari and then in the French Congo, where he qualified as a teacher. Gaining appointment as headmaster of a primary school in Bangui, the capital of the Central African Republic, he became active in the teachers' trade union, then affiliated to the Force Ouvrière, the French Socialist trade union federation. He took no direct part in politics, however, until he was elected in March 1957 to the Territorial Assembly for Ombella M'Poko on the M.E.S.A.N. ticket. From May 1957 to August 1958 he served as Minister of Agriculture, Cattle-Breeding, and Forestry in the Boganda administration, and from August to December 1958 as Minister of Administrative Affairs, being re-elected to the Assembly in December 1958 and becoming Minister of the Interior. In the de Gaulle referendum of the previous September, the Central African Republic, under Boganda's lead, had turned in a 98·1 per cent vote in favour of autonomy within the French Community and against complete independence from France, and on 1 December it proclaimed its membership of the Community.

The elections for the new fifty member Legislative Assembly in April 1959 were disrupted by Boganda's sudden death, and panic spread throughout the ranks of M.E.S.A.N. The elections themselves, however, passed off quietly, the poll was fifty-eight per cent, and the movement's candidates won forty-eight of the fifty seats. The new Assembly expressed its confidence in David Dacko as Prime Minister, though it soon showed that it was not prepared to be as docile towards him as its predecessors had been to Boganda. In October 1959 a motion of no confidence in his administration was introduced in the Assembly, and Dacko won the vote only by threatening to dissolve parliament altogether.

During 1960 disputes within M.E.S.A.N. increased till in June Abel Goumba, a former Minister of Finance, withdrew to form a rival party, the Mouvement pour l'Évolution Démocratique de l'Afrique Centrale (M.E.D.A.C.). Goumba's chief aim was to fight the strong presidential constitution proposed by Dacko, but this was passed by the Assembly in November after a long closed session. In December M.E.D.A.C. itself was dissolved and Goumba, together with other opposition deputies, arrested. Though Dacko would appear to have political power at present firmly in his hands, the situation in the Central African Republic is more fluid than in any of the other three territories, and the potential for a strong opposition exists within M.E.S.A.N. itself. Dacko has to a large extent followed the policy of Boganda, but he has neither the prestige nor the personality of his predecessor, whose shadow still lies over the politics of the Republic, darkening the efforts of a relatively ineffectual succession.

*

Most northerly of the four territories and by far the largest is the Republic of Chad, 495,000 square miles in area and with an estimated population of 2,730,000. It has few good internal communications, a handful of roads, and only one river system, while desert covers much of its northern half. Its economy is based almost entirely on the raising of livestock in the north and east, and the production of cotton in the south-west region, and its only wealth is that of its population, more than half of the total in the four territories together. Chadians appear aware of their territory's great economic weakness, a recognition that has doubtless played its part in encouraging cooperation with France and the territory's own neighbours. Racial tension, however, exists between the Moslem, once-dominant Arab strain in the North and the Negroes themselves, who from having been slaves now constitute the more prosperous and better educated élite in the towns and farmlands of the South.

In June 1947, the Parti Progressiste Tchadien (P.P.T.) was founded by Gabriel Lisette, a West Indian who had served in the French administration and been elected as the deputy for Chad to the French National Assembly. Centred in the South, the P.P.T. became the local section of the inter-territorial Rassemblement Démocratique Africain (R.D.A.) and rapidly increased its political hold over the country until, under Lisette's leadership, it constituted the first African government after the territorial elections in 1957. The Moslems in the northern region, however, grew increasingly suspicious of Lisette's domination, and in May 1959 Lisette was compelled to surrender the leadership of the party and of the government to one of his supporters, Tombalbaye.

FRANÇOIS TOMBALBAYE, now President and Minister of Finance, was born in 1918 at Bedaya, a small village in the south of Chad, into a family of Protestant traders belonging to the Sara-Madjingaye tribal group. After a few years of primary schooling, he passed his *brevet élémentaire* examination and then worked for several years as an assistant teacher. Becoming President of the Syndicat Autonome du Tchad, an independent trade union, he settled for a while in Fort-Archambault, where he organized the local branch of the Parti Progressiste Tchadien. In March 1952 he was elected on the P.P.T. ticket to the Territorial Assembly and in 1957 was elected again, to become Member and then Vice-President of the General Council of French Equatorial Africa.

In May 1959 he succeeded to the Premiership after growing opposition in the North, led by Hamad Koullamalah, had compelled the resignation of Lisette, and in August 1960, again under pressure from Koullamalah, he expelled Lisette from the Cabinet and exiled him from the territory altogether. In August too, he was elected President of the Republic, President of the Council of Ministers, and Minister of National Defence. Unrest in the North had meanwhile grown, and in February 1960 the local Moslem parties had fused to form the Parti National Africain (P.N.A.).

The P.N.A. seemed to represent a considerable threat to the P.P.T. régime, though it held only ten seats out of eighty-three in the National Assembly, to the P.P.T.'s sixty-seven. Tombalbaye therefore initiated negotiations with its leaders and, in March 1961, was able to announce a fusion of the two parties to form the new Union pour le Progrès du Tchad, which accordingly now holds seventy-seven of the eighty-three seats in the Assembly. Still faced, however, by the great problem of creating a permanent unity between the Sara South and the Moslem North, Tombalbaye strongly advocates – especially as his country is land-locked – some federation of the four Republics in Equatorial Africa.

★

Of all the four, the Republic of Congo, with its 129,000 square miles of territory and 795,000 inhabitants, is perhaps the most developed, though seemingly the poorest in natural resources.

The northern half is covered by dense forest, without mineral wealth or the vast supplies of okoumé wood so profitable a feature of Gabon. Only the Niari valley is really fertile, and though a few industries have been set up in the south, many more have failed than have survived. The territory's most profitable possession, indeed, is the river and railroad capital of Brazzaville, which contains one-seventh of the total population and serves as a junction for traffic along the Congo and Obangui rivers between the interior of Equatorial Africa and the sea. About one-third of the country's population live in small villages scattered throughout the northern forests and most of them belong to the M'Bochi tribe, while the further important tribal group of the Bakongo, inhabiting the north of Angola and the east of the formerly Belgian Congo as well, is represented mainly by the Lari branch.

Dominant today within the territory and politically active beyond its borders is the President, ABBÉ FULBERT YOULOU. Born in June 1917 of the Lari tribe at Madibou close to Brazzaville, Youlou early decided to enter the priesthood. In 1929 he enrolled at a seminary in Brazzaville, transferred to another at Akono in the French Cameroons, and then proceeded to Yaoundé, where he studied philosophy together with Barthélemy Boganda, later Premier of the Central African Republic. Having taught at the seminary of M'bamou in the Congo for a while, he studied theology at Libreville and Brazzaville and was ordained a priest of the Roman Catholic Church in June 1946, to become Vicar of St Francis Parish in Brazzaville.

Territorial politics at the time were dominated by the Mouvement Socialiste Africain (M.S.A.) – founded in 1946 as a local section of the French Socialist Party (S.F.I.O.), by a Frenchman, M. Cazaban-Mazerolles – which counted among its prominent African members Jacques Opangault. Most of the party's leaders came from the north, and the party itself in consequence possessed its primary support there.

Busying himself particularly with youth movements and in his work as almoner at the neighbouring hospital, Youlou became widely known and in 1956 stood for election as deputy to the French Assembly against Félix Tchicaya, the incumbent, and

Jacques Opangault. He was defeated, but his interest in politics was confirmed, and he was hailed throughout the south as the leader of the Lari. In the same year he formed the Union Démocratique de la Défense des Intérêts Africains (U.D.D.I.A.), as an opposition to the Mouvement Socialiste Africain, and started a magazine called *Cette Semaine*. In the municipal elections of November 1956 he scored considerable success and became Mayor of Brazzaville, while his close colleague, Stéphane Tchichellé, became Mayor of the seaport, Pointe Noire.

In the March 1957 elections to the Territorial Assembly, the U.D.D.I.A. and the M.S.A. each won twenty-one of the forty-five seats. The remaining three successful candidates were independents, and two gave their support to Opangault, the M.S.A. President, who was therefore enabled to form a government. Youlou himself became Minister of Agriculture in the new administration and in August affiliated his U.D.D.I.A. to the Rassemblement Démocratique Africain (R.D.A.). Though suspended by the ecclesiastical authorities in 1956 for having broken his vows, he continued to wear his habit and use the title of Abbé, as indeed he still does today. In September 1958 he campaigned during the de Gaulle referendum in favour of autonomy within the French Community and against the complete independence of the territory from France. When in November the Republic of Congo was proclaimed, one Opangault supporter in the Assembly defected to the U.D.D.I.A., so giving Youlou a majority and leading to his election as Premier.

Tension developed between the supporters of Opangault and those of Youlou, ending in widespread rioting at Brazzaville and Pointe Noire in January 1959 between the Lari and M'Bochi. Some 200 people were killed, the opposition was blamed, and its leaders, including Opangault himself, were imprisoned. In the elections of June 1959 Youlou won fifty-one of the sixty-one seats and became President of the Republic. Opangault, while still in jail, was also elected to the Assembly, and before independence on 15 August 1960 he reached an agreement with Youlou whereby he became Minister of State and the M.S.A. merged into the Youlou government party. Independence celebrations in Brazzaville were marked by posters exhorting the people to show their 'gratitude and friendship to France' and by the unveiling of a statue to General de Gaulle.

Youlou took the initiative in proposing a union of Central African Republics, but in May 1960 the negotiations broke down over the reluctance of Gabon to sacrifice its relative economic strength to a federation. Extremely antagonistic to Patrice Lumumba throughout the Congo crisis, he gave open support to Kasavubu, allowing him to use the radio station and airport at Brazzaville when the airport and radio station in Leopoldville were closed to both Congolese leaders by the United Nations Command. Meanwhile the reconciliation between Youlou and Opangault continued, and in January 1961 Youlou made his former rival Second Vice-President, with responsibility for Justice.

In the last months of 1960 Youlou became increasingly active at the Pan-African level and was host to two conferences at Brazzaville in an attempt to find a federal solution to the persisting crisis in the formerly Belgian Congo Republic. Indeed, the present Brazzaville bloc of twelve formerly French African States first took real shape at the Brazzaville Conference of December 1960. As Kasavubu began to cooperate with the United Nations after the death of Lumumba, however, and took strong measures to counter the secession of Katanga, Youlou switched sides and – whether as a consequence of economic aid promised him by the Katanga régime, or rivalry for the leadership of the Bakongo against Kasavubu – increasingly gave his open support to Moise Tshombe. When Tshombe was arrested by Kasavubu in April 1961, Youlou called for the immediate intervention of the United Nations Secretary-General and asked the other members of the Brazzaville bloc to back his protests against 'this act of banditry'. Though his sympathy with Tshombe threatened to compel his absence from the Monrovia Conference of Independent African States later in the month, he was reportedly swayed by Félix Houphouet-Boigny, President of the Ivory Coast and a dominant figure within the Brazzaville bloc, to attend. He failed, however, to get any sympathy at

Monrovia for Tshombe and, as a result of his stand, the Leopoldville régime closed the frontier with Brazzaville and stopped all official traffic between the two Congo Republics.

★

National frontiers in Africa are, as has often enough been said, largely artificial, the result of colonial rivalry and administrative convenience. The four territories of the former French federation of Equatorial Africa would seem to constitute the right material for a contemporary experiment in African unity. Yet it is debatable whether the Republic of Congo itself – or at least the southern part of it – is not more closely drawn towards the Bakongo in the formerly Belgian Congo Republic and in the northern regions of Angola than to federation with its northern equatorial neighbours. Indeed, it is the tensions within the territory itself and the rivalry for leadership of the Bakongo people that together probably account for Youlou's own political conduct.

The passion for African unity, however, is not limited by colonial attempts at federation or by subsequent demands for a revision to pre-colonial associations. Despite the internal tensions within it and its one united stand against hasty experiments in federalism, the Brazzaville bloc had led in a short time to a considerable degree of inter-State cooperation. The short history of modern independent Africa suggests that the disintegration of colonial unities is anything but identical with balkanization. The four States of what was once French Equatorial Africa might not yet have found the means to retain their close administrative connexion. There remains, however, every reason to suppose that they will in time together join a much larger African federation, which may well contribute to the unification of the whole continent.

12 The Test of Cameroun

On 1 October 1961 the Federal Republic of Cameroun came into being, combining the formerly French Republic of Cameroun, 166,489 square miles in area and containing a population of 3,225,000, with the formerly British-administered international trust territory of the Southern Cameroons, 16,581 square miles in area and containing 814,000 people. The date initiated a significant experiment – the reunification of a people divided by colonial rule, the integration of two countries despite the barriers of different administrative languages, political institutions, and recent histories. The main obstacle to African unity is considered by many to be the differences in language and culture between what was once French and what was once British Africa. Should the Federal Republic of Cameroun manage to survive, it cannot but influence further attempts to scale the wall that the European rivalries in Africa inevitably built.

In 1884 Germany took possession of the Cameroons, to the south-east of what was soon to become British Nigeria, and held the territory until it was defeated in the First World War. The League of Nations then established the area as an international trust territory, dividing its administration in 1919 between France and Britain. From then onwards the Cameroons became in effect two countries, one controlled by Britain in two administrative shapes – the Southern Cameroons, attached to the Eastern Region of Nigeria, and the Northern Cameroons, administered as part of Nigeria's Northern Region – while the other, by far the larger part of the territory, fell under absolute French control. The development of African nationalism, however, excited a desire for reunification in both British and French administered areas.

In 1947 the Union des Populations du Cameroun (U.P.C.) was founded in the French Cameroons to demand integration of the British and French territories and independence in accordance with Article 76 of the United Nations Charter. In 1952 the movement's leader, Reuben Um Nyobe, went to the United Nations to demand immediate reunification; the establishment of a Legislative Assembly for a United Cameroons, to be elected by universal adult suffrage through a single voters' roll; and the fixing of a date for independence. These representations met with no effective response, however, and the U.P.C. convened a meeting on 22 April 1955 of various organizations which together issued a common call for the ending of trusteeship, the building of a sovereign Cameroun, and a United Nations sponsored general election to a constituent assembly before 1 December 1955. Popular response to this proclamation provoked a wave of repression by the French authorities, several thousand Camerounians were reported to have been killed, and the U.P.C. itself – together with its supporting movements, the Union Démocratique des Femmes Kamerunaises (U.D.F.K.), and the Jeunesse Démocratique du Kamerun (J.D.K.) – was banned in July 1955, under a 1936 law passed to deal with fascist organizations.

On 12 July 1956 the U.P.C. launched a guerilla war of resistance to the French administration, calling for unity of all national groups in the country around four minimum demands: reunification of the British and French Cameroons, a popular referendum or democratically elected constituent assembly, a total amnesty for all political prisoners, and complete freedom of expression. The French government finally set a date for elections in December 1956, but as these were to be conducted under a state of emergency, the U.P.C. called for a boycott which was to a large extent effective. The movement meanwhile pursued the struggle with an 'army of national liberation', which waged sustained and bitter warfare, especially in the Bamiléké and Sanaga-Maritime regions, while the exiled U.P.C.

leaders, whose headquarters were in Cairo and later in Conakry, conducted an international campaign for the withdrawal of French troops and the reunification of the Cameroons in an independent republic. Reuben Um Nyobe himself remained to conduct rebel operations, but was killed in 1958. The U.P.C. lost its most popular leader, and much of the force of the movement disappeared with the establishment of an independent Cameroun Republic on 1 January 1960.

AHMADOU AHIDJO, first President of the Republic, was born in May 1922 at Garoua, the capital of the Northern Region. Son of a Fulani Chief, he was educated locally and at secondary school in Yaoundé, the capital, becoming in 1941 a radio operator in the Post Office. Leader of the Jeunes Musulmans movement, he was especially concerned to build up better understanding between the Northern and Southern sections of the country, and he more and more took an active part in national politics.

In 1947 he was elected for the Benue region to the Territorial Assembly, then still a purely consultative body, and in 1952 was re-elected when the Assembly was at last given certain legislative powers. In October 1953 he was elected to the Assembly of the French Union in Paris, and became first one of its Secretaries in 1954 and then Vice-President in 1956. In December 1956 he was again elected to the Territorial Assembly and immediately afterwards made its President.

An influential member of the Bloc Démocratique Camerounais (B.D.C.) – founded by a European, Dr Aujoulat, and led by André-Marie Mbida – he became Vice-Premier and Minister of the Interior in the first African government of the territory, formed in May 1957 under Mbida as Premier. The two leaders, however, were rivals for power, and the clash between them could not be long postponed.

Both Mbida and Ahidjo participated in the negotiations with France and the United Nations which led to the ending of the Cameroun's trusteeship status, but all the while the government was faced with an extremely difficult situation in the country at large. Since the 1956 elections, rebellion under U.P.C. direction had persisted in the country, particularly in the Sanaga-Maritime and Bamléké areas, although Mbida had employed the French army and increasingly savage measures to destroy the U.P.C. maquis.

In February 1958 he was at last defeated in the Assembly, principally because most of the members considered him too amenable to pressure from the French government and felt that some serious attempts should be made to negotiate with the U.P.C. Ahidjo, who was now leading his own party – the Union Camerounaise, based on his own Northern Region – was accordingly able to form a government, and while he continued to use French troops in order to crush the rebellion, he offered an amnesty to those terrorists willing to surrender. As a result, certain influential members of the U.P.C. – most notably Mayi Matip, who led the maquis in the Sanaga-Maritime area – abandoned terrorism and returned to constitutional politics. The section of the U.P.C. still active in the Bamiléké area and ultimately controlled by Félix-Roland Moumié from Guinea, continued, however, to fight.

Ahidjo was pressed to hold elections under United Nations supervision before independence, but he refused, and in 1959 he disbanded parliament altogether, to rule by decree. On 1 January 1960 the country became independent, and on 21 February a referendum was held to approve a presidential constitution. Moumié called for a boycott and Matip for a vote of 'no', but a seventy-five per cent poll gave Ahidjo an overall majority of some twelve per cent. Then, in the April 1960 elections to the National Assembly, the Union Camerounaise emerged with sixty-one of the 100 seats, and Ahidjo himself became President of the Republic on a vote of eighty-nine out of 100.

Under the new Premier, Charles Assale – a supporter of Ahidjo's, with considerable influence in the South of the territory – a coalition government was formed, though Mayi Matip and the former Prime Minister, Mbida, refused the ministries offered to them and remained in opposition. Tension accordingly continued and in October 1960, at the third Congress of the Union Camerounaise, Ahidjo again appealed for national unity and emphasized the need for rapid economic development. Attacked for being too moderate and for continuing to use French troops in order to suppress the lingering rebellion, his administration was only reluctantly recognized by Ghana and Guinea as that of a genuinely independent state. The impact of the U.P.C. itself, however, was considerably weakened in November 1960 with the death of Félix-Roland Moumié by poisoning, and though terrorism continued, it did so on a substantially reduced scale.

During 1960 Ahidjo held tentative talks with John Foncha, Prime Minister of the British-administered Southern Cameroons, over the unification of the two countries. The two territories of the British Cameroons, Northern and Southern, then went separately to the polls in February 1961, under United Nations supervision, to decide their future. In the Northern Cameroons, a poll of eighty-three per cent registered 146,296 votes for union with Nigeria, and 97,659 votes for union with the Cameroun Republic. In the larger Southern Cameroons, however, a ninety-five per cent poll recorded 233,571 votes for unification with Cameroun and only 97,741 votes for union with Nigeria.

JOHN NGU FONCHA, Prime Minister of the Southern Cameroons until its incorporation in the Cameroun Republic, was born in 1916 at Bamenda, a Catholic of the Meta tribe. Educated at Bamenda Government School and at St Michael's School in Buguma, he served as a pupil teacher from 1933 to 1936, and then attended St Charles Training College at Onitsha, where he obtained his Grade II Teacher's Certificate in 1939.

From 1940 to 1954 he was headmaster at various Catholic schools in Bamenda, taking all the while an ever-increasing interest in politics. From 1942 to 1945 he served as Secretary of the Bamenda branch of the Cameroons Youth League, from 1942 to 1954 as Founder President of the Bamenda Catholic Teachers' Union, and from 1945 to 1954 as President of the

Bamenda Board of the National Union of Teachers. From 1948 to 1951 he was Secretary of the Bamenda Improvement Union, and during 1949-50 he was organizer of the Bamenda section of the Cameroons National Federation, the political group established to give evidence to the United Nations visiting mission.

Conflicting political alignments, however, were forming over the issue of Cameroonian reunification. In 1951 Foncha left the Federation altogether to help form the Kamerun United National Congress (K.U.N.C.), on a policy of reunification with the French Cameroons, and in the same year he was elected to Nigeria's Eastern Regional Assembly. When the Kamerun National Congress (K.N.C.) was established by a merging of the Cameroons National Federation under Dr Emmanuel Endeley with the K.U.N.C., Foncha became Branch Secretary in the Bamenda district. The Kamerun National Congress, however, under Dr Endeley's leadership, evolved a programme aimed at divorcing the Southern Cameroons from the Eastern Region of Nigeria and forming it into a separate region within the Nigerian Federation. The K.N.C. swept to power in subsequent elections, and in 1954 the Southern Cameroons was accordingly established as a separate region of Nigeria, with Dr Endeley as its first Prime Minister.

Foncha, meanwhile, had grown ever more strongly convinced of the need for unification between the French and British Cameroons, and in 1955 he resigned from the K.N.C. to found the opposition Kamerun National Democratic Party, on a programme of Cameroonian reunification. Becoming President-General of the new movement, he campaigned strenuously on its behalf, and after it had won five seats in the 1957 elections, the K.N.D.P. achieved recognition as the official opposition. For the elections of January 1959, Foncha conducted his campaign almost entirely on a policy of unification with the French Cameroons, stressing the dangers to the Southern Cameroons of being swallowed by Nigeria, and when the K.N.D.P. emerged from the elections with fourteen seats to twelve for the opposition, he became Prime Minister.

After negotiations with Dr Endeley, as opposition leader, he agreed to a United Nations supervised plebiscite in February 1961 to give the territory a choice between unification with Nigeria and unification with the formerly French-administered and now independent Republic of Cameroun.

Then in July 1960, he reached agreement with Ahmadou Ahidjo, President of the Republic, over a federal-type association between the two countries, and the two leaders established a study group to examine the implications further. In November Foncha himself visited London to sound out the British government over whether it would surrender sovereignty to the Southern Cameroons should the plebiscite support unification, and he apparently received the undertakings he required. Certainly his political judgement was accurate, for the February 1961 plebiscite resulted in an overwhelming victory for the policy of the Kamerun National Democratic Party and enormously strengthened Foncha's personal position.

On 1 October British trusteeship of the Southern Cameroons came to an end, and in Buea, the small capital of the territory, a twenty-one-gun salute boomed, church bells chimed, and the Union Jack gave place to the flag – yellow, red, and green, with two gold stars – of the new Federal Republic of Cameroun.

The new constitution establishes Yaoundé as the federal capital, and redesignates the Cameroun Republic as Eastern Cameroun and the Southern Cameroons as Western Cameroun. It provides for a President to be elected for a five-year term, and contrary to general practice in West Africa, excludes Cabinet Ministers from membership of parliament. The President, as Chief of State, controls the armed forces and possesses considerable powers on the American model.

A National Federal Assembly of fifty members is to be elected by universal suffrage, with one member for every 80,000 people, so providing forty members for Eastern Cameroun and ten for the West. The Federal President himself appoints the two Premiers of the regions, who have then to be invested by their own legislatures. The Federal authority covers external relations, foreign affairs, trade, defence, security, and all centralized activities, while arrangements have already been made to establish a federal public service. Efforts have begun to teach English in West Cameroun and French in East Cameroun, but the problem remains of whether the two educational systems should be left separate or integrated at an immediate cost to standards.

John Foncha, Vice-President of the new Federal Republic and Premier of its Western Region, called on the people to rejoice that the Cameroun nation had been reborn. 'Greater efforts and conscientiousness in our work are required of us to make this experiment a success', he proclaimed on the day of unification. Ahidjo himself said that the new republic promised to be a laboratory for an African union of English- and French-speaking States. It would 'constitute a bridge between the two Africas, and its rôle cannot but influence future African gatherings.' He ended by calling for unity and appealed to elements in the Federal Republic, which he said were 'blinded by passion and envy', to help in the tasks ahead.

The Times reported on 26 October: 'Fears that 1 October would herald an increase in terrorist activity have so far proved unfounded, and the Camerounian army, which took over responsibility for internal security in West Cameroun from British troops, seems to be doing its job quite well. The fact that the terrorists have so far done little, however, does not necessarily mean that they are in eclipse.' Certainly the rebellion continues in the Bamiléké area, on the very border of what was the Southern Cameroons. France seems willing to continue with financial assistance, at present amounting to more than one-third of the Republic's annual £15 million budget, and this dependence on French aid, combined with the presence of a French battalion and French officers in the Cameroun army, remains one of the major arguments used by the terrorists to justify their continued rebellion. The U.P.C. claims that the republic is free in name only, and that its foreign policy – it is one of the most ardently pro-French in the Brazzaville bloc – is making this increasingly evident.

It would be a pity if this first experiment in African unity across the language frontier were to fail. Ahidjo himself recognizes that he must spread his influence throughout the South, where his opposition groups are based, if his régime is to possess any real stability, and certainly his survival for so long in so complex and explosive a situation is a measure of his shrewd political ability. But leaderless as it may seem now to be, the U.P.C. remains a rallying point for disaffection, and would soon enough find support in the former Southern Cameroons were the authoritarianism of the Ahidjo régime to continue substituting force for a programme of dramatic reform, likely to win widespread popular support. Reunification of the Camerounian people is less a triumph than a test for Ahidjo. For the sake of the exciting experiment which at the moment he guides, he must make every effort not to fail, and success cannot lie in the assistance of French forces to still disaffection. It can only come from a true participation of the reunified Camerounians in the evolution of a free and just society.

13 The Four Faces of Nigerian Nationalism

Of all the new nations that constitute contemporary Africa, it is Nigeria, the most populous, that is most dramatically the product of colonialism. Within an area of 373,250 square miles live over 35,000,000 people, speaking some 250 different languages and constituting numerous distinctive traditional groups, of which the Yoruba dominate the West, the Ibo the East, and the Fulani the North. Enjoying different climates and soil resources, with varying histories and political experiences, the principal peoples of Nigeria were welded together by British dominion and the resistance which that excited.

The reaction to pacification, completed by the end of the nineteenth century, was at the beginning fragmentary and localized, provoked by specific grievances, and speedily stilled by a show of force. It was the tiny intelligentsia, operating in the main through press and public meeting, that awoke first a racial and then a national consciousness.

From its founding in 1891 to the early 1930s, the *Lagos Weekly Record*, owned and edited by John Payne Jackson and then after his death in 1918 by his son Thomas Horatius Jackson, aroused resistance by its persistent assaults on British rule. Nigerians participated in the early Pan-African Conferences – the first at Paris in 1918–19, organized by the American Negro W. E. B. Du Bois and Blaise Diagne, the African Deputy for Senegal in the French Assembly; the second, at Lisbon in 1923; and the third in 1927 at New York.

Concurrently, the Universal Negro Improvement Association, founded and led by Marcus Garvey, a Jamaican Negro, was canvassing 'no other salvation for the Negro but through a free and independent Africa'. The Garvey movement registered spectacular success among Negroes in the United States, publishing a newspaper, *Negro World*, and producing branches in Africa itself, one of which sprouted at Lagos in 1920 with support from the *Lagos Weekly Record*. The movement collapsed with Garvey's deportation from the United States in 1927, but the cry of 'Africa for the Africans' which he had raised was to reverberate long after his own disappearance from active politics.

Influenced by such developments and by the growth of the Congress movement in India, a number of West African intellectuals established the National Congress of British West Africa in 1920, with a conference at Accra; but the movement failed to take real root in Nigeria, and it was the West African Students' Union, founded in London in 1925, which rapidly developed into a training ground for Nigerian nationalist leaders.

What political organization existed within Nigeria itself was confined to Lagos, stimulated in 1923 by the grant of four elected African members to a new Legislative Council for the Colony and Southern Nigeria, three of them for Lagos itself. Herbert Macaulay, popularly considered the 'father of Nigerian nationalism', from 1908 for almost forty years canvassed the cause of Africans against their rulers. Twice imprisoned – once for the misapplication of trust funds and then for criminal libel – he was personally disqualified from election to office, but his influence with the Lagos market women, his newspaper, the *Lagos Daily News*, and the Nigerian National Democratic Party (N.N.D.P.), which he founded in 1923 to fight the first elections under the new constitution, together gave him a considerable influence in Lagos politics. The N.N.D.P., despite its name, however, remained an entirely Lagos-based organization, though its frequent 'national' approach to political issues and economic grievances excited Lagos to see itself as a part of Nigeria, instead of as a distinct political entity with exclusive problems.

Yet until the late 1930s, there was little real nationalist activity in Nigeria, and in 1936 an Australian who had just resigned from the Nigerian Colonial Service could state that the territory has fewer problems than any other governing unit of the same population in the world. There is no problem of racial antagonism; there are no economic problems . . . there is no conflict between white capital and coloured labour . . . and there are no political problems, internal or external, of any kind. Social problems like caste, economic problems like agricultural indebtedness, political problems like nationalism, as in India, are all non-existent.[1]

Sanguine as this colonial commentary must have been, it did reflect the lethargy of nationalist politics at the time. Nigeria was half asleep. It was DR BENJAMIN NNAMDI AZIKIWE, or 'ZIK', who was more than anyone else to rouse it awake. His father, an Ibo from Onitsha in the East, was a clerk in the Nigerian Regiment at Zungeru in the North, and it was there that Zik was born in 1904. Educated at mission schools in Onitsha, Lagos, and Calabar, he worked from 1921 to 1925 as a government clerk in the Treasury at Lagos and then set off for further studies in the United States of America. Enrolled first at Storer College in West Virginia, at Howard University in Washington D.C., and then at Lincoln University in Pennsylvania, he was strongly influenced by what he saw and experienced of colour discrimination and the development of Negro nationalism in the country.

The period of his stay in America was one of unprecedented Negro activity – the Garvey movement was at high tide when he arrived – enforced by a newly militant Negro press. He studied journalism himself and was vividly impressed by the power of newspapers as organs of propaganda and protest. Working at various times as a coal miner, casual labourer, dish-washer, steward, and even as a boxer, to keep himself, he concentrated on history and political science, taking a post-graduate course at the University of Pennsylvania.

His experience of colour cruelty in the United States made him conscious of the discrimination endured by the black-skinned outside of Africa as well, and he resolved upon an international emancipation for all those of his race. At first he even attacked territorial nationalism as a distraction from the

1. James S. Coleman, *Nigeria: Background to Nationalism.*

racial struggle, summoning all the colonies of West Africa to united effort against the common European enemy. In 1934 he visited London, where he published *Liberia in World Affairs*, and then settled in the Gold Coast, where he spent three years as Editor of the *African Morning Post* and secured for himself a considerable reputation as a journalist and political propagandist. Prosecuted on a charge of libel for having published an article entitled 'Has the African a God?', he was eventually acquitted on appeal.

In 1934 Lagos was excited over African education in Nigeria, with the establishment of a Yaba Higher College unattached to any British university. The standards of the new college were regarded as inferior, and a number of the younger critics formed the Lagos Youth Movement to oppose the institution. Then, after agitation over the college had died down, the leaders stirred up resistance on other issues, like the failure to appoint Africans to senior posts in the civil service and legislative discrimination against African lorry drivers. In 1936 the name of the organization was changed to the Nigerian Youth Movement, and in 1937, when Azikiwe returned to Nigeria, he joined its Executive.

It was by his journalism, however, that Azikiwe gave a new impetus to Nigerian nationalism. He started a chain of newspapers, the most important of which was the *West African Pilot*, and revolutionized West African journalism by the daring and directness of his editorials and news coverage. Concentrating upon racial injustices and the need for positive action to emancipate Africa, he energetically spread his message throughout the territory, nursing circulation by provincial news coverage and by efficient distribution, and establishing four provincial dailies, in Ibadan, Onitsha, Port Harcourt, and Kano.

The Ibo in the East, some 5,000,000 strong, had been the last of the major groups in Southern Nigeria to be pacified and had remained outside the mainstream of Nigerian politics. It was the Yoruba in Lagos and the West who had dominated anti-colonial agitation and produced the movements of resistance. Azikiwe was accordingly able to bring to Nigerian nationalism not only a vigorous race consciousness and militantly popular press, but leadership of one of Nigeria's most powerful peoples. He at once became a symbol of Ibo – indeed of all non-Yoruba – political resistance to foreign rule, the spokesman of a truly country-wide nationalism.

The Nigerian Youth Movement, immeasurably strengthened by Azikiwe's influence and propaganda, won the Lagos Town Council elections and, in October 1938, defeated Macaulay's Nigerian National Democratic Party in the elections to the Legislative Council. In the same year it also published the Nigerian Youth Charter, which outlined the objectives of the movement as '... complete autonomy within the British Empire ... a position of equal partnership with other member States of the British Commonwealth ... and complete independence in the local management of our affairs'. By the end of 1938 the movement claimed a national membership of over 10,000 and nearly twenty provincial branches throughout the territory. In 1941, however, Azikiwe left the N.Y.M. over its nomination of one of his personal antagonists to a vacant Legislative Council seat, and he took almost all the Ibo members with him. Efforts to save the organization failed, and it only survived effectively in Ibadan, under the leadership of Chief Obafemi Awolowo, to become the basis of the present Action Group.

The outbreak of the Second World War opened a new phase in the history of Nigerian nationalism. The loss of British colonies in the Far East and the nationalist struggle in India eroded imperial prestige in the non-white world, while the Atlantic Charter, with its publication of 'the right of all peoples to choose the form of government under which they will live', excited nationalist sentiment everywhere in the colonial world. In 1942 Azikiwe founded the Nigerian Reconstruction Group, a study circle to examine the problems which Nigeria would face after the war, and he made plans to form a national political party. The following year he went to Britain to protest to the Colonial Secretary against the restrictions then imposed upon Nigerian students there, as well as to submit, with seven other journalists, a memorandum, *The Atlantic Charter and British West Africa*. This demanded the immediate abrogation of

Crown Colony government, immediate Africanization of the civil service, and ten years of representative government to be followed by five years of full responsible government before independence.

In August 1944 a group of Nigerian students and young intellectuals visited Azikiwe to complain that the youth of the country were prepared for the nationalist struggle but lacked real leadership. With the encouragement of Azikiwe himself and his press, they called a conference in Lagos to organize a national council that would 'weld the heterogeneous masses of Nigeria into one solid block'. On 26 August 1944 the inaugural meeting of this conference resolved to form the Nigerian National Council, 'believing our country is rightfully entitled to liberty and prosperous life . . . and determined to work in unity for the realization of our ultimate goal of self-government within the British Empire'. Though the Nigerian Youth Movement held aloof, the new party – soon afterwards renamed the National Council of Nigeria and the Cameroons (N.C.N.C.), to promote affiliation from Cameroonian associations in Lagos – united a vast number of literary, professional, tribal, social, and youth organizations with the old Nigerian National Democratic Party. Herbert Macaulay was elected President, and Azikiwe himself the Secretary-General. It was at this period that Azikiwe advocated a federation of eight states as the best political arrangement for an independent Nigeria, a proposal that he had first made in *Political Blueprint for Nigeria*, published in 1943.

On 6 March 1945 Governor Sir Arthur Richards presented proposals for a new constitution to the Legislative Council of Nigeria. These were approved after slight modification, and what came to be known as the Richards Constitution governed Nigeria until 1951. It was not so much the proposed division of the country into three regions that stirred nationalist sentiment into a storm of protest against the new constitution, since Azikiwe himself and many of his colleagues in the N.C.N.C., let alone Awolowo and the Nigerian Youth Movement at Ibadan, were canvassing various federal arrangements. The constitution was rushed through the Legislative Council; there had been no previous consultation with nationalist leaders; and the 'unofficial' members of the Council who gave their approval had long been repudiated by Nigerian nationalist opinion. The constitution ignored the demands made by the nationalists for a greater share in the management of their own affairs, and it provided no executive training of Nigerians for responsible self-government. Though the constitutional proposals promised an 'unofficial majority' in the Regional Houses of Assembly and in the central Legislative Council, a number of 'unofficials' were to be nominees of the governor, while chiefs and emirs, who owed their position to the government, were to be classed as 'unofficials' as well.

Azikiwe himself agitated vigorously against the new constitution, assaulting it with all the influence of his press. The rise in the cost of living during the war had not been relieved by any corresponding rise in wages, and labour unrest exploded in 1945 with a general strike supported by some 30,000 workers and lasting for thirty-seven days. The success of the strike, which only ended after the government had promised an impartial commission of inquiry into labour grievances and given assurances that there would be no victimization, enormously increased Azikiwe's stature throughout the country, since he had strongly supported the strikers in his newspapers.

In July 1945 Azikiwe's *West African Pilot* and *Daily Comet* were banned for misrepresenting facts, and Azikiwe himself went into hiding in Onitsha, claiming that he had been threatened with assassination. The masses of Nigeria believed that Azikiwe was in danger because of his efforts to emancipate Africa, and he became a national hero. With his own position much enhanced, his newspapers circulated more widely than ever. They were sympathetic to labour, the youth, clerks, teachers, and the educated non-Yoruba elements throughout the territory; they set themselves up as the guardian of African rights; and they furnished wide publicity for individual African grievances against the government. In 1946 the Zikist Movement was formed by a number of Azikiwe's admirers, to protect him against attack and act as a radical, 'ginger' group of young Nigerian nationalists.

At the end of April 1946 the N.C.N.C. leaders started a tour of Nigeria to raise funds for a delegation of protest to London, and large numbers of people were first made aware of Nigerian unity through the speeches and visits of the touring nationalists. Before its conclusion, Macaulay died, at the age of eighty-two, and Azikiwe became President of the N.C.N.C. in his stead. In June 1947 the protest delegation visited London without success, but this too increased the prestige of Azikiwe throughout the country.

In 1948 the unpopular Governor Richards retired, and Sir John Macpherson, his successor, promised an early revision of the Richards Constitution, speedier Africanization of the senior civil service, and the extension of facilities for higher education. During 1949, village, provincial, and regional conferences were held, and in January 1950 a general conference with representatives from all parts of the territory took place to discuss the regional recommendations. The majority voted to retain the existing three regions – Eastern, Western, and Northern – as the political divisions of Nigeria, while a subsequent select committee of the Legislative Council recommended the incorporation of Lagos into the West. The members of the central legislature were to be elected by the various Regional Assemblies.

The N.C.N.C. agreed to participate in elections under the new constitution, and in 1951 Azikiwe was elected from Lagos to the Western Region House of Assembly, while Eyo Ita became Leader of the N.C.N.C. Government in the East. The predominance of the newly formed Yoruba-controlled Action Group in the Western House, however, prevented Azikiwe's election from there to the Federal House, and remaining as Leader of the Opposition in the Western Assembly, he began to agitate against the constitution. N.C.N.C. Ministers in the Federal House stated, however, that the constitution should be given a trial, and in 1952 they were expelled from the party for disloyalty to the leader and his policies. The dispute none the less continued, with some of the Eastern Ministers, including Eyo Ita, supporting the rebels. As a result, a crisis developed throughout the Eastern Region, with the N.C.N.C. itself in opposition to a government drawn from among its members. In March 1953 the dissident elements of the party from both the Federal and Regional Houses split away to form the National Independence Party. In May the Eastern House was dissolved, and new elections gave the N.C.N.C. seventy-two of the ninety-seven seats, with only nine for the National Independence Party. Azikiwe himself joined the Eastern House, confirming his hold over the Region, and became first Chief Minister and then Premier.

After a year of operation, the Macpherson Constitution proved unworkable – not least because of Azikiwe's opposition to it – and on 30 July 1953 Nigerian political leaders met with representatives of the British Government in London to discuss constitutional changes and 'the question of self-government in 1956'. The conference resolved that Nigeria should become a truly federal state, with specific powers enjoyed by the federal government and residual powers given to the regional governments, rather than – as under the 1951 constitution – an essentially unitary state, the legislature of which was regionally elected. Elections to the Federal House were to be direct in the Eastern and Western Regions, while each of the three regional governments, possessing greater power and responsibility, would be controlled by a Nigerian 'Premier' and Ministers enjoying effective authority over their departments. Finally, full self-government would be granted in 1956 to those regions desiring it.

In 1956 the Foster-Sutton Tribunal was established to inquire into allegations that Azikiwe had improperly invested Eastern Region government money in the African Continental Bank, a concern in which he had considerable personal interests. Its report, published on 16 January 1957, concluded that his conduct had fallen short 'of the expectation of honest, reasonable people', and a few days afterwards the N.C.N.C. National Executive, while refuting the conclusions of the Tribunal, announced that it had advised the Premier – who had agreed – to transfer his rights and interests in the bank to the Eastern Regional Government. Azikiwe decided to dissolve the Eastern House, and new elections on 15 March 1957 returned him and his party to power with a large majority.

Certain elements in the Region, however, began to agitate for a change in the N.C.N.C. leadership. Aware of this, Azikiwe attacked the party organization for lack of efficiency at the N.C.N.C. Convention in April 1957, criticizing especially Dr Kingsley Mbadiwe, then Federal Minister of Commerce and Second National Vice-President of the N.C.N.C., and Kola Balogun, the party's General Secretary. In October of the same year Azikiwe assumed special powers and removed both from their offices. They then produced a resolution signed by thirty-one influential N.C.N.C. members demanding Azikiwe's own resignation. Both, together with those who had supported them, were then expelled from the party and set up the N.C.N.C. Reform Committee, which passed a further resolution demanding Azikiwe's dismissal. After a period of charge and counter-charge Azikiwe once more triumphed, largely because of his irresistible personality and enormous prestige. In July 1958 the dissidents formed the Democratic Party of Nigeria and the Cameroons, leaving Azikiwe supreme within the N.C.N.C. and the East.

At this time Azikiwe began negotiating an understanding on the federal level with the Northern People's Congress (N.P.C.), in the hope that he might through such an alliance become the Federal Prime Minister. After the federal elections in December 1959, however, though an N.C.N.C.–N.P.C. coalition was able to form the government, he himself became President of the Senate and then Governor-General.

A man of considerable learning, with a wide-reaching mind, greatly respected as the leader of Nigerian nationalism for many years, Azikiwe remains a considerable force in Nigeria, possessing a popular appeal, especially in the East, which makes it impossible for his political opponents to remove him. Though his position as Governor-General has lifted him above political contest, and the leadership of the N.C.N.C. – renamed the National Convention of Nigerian Citizens at the beginning of 1962 – has been assumed by Dr Michael Okpara, Azikiwe is still a power in Nigerian politics, the measure of which only events in the next few years can reveal. In December 1961, Sir Abubakar Tafawa Balewa, Federal Prime Minister, publicly gave his support to those advocating a republican Nigeria. Certainly, the change to a republic is unlikely to be long delayed, and Azikiwe may well be the first President.

*

The Northern Region of Nigeria covers more than seventy-five per cent of the territory's land surface and includes nearly sixty per cent of its population. More than forty per cent of its many different peoples speak Hausa as their mother tongue, the vast bulk are Moslem, and the area's Islamic culture has links, via the Maghreb and Egypt, with Mecca, the Arab world, and the East. Dominant politically and economically within the region for the past century and a half have been the Fulani, whose empire – centred on Sokoto – was established as a result of the successful *jihad* launched in 1802 under the leadership of a Fulani Sheik, Othman Dan Fodio.

The North lagged far behind the East and West in nationalist activity and sentiment; education there was traditional and Islamic, while the authoritarian political structure of the Hausa States – strengthened by Britain's energetically applied policy of indirect rule – crushed as 'inefficiency or insubordination' any signs of individual resistance or radicalism. The traditional ruling class – called the *Fulanin Gida* or Fulani House – was largely supported by the merchant and artisan classes in its opposition to any social and political reform. The peasant masses, or *talakawa*, the overwhelming bulk of the population, were politically inert until the early nineteen-fifties, and such nationalist activity as did take place was almost invariably the work of Southerners settled temporarily in the North.

The nationalist awakening, however, was soon to come as a response to Southern example. In 1945 a Zikist supporter of the National Council of Nigeria and the Cameroons, Mallam H. R. Abdallah, founded the Northern Elements Progressive Association in Kano, but when Abdallah himself was imprisoned shortly afterwards the organization disintegrated. Then, in 1949, a number of Northerners, including Abubakar Tafawa Balewa, the present Federal Prime Minister of Nigeria, founded the Jam'iyyar Mutanen Arewa – Hausa for Northern People's

Congress – as a cultural organization. For a short while it was the home of Northern radicals, but the growing influence over it of the traditional rulers made it evident that the organization would not lend itself to a campaign for political reform. In July 1950, therefore, a group of dissidents led by Mallam Aminu Kano broke away to form the Northern Elements Progressive Union, which successfully contested the Kano primary elections of 1951. In reaction the Jam'iyyar Mutanen Arewa formed itself into a political party as the Northern People's Congress (N.P.C.) in October 1951, receiving the immediate support of the powerful Sardauna of Sokoto and the Emirs, together with the encouragement of the British Administration.

Accomplishing absolute control of the North, with its fifty per cent share of seats in the Federal House of Representatives, the new party possessed a final say in the government of an independent Nigeria, since no group could command a majority without its support. After the federal elections of December 1959, it entered into coalition with the N.C.N.C., and its leader in the Federal House, SIR ALHAJI ABUBAKAR TAFAWA BALEWA, became Nigeria's Federal Prime Minister.

Born in 1912 of a Moslem family in Bauchi, the son of the district head of Lere, Sir Abubakar does not come, as do the majority of the Northern Region leaders, from the ruling Fulani people. Educated locally, he went to Katsina College, where he qualified as a teacher, and then returned home to teach at the Bauchi Middle School, passing the Senior Teacher's Certificate by private study. In 1945, together with Aminu Kano and a group of other Northern leaders, he spent one year at the London University Institute of Education, and experience of a world so different from the traditionalist Moslem North had upon him and his colleagues a dramatic political impact. Indeed, of this time in his life he was later to write: 'I returned to Nigeria with new eyes, because I had seen people who lived without fear, who obeyed the law as part of their nature, who knew individual liberty.'

Believing, however, not in revolution – as Aminu Kano did –

but in gradual reform, he returned to Nigeria to serve as a Native Authority Education Officer and, enjoying the trust of the traditional rulers, was almost immediately appointed to the first Northern Region House of Assembly, from where he was unanimously elected to the Nigerian Legislative Council. In the 1949–50 constitutional talks, he energetically advocated the special interests of the North and was regarded as the most militant of the Region's leaders in his opposition to the influence of the South. Meanwhile, however, he was pressing quietly but firmly for reform within the North, and in 1951 he introduced a motion in the Northern Region House which led to a select committee on local government. 'I believe in indirect rule,' he said. 'It allows us to retain good traditions. But I abhor the notion of a sole Native Authority which has the support of neither religion nor history. Ending that status is the most important reform.' It was largely the threat of Southern domination that was stimulating this Northern awakening, since conservatives and traditionalists were ready to cooperate with moderates in instituting changes rather than permit an identification of all reform with the militant Southern parties.

Sir Abubakar played a significant part in the establishment of the Northern People's Congress as a political party and was elected on its ticket first to the Northern House of Assembly and then from there to the Federal House of Representatives. In 1952 he became Federal Minister of Works, and his reputation within the Cabinet persistently grew. He became firmly convinced that Nigerian unity was possible and that it was his duty to work for it. In 1954 he became Federal Minister of Transport and, as First Vice-President of the N.P.C. and leader of the largest party in the House of Representatives, an obvious possibility for national leadership. In 1957 he became Chief Minister and was largely responsible for the formation of a national government, bringing the Action Group from the West into coalition with the N.P.C. and the N.C.N.C. Soon afterwards he became the first Federal Prime Minister, principally because he was an uncontroversial figure and efficient administrator, whose integrity protected him from personal attack.

Though widely respected throughout Nigeria and supremely skilful at keeping his Cabinet united behind him, Sir Abubakar possesses little popular following. The N.P.C. itself remains absolutely dominant in the North – in the regional elections of May 1961, it won 160 out of the 170 seats in the Northern House of Assembly – and its President, Alhaji Sir Ahmadu Bello, the Sardauna of Sokoto, appears content to remain Premier of the Northern Region. Were the Sardauna, whose energy and efficiency are accompanied by an aristocratic authoritarianism and Moslem fervour, to have attempted federal rule himself, it is conceivable that the strains would have been too great for the uneasy coalition of traditionalist North and radical South to survive. Sir Abubakar has, however, attempted to build a bridge between the North and South, resisting those pressures that he regards as too radical but recognizing too the constant need for reform.

Opposed to extreme Pan-Africanism and any hasty demands for West African federation, he has nevertheless adopted a strong stand over race rule in South Africa and the French atomic bomb tests in the Sahara. Attending the twenty-nation Conference of Independent African States at Monrovia in May 1961, he was generally observed as having exercised a dominant influence and undoubtedly increased his international standing as a result. He remains shrewdly attentive to the mood of public opinion within Nigeria itself, and negotiated an end to the unpopular Anglo-Nigerian Defence Agreement on 21 January 1962, after it had been in force for less than two years.

On 25 January a conference of twenty independent African states opened in Lagos. Called by the countries which had met at Monrovia in May 1961, it had been intended as the occasion for a dramatic reconciliation between them and the five states of the Casablanca bloc – Ghana, Guinea, Mali, Morocco, and the United Arab Republic. Under pressure from the Brazzaville bloc of pro-French states, led by the Ivory Coast, however, the Provisional Government of the Algerian Republic had not been invited. As a result, on 21 January, the Foreign Ministers of the Casablanca states had announced in Accra that they would not attend the Lagos meeting. In a joint statement, they had claimed that the failure to invite the Algerians was 'of such a character as may undermine the struggle of the Algerian people for their survival and independence at a critical stage in that struggle'. They had further maintained that 'the agenda and all necessary arrangements for the Lagos Conference were made unilaterally and without consultation with the Casablanca Charter states, thereby depriving [them] of the opportunity of making the necessary preparation with all the care and attention demanded by such a conference'. Partly in embarrassment at the failure to invite the Algerians, and partly in response to the reaction of the Casablanca states, Libya, the Sudan, and Tunisia had also withdrawn from the conference.

The Nigerian government hastened to announce that it had no objection to inviting the Algerians, but that invitations had been issued jointly by the whole Monrovia bloc. Yet, in many African capitals, it was Nigeria that was blamed for not having used its predominant status, as by far the most populous and powerful member of the Monrovia group, to compel the issuing of an invitation to the Algerians. Certainly some advances were made in the direction of African unity. An Organization of African States was inaugurated, with a constituent assembly composed of heads of state, meeting every three years, and a permanent council of ministers, to supervise the work of a secretariat. Disputes between African states were to be settled by a permanent tribunal, and resolutions launched a development bank, a private investment guarantee fund, an organization for health, labour, and social affairs, an educational and cultural council, and various commissions on specific practical issues. There is some distance between agreement and implementation, however, and it remains to be seen with what willingness the Monrovia states are prepared to travel it. What is less questionable is the effect that the continuing split between the Casablanca and Monrovia groupings is likely to have on all the countries involved, not least upon Nigeria itself. No Nigerian government can afford to be too closely associated with the Brazzaville bloc and its clear commitment to the West. Sir

Abubakar lost the gamble to bring Casablanca and Monrovia together at Lagos. The internal politics of Nigeria are unlikely to escape the consequences.

*

The Yoruba peoples who dominate the Western Region and, through the Action Group, the Federal Opposition in Nigeria, possess perhaps the longest history of political unity and a common culture in all West Africa. Overwhelmingly represented in Lagos, where nationalist activity in the territory began, they provided the most significant intellectual force resisting colonial rule until the coming of Dr Azikiwe and the stimulation that he gave to the Ibos in the East.

CHIEF OBAFEMI AWOLOWO, Leader of the Action Group Opposition in the Nigerian Federal Parliament, was born at Ijebu-Remo in March 1909, an Ijebu Yoruba and the son of a farmer. Educated at Anglican and Methodist schools in Ikenne and at the Methodist School and Baptist Boys High School in Abeokuta, he was forced to interrupt his studies through lack of money after his father's death. For a while he worked as a pupil teacher and then proceeded to Wesley College in Ibadan for teacher training. Leaving Wesley, he studied shorthand and typing and went to work for a German firm in Lagos, losing his job in the depression and returning to Wesley College as a clerk in 1932. In 1934 he again left Wesley, this time to become a trader and then a newspaper reporter, organizing in the late thirties the Nigerian Produce Traders Association and becoming Secretary of the Nigerian Motor Transport Union. Meanwhile, however, he studied in his spare time, matriculating in 1939 and gaining his Bachelor of Commerce degree in 1944, while he was editing the *Nigerian Worker*.

In June 1940 he became Secretary of the Ibadan branch of the Nigerian Youth Movement (N.Y.M.) and led the agitation for reform of the Ibadan Native Authority Administration Council, a campaign which resulted in the establishment of the Ibadan Native Authority Advisory Board in 1942. As the Ibadan leader of the N.Y.M., he condemned the concentration of all leadership in Lagos and attempted to spread control of the movement to other areas. After Dr Azikiwe and nearly all the Ibo members had walked out of the N.Y.M. in 1941, the Ibadan branch remained the only influential section, and Awolowo tried, with little success, to reconstruct the whole movement.

In 1943 he was a co-founder of the Trades Union Congress of Nigeria, and in 1944 he at last left Nigeria for London to fulfil his life-long ambition to study law. While in London he founded the Egbe Omo Oduduwa, a Yoruba cultural and political movement which was to help lay the foundations of the Action Group, and wrote *Path to Nigerian Freedom*, in which he outlined his federal approach to Nigerian nationalism.

> Under a true federal constitution each group, however small, is entitled to the same treatment as any other group, however large. Opportunity must be offered to each to evolve its own peculiar political institution. Each group must be autonomous in regard to its internal affairs. Each must have its own regional House of Assembly. . . .
>
> We need not be alarmed at the number of autonomous States which would thus emerge. The population of Switzerland is about four million; just about one-sixth of that of Nigeria. This country consists of four racial groups. These are divided into twenty-two cantons, each of which has its own Parliament and Government. . . . Canada, with a population of about half of that of Nigeria, has nine Provinces, each of which has its own Legislature. According to these and other well-known and well-tried constitutional precedents, even as many as thirty to forty Regional Houses of Assembly would not be too many in the future United States of Nigeria.

Qualifying in 1947, Awolowo returned to Ibadan and set up in practice, all the while continuing to work with the Egbe, of which he became General Secretary in 1948. On 28 April 1951, the Action Group was publicly inaugurated as a political party under his leadership, with a programme of 'freedom for all, life more abundant', and the new movement won the Western Region elections in 1951. Awolowo himself was elected for the Ijebu-Remo division, and from 1951 to 1954 he served as Minister of Local Government, carrying out a complete reform of local government structure and establishing a modern system of elective councils with seats reserved for traditional Chiefs. In 1953 Chief Anthony Enahoro of the Action Group tabled the motion in the Nigerian Federal House of Representatives 'that this House accepts as a primary political objective the demand of self-government for Nigeria in 1956'.

In October 1954, when the new constitution came into force, Awolowo became Premier of the Western Region, and attempting to build the Action Group into a country-wide party, he forged alliances with minority groups in other regions, collecting around him both in party and in government an able and efficient team. He gradually built the Action Group into the best political organization in Nigeria, using modern methods of mass persuasion, and during his period of office, he steadily improved educational and social services, as well as agricultural methods, in the Western Region. Contesting the federal elections in December 1959, he hoped to bring the Action Group to federal power, but he failed to make adequate impact outside the Western Region and became instead Leader of the Opposition in the Federal House of Representatives.

The Action Group is by far the richest of the Nigerian parties, but has only seventy-five seats in the Federal House, where it constitutes the official opposition. Principally backed by the Yoruba chiefs, cocoa farmers, and businessmen of the Western Region, the party's policy was initially moderate, and Awolowo himself claimed that he was 'unhesitatingly and unequivocally for the Western democracies', calling 'neutrality in international affairs ... an unmitigated disservice to humanity'.

In attempting to accommodate itself to the demands of a national opposition and in recognition of the radical strain that runs through the Nigerian intelligentsia and youth, the Action Group has, however, increasingly moved away from this policy. In November 1960 Awolowo himself issued a plea in the Federal House of Representatives for speedy nationalization. In June 1961 he visited Ghana for consultations with Dr Nkrumah, and stated on his arrival at Accra airport that a target date should be set for the complete freedom of all African countries, which should break their foreign defence ties and other external alliances. Returning to Lagos, he announced that Nigeria should join the Ghana-Guinea-Mali Union, generally regarded as the militant wing of African nationalism, and that the rôle of Nigeria in African affairs did not inspire confidence among African nationalists. He claimed that Nigeria was seriously distrusted because of her military alignment with Britain, and that she should not have attended the Monrovia Conference, 'which was convened through the financial backing of certain Western powers'. Sharply competent and modern in outlook, Awolowo is clearly attempting to erase the belief that the Action Group is entirely Yoruba in aspect and aspirations, or that he himself represents tribal and conservative interests within Nigeria.

*

Such are the three faces of Nigerian nationalism – Azikiwe, Abubakar, Awolowo. The present structure of Federation – despite the recent establishment of a fourth region, the Mid-West State – seems clear enough, but it is a federation of seemingly static one-party rule, with each of the three main political movements absolutely dominant within its particular home region (the N.C.N.C. is expected to control the new Mid-West State). All attempts to extend the influence of one party from its own region to another have failed, and it seems clear that none of the three movements in its present form possesses a policy or leadership capable of providing it with a national following.

Two groups in Nigeria are of potential importance, and neither is necessarily attached to any of the three major movements. Federal education policy aims at the provision of some 80,000 men and women to direct the development of the schools, hospitals, roads, factories, and other projects required to raise Nigeria's standard of living. These will possess an importance far beyond their numbers and are likely to be most vocal in demanding the radical reforms which none of the major movements at present promises. Significant too are the large numbers of those leaving primary schools – all regional governments are devoting from one-third to one half of their annual expenditure to primary and secondary education – who under present circumstances will experience the greatest difficulty in finding satisfactory employment. They too are likely to constitute considerable pressure for a national party based on the sort of economic planning that is likely to provide them with economic security.

Complaining that no movement in Nigeria today is giving to the country the 'spirit of dynamism and unity, of popular socialism' that Nigeria needs in order to lead 'the resurgence in the social and political life of Africa around her', Mokwugo Okoye, radical youth leader of the N.C.N.C., claimed in *Africa South* (Vol. 6, No. 1, Oct.–Dec. 1961) that this resulted from a failure in leadership.

> Ours is a large country and a rich one. Neither its size nor its riches, however, can bring a better life to its people, and so to peoples all over Africa, if its leadership lacks the determination and the vision. The Nigerian crisis is a crisis of leadership. It cannot be long before the people of Nigeria find men able to translate their aspirations into achievement.

Certainly none of the three faces of Nigerian nationalism appears at the moment capable of uniting all Nigeria behind it. Yet the pressure for such unification persistently mounts. Will one of the three come to terms with it and so become its symbol? Or will it be a fourth, the features of which we do not at the moment recognize?

14 Kwame Nkrumah of Ghana

FRANCIS NWIA KOFIE KWAME NKRUMAH was born into the Nzima group of the Akan tribe at Nkroful in the Western Province of Ghana – then known as the Gold Coast – near the territory's border with the Ivory Coast. His precise date of birth is unknown, though it was probably in September 1909 and certainly on a Saturday, since Kwame is the name Akan mothers give to those of their children born on that day. Nkrumah himself sifts various sources in his autobiography to arrive at Saturday, 18 September 1909 as his most likely date of birth.

Nkrumah's autobiography, published in 1957, is dedicated to his mother, and the book everywhere reflects the love that he always felt for her.

> Certainly my mother rarely denied me anything and doubtless I took advantage of this, but I believe that she tried not to make her affection too obvious because whenever she was serving our meals, she always gave me mine last. I insisted on sleeping in her bed until, of my own free will, I decided to join my half-brothers, and I remember how I used to be angry when my father came to sleep in our bed and I insisted on sleeping between them. Several times he tried to explain to me that he was married to my mother, but I told him that I also was married to her and that it was my job to protect her.

His father was a goldsmith in Half Assini, some fifty miles from Nkroful and on the border with the Ivory Coast, and when Nkrumah was almost three years old, his mother took him there to join his father.

He early came under the influence of a Roman Catholic priest, a German called George Fischer, who relieved his parents of most of the responsibility for his primary education; his mother had herself been converted to Catholicism, and he was soon baptized into the Roman Catholic Church. Educated at Catholic mission schools for eight years, he then served as a pupil teacher for one year at Half Assini and in 1926 went to the Government Training College in Accra (later incorporated into Achimota College), where he studied teaching and graduated in 1930. Having taught at a variety of schools, he left for the United States in 1935, with assistance from an uncle in Lagos to swell his savings. He had already become a passionate nationalist, largely from reading articles written in the *African Morning Post* by Dr Nnamdi Azikiwe, now Governor-General of Nigeria, who lived in the Gold Coast and edited the paper from 1934 to 1937.

In 1939 he graduated from Lincoln University with a major in Economics and Sociology, but stayed on to study Theology. Having obtained post-graduate degrees in Education and Philosophy from the University of Pennsylvania, he was appointed Lecturer in Political Science at Lincoln University and while there was elected President of the African Students Organization of America and Canada. Coming across the works of Marcus Garvey – the Jamaican Negro who had established the Universal Negro Improvement Association to canvass 'no other salvation for the Negro but through a free and independent Africa' – he was drawn to the whole concept of an Africa emancipated from foreign rule and united in a common aspiration. At last, in May 1945, he left New York for London, to study Law and complete his thesis for a Doctorate in Philosophy, and there rapidly became involved in active politics. 'These years in America and England', he was to write in the preface to his autobiography, 'were years of sorrow and loneliness, poverty and hard work. But I have never regretted them, because the background that they provided has helped me to formulate my philosophy of life and politics.'

England excited him.

> Nobody bothered about what you were doing and there was nothing to stop you getting on your feet and denouncing the whole of the British Empire. In fact one of my pleasures in London was to buy a

copy of the *Daily Worker*, the only paper I really enjoyed reading, and push my way into the Underground with the businessmen. There, surrounded by copies of *The Times*, the *Daily Telegraph*, and the *Manchester Guardian*, I used to unfold my *Daily Worker* as ostentatiously as I could and then watch as pairs of eyes were suddenly focused on me. But the gaze of these bowler-hatted gentlemen was not in any way hostile and the atmosphere was always one of mild amusement.

The West African Students Union, founded at London in 1925, had rapidly developed into a training ground for the coming leaders of West African nationalism. Nkrumah himself became Vice-President, and in this post he worked closely with George Padmore, by whose writings he had already been influenced during his stay in America. One of the Secretaries of the Fifth Pan-African Conference at Manchester, where plans were made to win independence in Africa through the organization of mass parties and the use of 'positive action', he was elected General Secretary of the Working Committee established after the Conference and Secretary of the West African National Secretariat. Recognizing the necessity for a newspaper as an official organ of the Secretariat, he established *The New African*, but this ceased publication soon after its first issue in March 1946 through lack of sufficient funds. He visited Paris, where he met the African Deputies in the French National Assembly – Léopold Senghor and Félix Houphouet-Boigny amongst others – and planned with them a West African Conference in London. He was, however, soon to be summoned home.

In August 1947 a group of intellectuals in the Gold Coast, led by Dr Joseph Danquah, a member of the Gold Coast Legislative Council, had formed the United Gold Coast Convention (U.G.C.C.) to agitate for constitutional reform. Ako Adjei, later to serve as an important member of the Ghana Cabinet after independence, had been President of the West African Students Union in London from 1945 to 1947 and, on his return to the Gold Coast, had played an influential rôle in the foundation of the U.G.C.C. Approached to become the movement's General

Secretary, he declined, and successfully proposed that Nkrumah be invited to fill the post instead. He then wrote himself, urging Nkrumah to return to the Gold Coast and take up the appointment, and after crushing his doubts that he would be able to work with the cautious intellectuals in control of the Convention, Nkrumah set sail for home on 14 November 1947.

'When I took up my appointment as General Secretary,' he wrote in his autobiography, 'I found, on going through the minute book, that thirteen branches had been formed throughout the country. On looking further into the matter, however, I discovered that this was entirely incorrect. In actual fact just a couple of branches had been established and these were inactive.' He accordingly set out to organize the Convention from the bottom upwards, establishing a powerful mass party. In February 1948 a boycott of European and Syrian traders, organized by Chief Nii Kwabena Bonne in an attempt to bring down the price of imported goods, combined with a demonstration of ex-servicemen to excite severe rioting on the 28th, in which twenty-nine Africans were killed and 237 injured. The U.G.C.C. was blamed for the disturbances, and on 12 March the major leaders were arrested. Nkrumah himself was detained at Lawra in the Northern Territories but released to give evidence before the Watson Commission, which had been appointed to investigate the disturbances and which resulted in the establishment of the Coussey Committee to recommend a new constitution.

The policy split between Nkrumah and his colleagues in the Working Committee of the U.G.C.C., evident from the beginning, meanwhile persistently widened. During the first days of his detention, when he had been held with Dr Danquah and four other members of the Committee in Kumasi prison, he experienced for the first time the sharp hostility of his associates. 'There appeared to be a general belief amongst them that the whole tragedy of our arrest and suffering was my fault, and they began to make it plain that they regretted the day they had ever invited me to take up the Secretaryship of the U.G.C.C.' The Working Committee demoted him from General Secretary to Treasurer, but he continued his work as soon as he was released from detention and in September 1948 founded the *Accra Evening News* as the organ of the nationalist movement.

At the same time he established the Committee on Youth Organization (C.Y.O.), which quickly developed into a movement paying allegiance to his personal leadership rather than to the U.G.C.C.

> The aim of the Committee on Youth Organization was not to work against the Working Committee of the U.G.C.C., but rather to form itself into a youth section of the national movement. The members of the Working Committee, however, objected strongly to its formation. ... basically they opposed it because it was composed of the less privileged, or radical, section of the people and voiced the economic, social and political aspirations of the rank and file. It went completely against their more conservative outlook. They thought, and rightly so, that I was responsible for this organization of the youth and this fact strengthened their desire to remove me from office. Unfortunately for them, they disclosed their intention of doing this and thereby brought about open conflict between the supporters of the C.Y.O. within the U.G.C.C. and the Working Committee. It became obvious to all that these men who had, until that moment, complete control of the national movement, were anxious to be rid of me because I represented the radical and progressive section of the movement.

The C.Y.O., with the encouragement of Nkrumah, decided to break with the U.G.C.C. altogether, and on 12 June 1949 it formed the Convention People's Party (C.P.P.) as an entirely new political organization with a six-point programme:

1. To fight relentlessly by all constitutional means for the achievement of full 'Self-Government Now' for the chiefs and the people of the Gold Coast;
2. To serve as the vigorous conscious political vanguard for removing all forms of oppression and for the establishment of a democratic government;
3. To secure and maintain the complete unity of the chiefs and the people of the Colony, Ashanti, Northern Territories, and Trans-Volta;
4. To work in the interests of the trade union movement in the country for better conditions of employment;

5. To work for a proper reconstruction of a better Gold Coast in which the people shall have the right to live and govern themselves as free people;
6. To assist and facilitate in any way possible the realization of a united and self-governing West Africa.

On 20 November the C.P.P. convened a Ghana Peoples Representative Assembly of all organizations, except the tribally elected territorial councils and the U.G.C.C., and this rejected the moderate constitutional reforms recommended in the Coussey Report of the previous month, demanding instead full dominion status for the Gold Coast. The C.P.P. warned that it intended to resort to 'positive action', and in January 1950 disturbances broke out in the territory. A state of emergency was declared, the C.P.P. leaders were arrested one after another, and on 21 January Nkrumah himself, together with other leaders of the organization, was detained in James Fort prison. The C.P.P., however, continued its political organization and gained sweeping victories at the municipal elections in Accra, Kumasi, and Cape Coast. The first general election then took place in February 1951, and the party emerged triumphant, with thirty-four out of a possible thirty-eight elected seats in a House of eighty, and possessing majority control of the Assembly through the support of some of the nominated members. Nkrumah himself, while still in detention, was elected for the constituency of Accra Central, winning 22,780 votes out of the 23,122 polled.

On 12 February he was released to become Leader of Government Business and soon afterwards showed his qualities by taking strong measures to eradicate swollen shoot disease in the cocoa plants, although this seemed likely to lose him popularity with the farmers. In March 1952 his title was changed to Prime Minister, and in the local government elections of the same year the C.P.P. gained ninety per cent of the seats. The party meanwhile continued to press for full self-government, and in 1953 a government White Paper on constitutional reform was published, evolved after consultations with chiefs, political parties, and various other representative groups. At the 1953 C.P.P. conference, Nkrumah was elected Life Chairman and

Leader of the party, and it was decided that the government should ask for independence of the Gold Coast as a dominion within the Commonwealth.

On 11 July Nkrumah's motion for independence was carried unanimously in the Assembly. New elections were held in June 1954, and the C.P.P. won seventy-two seats out of 104, while a new Northern People's Party secured twelve; the remaining twenty seats were mostly filled by independents who later attached themselves to the existing parties, bringing the C.P.P. representation to seventy-nine, or over seventy-five per cent. The Nkrumah government objected to recognition of an official opposition, claiming that the Northern People's Party had no national basis, but this contention was overruled by the Speaker.

In August 1954, after Nkrumah had introduced measures to peg the price of cocoa at 72s. per load of 60 lb., well below the current world price, a strong opposition group, called the National Liberation Movement (N.L.M.) and centred in Ashanti, gathered against him, with the aim of establishing a federal form of government. Disturbances in Ashanti, with the destoolment by the Asanteman Council of those chiefs sympathetic to the administration, stimulated Nkrumah to take strong measures, including the passing of an ordinance which gave destooled chiefs the right of appeal to the Governor. Nkrumah then appointed a select committee to look into the whole issue of a federal or unitary government for the Gold Coast, but the opposition boycotted its proceedings. The committee finally reported against federation, but the British Colonial Secretary announced that independence would not be granted until the country was calm and fresh elections had resolved where power should finally rest. A new constitutional adviser, Sir Frederick Bourne, was appointed, who recommended the devolution of certain powers to regional assemblies, and in February 1956 a representative constitutional conference at Achimota accepted nearly all the Bourne proposals, including the establishment of an Upper House of Chiefs for each region, with power to review social and cultural legislation.

The N.L.M. continued to campaign outside the Assembly, disturbances persisted in Ashanti, and the Colonial Secretary expressed himself unable to agree that there was national support for the new constitution. Nkrumah himself was unwilling to hold any general election before independence in case there was violence, but he was persuaded, by fear that Britain would withhold self-government, to announce elections in July 1956. The C.P.P. won seventy-one seats, later increased to seventy-two, out of 104, giving Nkrumah the mandate he required. The Opposition, however, which had won a majority vote in the cities of the north and in Ashanti, boycotted the Assembly when it met to discuss the government motion for immediate independence, and Dr Busia, leader of the National Liberation Movement, went to London to demand a delay. The British government none the less agreed to independence on 6 March 1957, together with the incorporation into Ghana – to which the country now changed its name – of British Togoland, a United Nations Trust Territory under British administration which had opted for such a union in a United Nations sponsored plebiscite during April 1956.

In the preface to his autobiography, first published on the same day as Ghana's independence was declared, Nkrumah analysed his political objectives.

> Capitalism is too complicated a system for a newly independent nation. Hence the need for a socialist society. But even a system based on social justice and a democratic constitution may need backing up, during the period following independence, by emergency measures of a totalitarian kind. Without discipline freedom cannot survive. In any event the basis must be a loyal, honest, hard-working and responsible civil service on which the party in power can rely. Armed forces must also be consolidated for defence.
>
> [Ghana's] independence will be incomplete, however, unless it is linked up with the liberation of other territories in Africa. Ghana now joins the independent states of Egypt, Ethiopia, Liberia, Libya, Morocco, the Sudan and Tunisia. Elsewhere the continent is ruled by not less than six European powers.

In 1957 the C.P.P. government passed the Deportation Act,

permitting the deportation of any person whose presence in Ghana was not conducive to the public good, while the Preventive Detention Acts of 1958 and 1959 gave the government power to detain for up to five years without trial. The National Assembly (Disqualification) Act of 1959 excluded from the Assembly anyone absent for more than twenty consecutive sittings without the prior permission of the Speaker, and the opposition leader, Dr Busia, who was lecturing in Holland at the time, immediately came under the axe of the new law.

Nkrumah soon took the initiative in furthering the concept of Pan-Africanism. He called a conference of independent African States at Accra in 1958 and the first All-African Peoples Conference, on a non-governmental level, in December of the same year. When Guinea broke with France in September 1958, Nkrumah immediately offered her £10 million for urgent needs, and in May 1959 a Ghana-Guinea Union, which loosely united the two countries, was established. In September 1960 the association of Senegal and Soudan in the Federation of Mali broke up, Senegal withdrew, and Soudan changed its name to the Republic of Mali. Nkrumah visited Bamako for discussions with Modibo Keita, Mali's President, and announced on his return to Accra on 27 November 1960 that Ghana would give Mali a long-term loan and that the two countries would establish a political association. On 24 December the union of Ghana, Guinea, and Mali was proclaimed, and though no formal political ties have so far been established, there are quarterly meetings of the three Heads of State.

During the Congo crisis of 1960–61, Nkrumah consistently supported the cause of Patrice Lumumba as the democratically elected Premier of the Congo Republic, sponsoring his right to represent the new State's Central Government at the United Nations and demanding his immediate release after his arrest by Colonel Mobutu's troops on the warrant of President Kasavubu. As a consequence of his dissatisfaction with the conduct of the United Nations Congo Command, Nkrumah approached nine African States at the end of November 1960 – Ethiopia, Guinea, Liberia, Libya, Mali, Morocco, Sudan, Tunisia, and the

United Arab Republic – to establish with Ghana a joint High Command, in order to provide aid to any African territory that might find itself in a situation similar to that which the Congo experienced on achieving its independence. In January 1961 he met with the Heads of State from Guinea, Mali, Morocco, and the United Arab Republic – together with the President of the Provisional Government of the Algerian Republic, the Foreign Minister of Libya, and the Ceylon Ambassador to Cairo – at Casablanca. The Casablanca Conference gave strong support to the Front de Libération Nationale (F.L.N.) in Algeria, and to Lumumbist forces in the Congo, and adopted an African Charter which condemned 'neo-colonialism' and established economic, cultural, and political committees for cooperation, as well as an African Consultative Assembly and a joint African High Command.

In March 1961 Nkrumah attended the Commonwealth Prime Ministers Conference and was widely reported in the press as having threatened that Ghana would have to withdraw from the Commonwealth if South Africa remained a member. Certainly Nkrumah was among the most bitter critics of South African racial policy at the Conference and must be regarded as having played a substantial part in the decision of Dr Verwoerd, Prime Minister of South Africa, to withdraw his country's application for readmission to the Commonwealth after South Africa became a republic at the end of May.

Nkrumah's increasingly neutralist line in international affairs soon brought him under heavy fire in the West, and he was accused – by Christian Herter, American Secretary of State in the dying days of the Eisenhower administration – of having taken Ghana into the Communist bloc. Visiting President Kennedy in Washington during March 1961, he replied to a member of the press who had asked him whether or not he was a Communist:

> In Africa we are trying to create a society in which private capital and certain state-controlled agencies can both operate. Be careful. Do not equate Communism or being Communist with African nationalism. We are anti-colonialist and we shall always remain so until all the

colonialists are gone. How could my country be a satellite of another country when we believe that? It is very unfair to be accused of being Communist on the basis of anti-colonialism.

In July and August 1961 he did a tour of Communist States, visiting the Soviet Union, China, and Eastern Europe. On 29 July, at a state reception in Budapest, he spoke of '100 years of colonialist oppression', and the British Minister to Hungary withdrew in protest. *The Times* editorialized:

It would be rash to conclude from the speeches that Dr Nkrumah is embracing Communism. His liking for a policy of socialization is known and he obviously suits his remarks to his audience. Essentially, however, Kwame Nkrumah is an ambitious leader. He wishes to remain in the saddle in Ghana and to continue to guide the movement for African unification. He would be helped in neither of those aims by exchanging the 'colonialist yoke' for control from Moscow.

On 19 August he signed in Peking a treaty of friendship, containing agreements on economic and technical cooperation, between the governments of China and Ghana. Nkrumah expressed support for China's right to United Nations representation and stated:

Today we hear of new propositions. We hear of the European Economic Market; we hear of Euro-Africa, which does not make sense. Africa is Africa, Europe is Europe. There must be friendship between Africa and Europe; but it must be based on freedom and equality and not on exploited and exploiter. We shall not stop there but will continue to talk of political unification of the African continent, because unless and until the independent States of Africa are united in a single nation, the exploitation of Africa by Europe will never end. If Africa's sixty States are united politically, they will find a way to their own economic emancipation and to an African economic plan for the whole continent....

At the beginning of September he attended the twenty-five-nation[1] conference of uncommitted countries at Belgrade, having been a prominent force behind its organization, and in response

1. Twenty-four independent States and the Provisional Government of the Algerian Republic.

to growing East-West tensions over Berlin and the Soviet decision to recommence the testing of nuclear weapons, he included in his speech to the delegates an invitation to the leaders of the United States of America and the Soviet Union to negotiate their differences in Accra.

Nkrumah's foreign policy, however, and the influence that he can expect it to have, must inevitably depend upon conditions within Ghana itself. The first real test of his popularity since independence took place in April 1960, when a referendum was held to approve the new republican constitution and to choose a President. The constitution was overwhelmingly accepted, and Nkrumah himself elected President against his old rival, Dr Danquah, by some ninety per cent of the votes. Anyone who was in Ghana at the time will testify to the massive popular support he manifestly enjoyed. *The Times* of 13 June 1961 reported, in the first of two articles on Ghana today:

> President Nkrumah's popularity in the country, which at times comes near to adulation, appears to be untouched, but it is that feverish kind of popularity which could be shattered overnight. The people immediately around him also accept his leadership, but more and more they accept it only on condition that he lead on their terms. The President's most urgent task is to reconcile all factions, even those that he no longer trusts. Unfortunately, and dangerously, those whom he does not trust, he rejects. The possibility of revolution lies among the rejected, whoever they turn out to be.

This analysis contains an element of truth. Under the umbrella of Nkrumah's personal popularity, it is the C.P.P. that exercises power in contemporary Ghana, and the C.P.P. itself is a coalition of different – sometimes conflicting – pressure groups. Lobbies within the government canvass the interests of the trade unions, the cocoa farmers, and private capital. More and more Nkrumah has felt himself forced to assume absolute authority over various sectors of the State where collision between different groups in the government could no longer be concealed. On 8 April 1961, in a dawn broadcast to the people of Ghana, he gave what he described as a 'homely chat', in which he strongly criticized members of the government and the C.P.P. who were using their positions to enrich themselves. He called for a speedy end to corruption and self-seeking.

I have had occasion to emphasize the part which private enterprise will continue to play in our economic and industrial life. A different situation arises with Ghanaian businessmen who attempt to combine business with political life. . . . Any party member of parliament who wishes to be a businessman can do so, but he should give up his seat in parliament. In other words, no minister, ministerial secretary, or party member of parliament should own a business or be involved in business, Ghanaian or foreign. . . . Members of parliament must remember at all times that they are representatives of their constituencies only by reason of their party membership and that on no account should they regard constituency representation as belonging to them in their own right.

This is not the time for unbridled militant trade unionism in our country. Trade union officials must shed their colonial character and their colonial thinking. The approach of the Trades Union Congress to our national issues should be reasoned and constructive in accordance with our present circumstances.

Statements which may be regarded as government policy statements are those which I make myself personally and those which are clearly stated in the text to be the official policy of the government. In recent months people in Ghana and abroad have frequently been confused and government's policies made uncertain as a result of unauthorized statements which have been made by persons employed by the government or quasi-government bodies.

Coming to the integral organization of the party, I consider it essential to emphasize once more that the Trades Union Congress, the United Ghana Farmers' Council, the National Cooperative Council, and the National Council of Ghana Women are integral parts of the Convention People's Party, and in order to correct certain existing anomalies the Central Committee has decided that separate membership cards of the integral organizations shall be abolished forthwith. The membership card of the party will be the only qualification for membership within these organizations.

On 1 May, addressing a huge rally in Accra, he announced that he was taking over full executive direction of the C.P.P. as Chief Secretary and Chairman of the party's Central Committee. The country, led by the party, was entering a 'new political revolution regarding the struggle for the total liberation of the African continent', while at home the country had begun 'a new phase of the industrial and technical revolution'.

The 1961 budget was introduced in July with a spirited attack by Nkrumah on those who spoke of a 'financial crisis'. He said that the estimated value of exports had increased by eight per cent during the past year, while gross national production had grown by not less than five per cent. Ghana's sterling assets – which had been some £250 million at independence – still amounted to £100 million, which was equal to two and a half times the currency circulation. His confidence, however, would appear to have been belied by the decision of the Ghana government – reportedly on the advice of a Cambridge economist, Nicholas Kaldor – to introduce in the same month a compulsory savings scheme to help balance the £128 million budget for the current financial year. Under the scheme, salary and wage-earners were required to save five per cent of all monthly incomes over £10 in national development bonds, to mature in ten years at 2½ per cent interest a year, while professional workers and the self-employed were to contribute ten per cent for ten years in bonds yielding four per cent interest. Ordinary workers were to have their compulsory savings deducted at source.

This new measure led to vigorous protests in many parts of the country, and the beginning of September saw a strike of some 4,000 Ghana port and railway employees at Takoradi, a harbour town some 140 miles west of Accra.

On 10 September the Ghana government declared a limited state of emergency for the Sekondi-Takoradi area, assuming powers to prohibit meetings, requisition vehicles, control traffic, and imprison saboteurs. John Tettegah, Secretary-General of the Ghana Trades Union Congress, said that the strike could be construed as 'counter-revolution', and that 'a mob bent on indulging in an illegal strike' could not be supported. A special conference of the C.P.P. urged the government to 'deal ruthlessly with any unruly activities in the country'. Nkrumah broke off his holiday in the Soviet Union and returned to Ghana on 16 September, lifting the limited state of emergency and appealing to the strikers to return to work.

On 22 September he assumed control over Ghana's armed forces as Supreme Commander and dismissed General Henry Alexander, a British officer, from his post. An official statement issued the night before affirmed that all positions of command in the Ghana army would be held by Ghanaians in the future, while 'necessary appointments' would be made by the Supreme Commander. There were rumours that the United States was reconsidering its offer of $133,000,000 (some £47,500,000) for the Volta River project, and *The Times* claimed:

> The internal financial situation in Ghana does not contribute to American confidence, and there have been press reports suggesting that enthusiasm for the project is waning in Washington. However, the aim appears to be to persuade Ghana to undertake sensible financial measures to improve her economy rather than anything more extreme.

Striking railway and port workers in both Takoradi and Sekondi went back to work in response to Nkrumah's call, and normal train services – seriously affected for eighteen days at a cost to the country of something like £1,000,000 – were resumed. The *Observer* of 24 September reported:

> There is anger about corruption, ostentatious living, and spending among top party people. This anger is increased by the fact that Dr Nkrumah has publicly denounced these activities but has so far taken no action to deal with the guilty parties. . . .

On 28 September, Nkrumah announced that he had asked six members of the government, including two of his chief lieutenants – K. A. Gbedemah, Minister of Health, and Kojo Botsio, Minister of Agriculture – to resign because of their 'varied business connexions'. Nkrumah added:

> Although there is no evidence to support any allegation that these business interests led to any irregularity in their ministerial conduct, I have come to the conclusion that it is undesirable that men with varied business connexions should be members of a government which must from now on be increasingly animated by socialist ideals.

Six other members, including four Ministers, had agreed to

surrender to the State private properties in excess of more than two houses, together valued at £20,000, more than two cars, and plots of land totalling more than £500. The *Observer*, under a head-line 'Nkrumah's "Purge" Stuns the Country', reported on 1 October:

> This week's upheavals have stunned Ghana after a period in which the people seem to have surrendered themselves entirely to rumours. ... Even those who had expected the President to act on his dawn broadcast of last April, when he said that no M.P. would be allowed to own property worth more than a certain amount, had not expected that both Mr Gbedemah and Mr Kojo Botsio would be sacked.

On 29 September the President's Office announced a bill to provide for the establishment of a special division of the High Court to deal with crimes against the State. Then on 3 October, the Ghana government ordered the arrest of fifty people, including Dr J. B. Danquah and Joe Appiah, M.P., opposition leaders, under the Preventive Detention Act. Liberal opinion in Britain was pained, and the *Guardian* commented:

> There is no attempt to belittle the internal problems with which Dr Nkrumah was faced on independence; he has succeeded quickly where a weaker man might have failed in giving Ghana a political cohesion.... In many ways Ghana is more vigorous than was the colonial Gold Coast. But Nkrumah's precept in colonial days was 'Seek ye first the political kingdom': he has both sought and found it, and having found it has kept it to himself.

A Ghana government statement issued on the same day alleged 'clandestine and dangerous activities of certain individuals in the country', deliberately calculated to 'subvert and endanger the security of the State'. Two days later, after talks in Accra, Nkrumah and Duncan Sandys, British Secretary of State for Commonwealth Relations, issued a statement appealing to Britons and Ghanaians alike to 'take the utmost care to avoid misinterpretation of each other's policies and intentions'. Relations between the two countries had deteriorated rapidly during the previous weeks, substantially as a consequence of Ghanaian press attacks on British policy towards the Congo and British press treatment of the crisis within Ghana itself.

The Queen, Elizabeth II, as Head of the Commonwealth, was due to pay a state visit to Ghana early in November. A few weeks before her departure, however, a section of British opinion, receiving the richest publicity in the right-wing press, demanded the cancellation of the tour, on the grounds that it might be interpreted as support for Nkrumah's actions against his opposition and would endanger the life of the Queen. There were press reports – subsequently proved to have been without foundation – that Nkrumah was hiding from the public in Accra and had even withdrawn for safety to a military camp. On 4 November two dynamite explosions took place in Accra, damaging the bronze statue of Nkrumah, and demands in Britain rose for a cancellation or postponement of the royal visit. The following day Duncan Sandys flew off to Accra, and on 7 November he toured what was to be the royal route with Nkrumah himself, to a tumultuous reception. The *Guardian* published a report from its special correspondent David Holden, who cabled from Accra on 6 November:

> In defiance of the betting among a somewhat wishful-thinking British press corps here last night Mr Duncan Sandys, the Secretary for Commonwealth Relations, arrived here this morning apparently not to tell President Nkrumah the tour must be cancelled, but to perform a sort of confidence trick to assure the British public that the danger to royal life has been exaggerated. . . . It is hard to discharge some sections of the British press from responsibility for arousing disquiet about the Queen's security for political reasons.

The royal visit began on 9 November and was generally admitted afterwards to have been an unalloyed success.

On 11 December 1961, the Ghana government published a White Paper – in explanation of the arrests in early October of various politicians – alleging that the opposition United Party had conspired with individuals in the C.P.P. to overthrow the government of President Nkrumah. The White Paper claimed that the conspiracy had been led by Dr Busia, former leader of the United Party, and that President Olympio of the Togo Republic had been involved. The most startling of the charges, however, was against Victor Yaw de Grant Brempong – Personal

Assistant to Gbedemah, one-time Minister of Finance and then of Health – who was accused of having attempted to obtained explosives from the army through bribery. British newspaper correspondents were also attacked for having published 'a whole series of untruths which they not only knew to be false, but which, on occasion, they had themselves invented'. Busia, Olympio, and Gbedemah all subsequently refuted the allegations against them.

The *Economist* of 16 December commented:

> The White Paper's weakest, and blackest, point remains its attitude to bringing the facts out in open court. It offers two explanations of this: that it is usually impossible to prove the guilt of the leaders of conspiracies, and the subordinates therefore suffer; and that it is better to detain conspirators until the day of reconciliation than to find them guilty of treason and, perhaps, hang them. This argument is casuistry worthy of the most devious neo-colonialist.

The White Paper itself had included a strong defence of the Preventive Detention Act. It had pointed out that 'however undesirable such a law may be as part of the permanent system of government', the strains experienced by a country fresh to independence might be greater than those experienced in a developed country at war – when, it was generally agreed, preventive detention was justified.

On 16 December 1961 the United States government at last proclaimed its intention to provide loans totalling £47,500,000 for the Volta River dam and its associated aluminium factory. The bulk of that sum would go to a consortium of private American companies to supply and operate the aluminium smelter which would use power from the dam, while £13,215,000 would be lent to Ghana for the dam itself. The dam was expected to cost £70 million in all, and the remainder of the sum required would be provided by the International Bank of Reconstruction and Development (£17 million), Britain (£5 million), and Ghana itself, which would grant £35 million, or the same as the total supplied by outside sources.

On 30 December the *Economist* commented:

Before the decade is out, Ghana will be producing twenty times as much electricity as it does now (and perhaps selling some of it across its borders); it will possess the world's largest man-made lake; it will be in a position to export iron, grow rice, and, perhaps, produce 10,000 tons of fish a year. With luck, the abundant electricity could attract other industries to Ghana. It is the most significant event in Ghana's – and perhaps West Africa's – history.

On 10 February 1962 Nkrumah formally opened Tema, the country's £18 million new harbour. Work on the port had begun in September 1954, and at peak periods during its construction more than 3,500 men had worked on the project, some of them in the hills 20 miles away, quarrying more than 10 million tons of rock. The port encloses some 400 acres of water, has a fishing harbour, and will eventually possess five quays and fifteen berths. Nkrumah proclaimed at the ceremony that Tema would be a 'free port' for countries like Mali and Upper Volta which wished to use it.

Accompanying Ghana's efforts at speedy industrialization has been her attempt to diversify her markets and her sources of capital investment. The overwhelming bulk of trade is still with the West – trade with the East was worth only £12 million, out of a total £245 million, in 1960. The twelve industries at present functioning at Tema, and many of those planned, are Western-financed. The Communist States, however, have recently granted Ghana a total of some £100 million in credits for the construction of new industries, all to be planned and eventually built by their own technicians. These funds, bearing a maximum interest rate of 2½ per cent, are repayable at varying periods of up to 10 years, nearly all in Ghana currency – cocoa shipments, in effect. Largest of the projects, the hydro-electric scheme at Bui on the Black Volta, to provide electricity for the Northern Region and possibly for export to neighbouring territories, is a Soviet project recently approved. And the Soviet Union has also agreed to undertake a geological survey of the whole country at a cost of £3 million. Hungary, which has provided credits of £2½ million at 2½ per cent, Poland with credits of £10 million for ten years, Czechoslovakia with £10 million at 2½ per cent,

Bulgaria with £2 million at 2½ per cent over 10 years, and the People's Republic of China with credits of £7 million, have agreed to build various factories for the manufacture of such different products as tyres and plywood, pencils and soap, aluminium cable and tomato juice, cigarettes and carpets.

In February 1962, Krobo Edusei, Ghana's Minister of Industries, explained to the National Assembly that the government had 'no alternative' but to seize the initiative in building industries, since there was no middle class in Ghana with the necessary capital and experience to take the lead. The people themselves would have to save a greater portion of the national income for investment, in the certainty that new industries, able to use cheap Volta power, had a promising future. The job of furthering industrialization, the Minister maintained, was none the less one for private enterprise as well as for the government. What the government wanted to avoid was a position where the more profitable sectors of industry were monopolized by private capital, or where Ghana relied on outside capital to a dangerous degree. The government would accordingly continue to provide all the protection and facilities that private enterprise needed, but in return it would expect improved quality, reasonable prices, the use of local raw materials, the training of Ghanaians, and better labour relations. That was socialism of the 'distinct Ghana brand'.

Nkrumah's place in African history is already secure. The leader of the first independent black State in Africa to struggle out of colonialism, he inspired Africans throughout the continent to believe that they were capable of emulating his example. It is difficult to describe the effect, for instance, that his emergence on to the world stage had upon Africans enduring the race rule of Dr Verwoerd. In addition, though often antagonizing by too speedy and energetic a partisanship, Nkrumah must surely rank as the African leader who has done the most concretely to further the ideals of Pan-Africanism. He has given office and travel facilities, as well as financial aid and asylum, to political refugees from other parts of the continent. Instead of nursing the resources of Ghana, he has directed a substantial proportion towards assisting governments and movements whose objectives he has – however capriciously, on occasions – considered as contributing to his ultimate goal of a free and a united Africa.

Yet it is impossible to deny that his stature outside of Ghana is less than it was during the first days of his triumph, while his power inside – however greater it may be on paper – is more precariously balanced than it has ever been since 6 March 1957. He certainly lacks the intellectual vigour of Sékou Touré, which has given to Guinea's President so passionate a personal following among so many of the younger African intellectuals. He has certainly made enemies in Africa amongst many of those whom he might very easily have made his friends, had he substituted argument and the pressures of example for peremptory demands and attack.

There are, however, few African governments which have not dealt with their opposition leaders every bit as ruthlessly as the Ghana government has dealt with its own. Though the Preventive Detention Act is an ugly law, and has stripped several hundred political opponents of their right to trial, there are neither firing squads nor torture chambers in Ghana today. Those commentators who are already classing Ghana as a tyranny not only misunderstand the course of popular government in Africa, which increasingly denies the need for an official opposition, but cast considerable doubt on their sane sense of proportion in a world that contains such societies as Haiti, Hungary, Portugal, Spain, and – if the conduct of the army and police is any measure – that heartland of Western civilization, France. It is difficult to escape the conclusion that Nkrumah's neutralism is more on trial in the Western press than any oppression of his domestic opposition.

All the same, Nkrumah has added nothing to the image of 'freedom and justice' in Ghana by having muzzled the *Ashanti Pioneer*, while encouraging the government press to degenerate into a shrill and interminable flattery. Though discontent with Nkrumah's rule may have grown, it has clearly not fortified a weak and popularly isolated opposition. It is therefore reasonable to wonder whether the government of Ghana is not sacrificing more of the good-will of liberal democrats outside of Africa than it has any reason to do.

The basic cause of Nkrumah's present decline has been his unwillingness – or his incapacity – to maintain a vision whole. Within Ghana he has increasingly arbitrated rather than led, balancing instead of fusing, failing to give personal and coherent impetus to the creation of the new society which he has so long claimed to want, but the precise form of which he has seemed unable to resolve. This internal indecision is echoed in his Pan-African policies, where he has far too often sacrificed the discipline of his score to the advice and personal intrigue whispered in his ear.

Nkrumah may be losing, but he has by no means lost. His is a failure of intellect, not of imagination. Perhaps he will yet take the leap from personality to programme, stripping Accra of its often Byzantine atmosphere and welding his people together into an enthusiasm which is the fundamental constituent of unity and sacrifice. The obituaries that have already been planned are perhaps a little premature. Nkrumah has already contributed more to the continent that he so patently loves than any of those – inside and outside of Africa – who find it so easy at the moment to belittle him.

15 Félix Houphouet-Boigny of the Ivory Coast

Far and away the most splendid residence in Africa is that of the Ivory Coast's President, M. Houphouet-Boigny. . . . Over £3 million has already been spent – out of French aid funds – and further work on the landscaping of the grounds is likely to cost a further million at least. In keeping with Houphouet's unflamboyant nature, the palace doesn't look so extraordinary from the street. It is in three separate buildings: the Presidency, the Residence, and the reception halls. Not until the dinner-jacketed guest penetrates to the latter, past fountains, cascades, statues, and descends a regal staircase into a vast marble reception hall, there to shake hands with his host and his beautiful wife, does the extent and beauty of the place register. Nothing is missing: from chandeliers and antique-style furniture in subtly contrasted colours to embossed chinaware and cutlery for over 1,000 guests, and a single table that seats hundreds. . . . Many visitors – both tax-paying Frenchmen and delegations from less favoured African states – were, I am told, shocked at such extravagance. But an Ivorian journalist who inspected the palace on the day after the big reception, exclaimed: 'My God, anyone could live here – the Queen of England, President Kennedy. It makes me feel thrilled to be an Ivory Coast citizen.'

So wrote a correspondent in *West Africa* of 26 August 1961. The splendour of Houphouet-Boigny's palace is a measure of Houphouet-Boigny's personality and a guide to the policy and place of his government in Africa. In any list of African leaders, Houphouet-Boigny must rank in the top handful. Indeed, if a bloc of modern African states exists, pro-Western and maintaining close political and economic links with France, Houphouet-Boigny is more than anyone else responsible. His history is the history of France's *rapprochement* with Africa, and his policies constitute an alternative to the vigorous African nationalism of the Casablanca states. African militants deplore and deride those African leaders who, they feel, have acquired independence only on paper and act as agents of contemporary French colonialism. Houphouet-Boigny alone, however loudly he is deplored, defies derision. He is nobody's puppet; and if he maintains the strongest links with France, he does so because he believes that such links are to his clear advantage. He is not only the principal advocate of cooperation with the former colonial powers, he is the leader of those leaders in Africa who consider the development of national sovereignty to be more pressing and profitable than the passion for speedy African unification. The architect of the Brazzaville and so of the Monrovia bloc, his policy is the antithesis of Dr Nkrumah's, canvassing the close cooperation of independent African states instead of their federation or union.

The initial stimulus to political development in the Ivory Coast was – so differently from Senegal, where political frustration excited the urban élite to agitate for gradualist reform – the economic grievance of the African planters. Even before the Second World War, a new class of African cash crop farmers had been generated by cocoa and coffee cultivation. Where the British government in the Gold Coast next door had ensured that economic change would remain entirely indigenous, the French administration in the Ivory Coast attracted European planters, more than 200 of whom established themselves along the southern coast of the territory and the line of rail. During the thirties, forced labour supplied the European estates with their African workers, while the Vichy administration during the war discriminated crudely in favour of the European settlers, paying them the highest prices for their crops, giving them priority to imported goods, and offering them a premium for every hectare under cultivation. A natural consequence was to ally the African planters with African workers, traders, civil servants and chiefs, producing an anti-colonial movement with a predominantly agrarian base. It was this movement that Houphouet-Boigny was to lead.

FÉLIX HOUPHOUET was born in October 1905 at Yamoussokro into a prominent Baoulé family. Son of a prosperous planter, he was schooled at Bingerville and in 1918 enrolled at the medical school in Dakar, Senegal. After qualifying as a medical assistant in 1925 he practised for fifteen years, becoming in 1940 chief of his home district and a planter in his own right. Angered by the discrimination which African planters in the territory were encountering, he founded and became President of the Syndicat Agricole Africain (S.A.A.) in 1944, a sort of African farmers' trade union that included within its membership some 20,000 of the more substantial African planters. Rapidly establishing itself as the only effective protest organization in the territory, with a network of local branches, it agitated vigorously against forced labour and called upon its members to recruit only voluntary workers.

Then, at the end of 1945, Houphouet formed the Parti Démocratique de la Côte d'Ivoire (P.D.C.I.), which combined the structure and financial strength of the S.A.A. with the ideas of the urban radicals, many of whom belonged to a study circle at Abidjan, started by the French Communists to analyse the application of Marxism to the problems of contemporary Africa. From 1946 onwards, accordingly, the Ivory Coast established itself as a rival centre of political activity to Senegal, and indeed appeared to the French authorities as the focal point of anti-colonial fervour.

Houphouet himself was elected in November 1945 and June 1946, for the Ivory Coast and Upper Volta, to the French Constituent Assemblies. The African parliamentarians in Paris decided to distribute their allegiance among the various metropolitan parties, and Houphouet sat with the Union Républicaine et Résistance, which was itself allied with the Communist Party. The first draft constitution of the Fourth Republic was defeated by referendum, while the second, which was accepted, contained substantially less liberal proposals for the colonies. Dismayed by the proposals themselves and by the implications of the difference between the two constitutions, all the African deputies agreed to meet in October 1946 at Bamako in French Soudan to discuss the formation of a mass political party.

The French Socialists, afraid that the conference would be

Communist controlled, persuaded those Africans associated with them – notably the Senegalese leaders, Léopold Senghor and Lamine Guèye – not to attend, so that the new inter-territorial movement, the Rassemblement Démocratique Africain (R.D.A.), was formed without them, on a policy of emancipating 'Africa from the colonial yoke by the affirmation of her personality and by the association, freely agreed to, of a union of nations'. Houphouet was made its first President, a post to which he was consistently re-elected in the years to come, while the P.D.C.I. became the virtual headquarters of the movement. In November 1946 Houphouet was elected to the French National Assembly for the Ivory Coast, and celebrated his success by adding to his name the word 'Boigny', meaning – in Baoulé – 'irresistible force'.

The R.D.A. was from its establishment advised and actively supported by the Communists in Paris, and the French administration, particularly after the Communists had gone into opposition, grew increasingly hostile to the movement, engendering and nourishing rival organizations, persecuting P.D.C.I. supporters, repressing demonstrations, manipulating elections, and dismissing chiefs and civil servants who supported the R.D.A. In reaction the R.D.A. organized women's demonstrations, boycotts of all European goods sold by expatriate firms, and a strike of domestic workers in settler homes. Resistance became, in 1949–50, especially serious in the Ivory Coast, and it was savagely repressed there by the administration. On 24 January 1950 a warrant was issued for Houphouet-Boigny's arrest, but he was protected by his parliamentary immunity; then, on 30 January, at Dimbokro thirteen Africans were killed and fifty wounded in a clash with the police. By 1951, according to official figures – which Thomas Hodgkin and Dr Ruth Schachter describe in their book *French-Speaking West Africa in Transition* 'as certainly an underestimate' – fifty-two Africans had been killed, several hundred wounded, and some 3,000 imprisoned.

Soon after the Dimbokro clash, the administration clamped down upon all political activity in the territory, and the R.D.A. became increasingly isolated. Repression itself left an indelible mark on the organization of both the P.D.C.I. and the R.D.A. The structure was radically weakened by mass arrests and fell completely into the hands of Houphouet-Boigny. Rancour grew up between those who had fought and those who had collaborated. Above all, Houphouet himself decided that the struggle was disproportionate to the results it might achieve, and he resolved upon a policy of cooperation with the French administration. In October 1950 he stated in the French Assembly that the R.D.A. had broken its links with the Communists; 'the R.D.A.', he said, 'is a purely African party, and it will remain as such.' The majority of the territorial parties followed his lead; those which did not, withdrew from active participation in the movement, though they were not formally expelled until 1955. The Secretary-General, Gabriel d'Arboussier, who bitterly opposed the decision, was dismissed.

In June 1951 new elections were held to the French Assembly, and though Houphouet himself was re-elected, the R.D.A. emerged with only three deputies. *L'Afrique Noire* of 6 December 1951 reported him on his new policy:

> We are not and we have never been Communists. Our deputies have abandoned their attachment to the Communist Party for two reasons: first, because Communism is not the goal of the R.D.A.; and second, because the class struggle which lies at the base of Communism has no meaning in a classless society. A new page has been turned; on it let us write a resolution to make Africa the most splendid and the most loyal territory in the French Union.

In the following years Houphouet concentrated on rebuilding the organization of the R.D.A. and the P.D.C.I., refusing to change his new policy of cooperation with the administration despite the opposition of radical critics. His new programme meant in practice a union with the French business community, and during the fifties confidence in the political moderates of the P.D.C.I. and in Houphouet himself encouraged a flow of public and private French capital into the territory. By 1956 the Ivory Coast had become by far the largest exporter of all the territories in French West Africa, providing forty-four per cent of the area's total, to Senegal's thirty-five per cent. Since the territory appeared to receive an inadequate return for its contribution to the federal revenue of French West Africa, a strong anti-federalist movement developed of which the P.D.C.I. became during the late fifties the principal exponent.

Gradually the R.D.A. rebuilt itself, and in January 1956 its supporters won nine seats in new elections to the French Assembly. In November of the same year Houphouet himself became Mayor of Abidjan, and the French government, acknowledging the strength of the R.D.A. and the unrivalled influence over it that Houphouet possessed, gave him a portfolio with Cabinet rank, which he retained until 1959. As a Minister in the French government, he played a significant part in the framing of the *loi-cadre*, which – through a new constitution – gave universal suffrage and Executive Councils with considerable responsibility to each of the territories in French Africa. In return, Houphouet's loyalty to the French administration was complete; he was a member of the Mollet Cabinet which launched the 1956 Suez invasion and the spokesman for France at the United Nations over the Togo dispute in January 1957. In March 1957 elections were held to the territorial assemblies in French Africa, and these not only constituted an overall triumph for the R.D.A., but revealed that within the Ivory Coast itself Houphouet's opponents could achieve only five per cent of the vote.

Gradually, however, the R.D.A. itself was dividing between those, sustained by the powerful Guinea and Soudan sections, who agitated for a French West African federation as a necessary step towards effective independence, and those like Houphouet who felt that each individual territory should remain distinct and promote its own relationship with France. At the third R.D.A. Congress, held at Bamako in September 1957, the Ivory Coast leadership canvassed strongly for the principle of individual autonomy within a French African Community. Conscious that the French government was opposed to federation, and unwilling to spread the riches of the Ivory Coast to other poorer territories in French Africa, Houphouet defied all federalist demands and was none the less re-elected President.

It was therefore natural that in the de Gaulle referendum of

September 1958, Houphouet should have campaigned for autonomy within the French Community and the continuance of close economic ties with France, instead of for the complete independence which Guinea overwhelmingly chose.

After the referendum, attempts were made to form a federation of Senegal, Soudan, Upper Volta, and Dahomey. These Houphouet resolutely opposed, and in the end he succeeded in winning Dahomey and Upper Volta away to a much looser union, called the Conseil de l'Entente, which the Ivory Coast established with the two countries and Niger on 29 May. Conceived as a loose form of association, it was the reply of the particularists to the Mali Federation between Senegal and Soudan and the Ghana-Guinea Union. In addition, it provided the Ivory Coast with a clear sphere of political influence, since she was the wealthiest of the four territories in the Entente and the only one under the effective control of a mass party. The Conseil had its first meeting in May 1959 and resolved on technical coordination in such fields as justice, finance, the civil service, labour, and public health; it then established a customs union and launched a development scheme, financed from contributions equivalent to ten per cent of the revenues of each of the four constituent territories.

In April 1959 Houphouet resigned from the French government and returned to the Ivory Coast in order to concentrate on territorial politics, partly because the R.D.A. had weakened with the independence of Guinea and the formation of the Mali Federation and partly because of growing opposition to his régime from more radical elements within the Ivory Coast itself. He called a special youth congress, tightened the party structure, and, after elections in which the P.D.C.I. won all the seats, included more young men in his cabinet. In July he was named by de Gaulle as one of the Advisory Ministers of the French Community, and he stated: 'If it were only a question of our economic development, we should turn to other people richer and more powerful. We have chosen the Community for sentiment rather than reason. We wish to achieve with the French a strong Community based on equality and fraternity.'

At the end of 1959, however, President de Gaulle agreed to re-form the Community in order to allow the Mali Federation to become independent within it. Houphouet was so angered by this decision, which seemed to him a surrender of the policy which he had so assiduously cultivated, that he and the leaders of the other three countries in the Entente also demanded independence, refusing to sign agreements first with France and so leaving the Community. The Ivory Coast became independent on 7 August 1960, and on 27 November Houphouet was re-elected President by ninety-eight per cent of the votes, while the P.D.C.I.'s single list of candidates for the National Assembly – no other party contested the election – was approved. In accordance with his policy of bringing potential opposition into the leadership of the party, he included in his single list several trade unionists and students who were known to be critical of his régime.

The change in the Ivory Coast's status did not, however, injure the territory's relations with France, and Houphouet continued to pursue his policy of friendly cooperation with the government of the Fifth Republic.

Believing that the independent African states should assist in bringing the Algerian war to an end without alienating France, Houphouet proposed a meeting of French-speaking African leaders. On 24 October 1960, accordingly, the heads of state from the Republic of Cameroun, Central African Republic, the formerly French Republic of Congo, Dahomey, Gabon, the Ivory Coast, Mauritania, Niger, Senegal, Chad, and Upper Volta met at Abidjan, to meet again, together with the President of the Malagasy Republic, at Brazzaville, capital of the former French Congo, in December. The twelve states soon became jointly known as the Brazzaville bloc, because it was at their Brazzaville meeting that the leaders resolved on common long term objectives, announcing that they would stay in existence as a group, to cooperate on economic problems and external policy.

All shared a desire to remain on the friendliest terms with France; all condemned Soviet policy and rejected any Communist presence in Africa, through economic aid or in any other shape; and all were seeking compromise solutions to both the Congo and Algerian crises. Finally, all were united in their opposition to political unions among the independent African states, and though they favoured the closest cooperation with each other, they all followed Houphouet's lead in claiming that common political institutions in independent Africa were both risky and needless.

At the end of April 1961, the French Premier and the heads of state from the four Entente countries signed, after long negotiations, agreements of cooperation covering technical and military assistance, economic and judicial affairs, higher education, cultural relations, civil aviation, and postal communications. Upper Volta alone did not sign the general defence pact.

In May 1961 a conference of independent African states took place at Monrovia under the sponsorship of Liberia, the Republic of Cameroun, Nigeria, and Togo. Twenty of the twenty-seven independent African states sent delegations; only the 'Casablanca bloc' – Ghana, Guinea, Mali, Morocco, the United Arab Republic – and the Sudan refused to attend. The formerly Belgian Congo Republic was not invited, to avoid any dispute over the legitimacy of its representation. Though President Tubman of Liberia and Sir Abubakar Tafawa Balewa, Prime Minister of Nigeria, played the most prominent parts at the conference itself, there seems little doubt that it was the policy of Houphouet around which the various leaders coalesced.

The Monrovia group, which made plans to meet regularly and expressed the hope that the Casablanca states 'might find it convenient to attend later meetings', fundamentally upheld the particularism of Houphouet and his concentration upon economic cooperation rather than political union. 'The unity that it is aimed to achieve at the moment', a resolution stated, 'is not the political integration of African states but unity of aspiration and action.' The conference proposed the consideration of plans for economic, educational, cultural, scientific, and technical cooperation, as well as coordination in the fields of communication and transportation. Certain principles for a permanent association were agreed: non-interference in the domestic affairs of other states, though national movements in colonies should be given every encouragement; the political equality of independent African states; freedom to accept or reject political unions; and respect for the territorial integrity of the independent African states.

The Ivory Coast was not invited to the conference of uncommitted nations at Belgrade in September 1961, and during his official visit to Paris in June 1961 Houphouet-Boigny had publicly expressed his disappointment at this. Apparently the sponsors of the Belgrade Conference did not regard the Ivory Coast as uncommitted.

Certainly, while France continued to pursue a policy of colonialism in both Algeria and Tunisia, Houphouet's continued association with the Fifth Republic could only be interpreted by the uncommitted states of the Afro-Asian world as a commitment to the West. In the General Assembly debate on the Bizerta dispute, the Ivory Coast refused to condemn France and abstained in the company of Britain and the United States, Portugal, and the Republic of South Africa, against the whole Soviet bloc and the vast majority of the Afro-Asian states.

More significantly, in its long term repercussions, the Ivory Coast took the lead in opposing the representation of Algeria's Provisional Government at the Lagos Conference of African States in January 1962. In protest at the decision of the Conference to exclude Algeria, the Casablanca states – Ghana, Guinea, Mali, Morocco, and the United Arab Republic – refused to attend, as did Libya, the Sudan, and Tunisia. The Africa Correspondent of *The Times* cabled from Lagos on 24 January:

> The general attitude is that the undignified squabble of the past two days has shown the so-called Brazzaville states – those which have retained close links with France – in their worst light. Even if the Brazzaville states' resistance to the Algerians was not directly instigated by France, it is pointed out that the situation is a necessary outcome of their association with the former colonial power. It is suggested that the dispute may already have made the conference valueless; certainly it has rendered questionable the whole basis of the Monrovia group of states.

In the last analysis, of course, Houphouet-Boigny's strength is his power within the Ivory Coast. His refusal to accommodate himself to the growing African pressures for continental unity and neutralism might have antagonized the political intelligentsia and the radical youth at home, as well as exciting the opposition of militant nationalist opinion elsewhere in the continent. His future, however, in the near term at least, would appear rather to depend upon his capacity to satisfy popular demand within the Ivory Coast itself for a better life under independence.

With massive French assistance, the turnover of industries rose from £10 million in 1957 to £16 million in 1960, and the budget from £15 million to £42 million between 1958 and 1961. The value of exports has mounted from £35·7 million to £54·8 million, despite a calamitous fall in the world price of coffee, and imports of £43·7 million leave a comfortable surplus in the balance of trade.

Prosperous governments do not, however, necessarily mean prosperous people. Apart from a slow Africanization of the civil service, the French have stayed, as have their businesses and their profits. When *West Africa* asked Houphouet-Boigny, as reported in its issue of 19 August 1961, why there was no equivalent of the Ghanaian and Nigerian Marketing Boards in the Ivory Coast, he replied simply: 'We have a liberal economy, we do not believe in that sort of thing.' During a policy speech in January 1961, he claimed that his ambition was to make the Ivory Coast a modern state. 'To combine this aim in a framework of real freedom and brotherhood, we shall concentrate on the necessity of feeding, clothing, teaching, healing, and housing the Ivorians.' Perhaps.

The concept of a 'liberal economy' and the requirements of economic advance have already collided. The Ivory Coast's Minister of Information, Mathieu Ekra, reported that there had been a capital inflow of £14 million during 1961, while £28 million had been repatriated in profits. To stop this 'financial haemorrhage', the Ivory Coast government declared that all businesses would be required to pay an additional 10 per cent of their profits to the state unless they could show that they had reinvested twice that amount in industries approved by the government. Outlining a development plan to diversify crops, improve animal husbandry, and exploit mineral deposits, Houphouet-Boigny announced a bill to acknowledge the state 'as the sole proprietor of all uncultivated land', and provide that the state would 'share out to all citizens all available land to ensure better production'. At a time when further effort was to be required from all farmers, the President maintained that it was only fair that 'those of us who have been a rather privileged class in comparison with the peasantry should also make sacrifices'. These sacrifices would include a 'national contribution' or special levy of 10 per cent on all salaries and wages above 150,000 francs C.F.A. a month, an end to free houses for civil servants, and the abolition from 1963 of most free cars for civil servants and Ministers.

The people of the Ivory Coast will undoubtedly wish to see in the coming years whether the prosperity of their country means that they will indeed be suitably fed, clothed, taught, healed, and housed. If 'a liberal economy' – despite the expatriate profits that it seems to entail – can accomplish this, Houphouet will perhaps be able to afford his contempt for 'economic nationalism'. He may even be able to brave the hostility of those who see in his relationship with France a colonial subservience. He stands at the opposite pole of African development from Sékou Touré in Guinea. His success, as his failure, will have continental implications.

16 The Missing Link of Upper Volta: Maurice Yaméogo

Immediately to the north of Ghana and the south of Mali, between the Ivory Coast to the south-west and both Niger and Dahomey in the east, lies the Republic of Upper Volta, with a population estimated in mid-1959 of 3,537,000 and an area of 105,900 square miles. It has been described as '*le maillon manquant*' – 'the missing link', for a union between Upper Volta and Ghana would not only isolate the Ivory Coast from its allies in the Conseil de l'Entente, but would join Ghana with Mali and Guinea at last in territorial as well as in economic and political proximity. The experiment in militant Pan-Africanism would receive an enormous boost, making possible for the first time a really effective union of the participants, while delivering a serious blow to the particularism of the Brazzaville bloc. In many ways therefore, the person of Maurice Yaméogo, President and Minister of Foreign Affairs in the Republic of Upper Volta, is important to the future direction of African politics.

Born in December 1921 at Koudougou in Upper Volta, a member of the Mossi tribe strong in the northern part of the territory, MAURICE YAMÉOGO was educated at secondary school in Pabret and then became a civil servant. In 1946 he was elected to the Territorial Assembly, and in 1948 to the Grand Council of French West Africa. For many years a member of the Confédération Française des Travailleurs Chrétiens, the Christian trade union movement, he became Vice-President of its Upper Volta section in 1954 and in the same year began taking an active part in the Rassemblement Démocratique Africain (R.D.A.), the inter-territorial movement led by Houphouet-

Boigny of the Ivory Coast. He decided to form his own party, however, and in 1957 he launched the Mouvement Démocratique Voltaique (M.D.V.). In the elections of March that year to the Territorial Assembly, conducted in terms of the new *loi-cadre* constitution, the local section of the R.D.A. won thirty-seven seats out of seventy and the M.D.V. twenty-six, while the remaining seven were scattered among smaller parties.

After negotiations, the R.D.A. and the M.D.V. agreed to form a coalition government under Ouezzin Coulibaly, one of Houphouet-Boigny's closest associates and supporters, and with five Ministries allotted to the M.D.V., Yaméogo himself became Minister of Agriculture. Then, in December, the M.D.V. and a section of the R.D.A. broke away from the coalition, leaving the government with a minority of the Assembly behind it. Ouezzin Coulibaly refused, however, to resign and gained a new majority when some of the M.D.V. deputies, led by Yaméogo, agreed to join the R.D.A. themselves.

Yaméogo became Minister of the Interior in the reformed cabinet, and when Ouezzin Coulibaly died at the end of 1958 was – after some negotiations – elected Premier. He then formed a coalition between the governing R.D.A. and the various opposition parties allied to the inter-territorial Parti du Regroupement Africain – the federalist movement led by Léopold Senghor of Senegal – with the object of creating a Mali Federation of Soudan, Senegal, Dahomey, and Upper Volta. Economic pressure from the Ivory Coast against the venture was too strong, however, Dahomey and Upper Volta were forced to withdraw, and the Federation was constituted by Senegal and Soudan alone. Yaméogo's decision to bow before Houphouet-Boigny's antagonism enraged the opposition parties in Upper Volta, still loyal to Senghor's Parti du Regroupement Africain, and they broke away from the coalition. Elections were accordingly held in April 1959, and Yaméogo won a crushing victory – his new grouping, the Union Démocratique Voltaique (U.D.V.), emerged with sixty-four of the seventy-five seats – to form a homogeneous government of his supporters. At the same time he took Upper Volta into the Conseil de l'Entente, a loose association formed by the Ivory Coast, Niger, Dahomey, and Upper Volta, formally established on 29 May and dominated by Houphouet-Boigny. In January 1960 he banned the major opposition party, the Parti Républicaine de la Liberté, and in July, stating that they were 'agitators who represented nothing', he arrested all its significant leaders but Nazi Boni, the founder, who escaped to Bamako in Mali. On 4 August Upper Volta became independent, and Yaméogo himself, already President of the Republic, took over as well the Ministry of Foreign Affairs.

It soon became clear that he intended to follow a political line independent of Houphouet-Boigny's, particularly over relations with France, and he began negotiating with the governments of Mali and Ghana. At the end of May 1961, indeed, after two days of talks in Accra, Yaméogo and Nkrumah agreed to take 'immediate effective measures' to strengthen the ties between their two peoples, including the abolition of customs barriers between Ghana and Upper Volta, the improvement of communications between the two States, and the provision of free movement for both people and produce between them.

Despite the differences in history and language, a union between Ghana and Upper Volta is economically desirable. Ghana buys most of Upper Volta's exports, mainly cattle and excess rice, while traders from Upper Volta visit Ghana for textiles and other essential products. Much of the customs work done before the decision of 27 June to remove trade barriers had, indeed, been the repression of smuggling. Many thousands of workers from Upper Volta are employed in Ghana, and the repatriation of their salaries helps to meet the permanent deficit in Upper Volta's economy.

Rumours among businessmen in Abidjan reflected a serious political collision between Houphouet-Boigny and Yaméogo, but the Tunisian weekly, *Afrique Action*, reported that Yaméogo had kept the Ivory Coast government informed of all his negotiations with Nkrumah. Houphouet-Boigny, the weekly continued, was well aware that he could not help Upper Volta over its economic difficulties and that the disproportionate popular living standards between the Ivory Coast and Upper Volta constituted an obvious source of conflict between the two countries. He believed that the links which united the States in the Conseil de l'Entente were sufficiently subtle to permit them to find original solutions to their individual problems. Paris was less sanguine, however, and Britain's *Financial Times* reported early in July:

> Concern is felt in Paris at the formation of a customs union between Ghana and Upper Volta, which also belongs to the franc area and the French West African Customs Union. Ghana would also give Upper Volta, its poor neighbour, a loan of 2,500 million C.F.A. francs to compensate it for the loss of revenue from import duties. Quite apart from the incompatability of Upper Volta's simultaneous membership of two different customs unions, there is the danger that it will be attracted into the neutralist political union of Ghana, Guinea and Mali which has just been set up . . . by and large, it is clear that Ghana and the other 'Casablanca' powers are determined to try to attract the newly independent African States away from what they regard as the undue political influence exercised in Africa by the Common Market.

In January 1962, Nazi Boni, former opposition leader, announced in Senegal that he would return to Upper Volta in response to an appeal from President Yaméogo, who had asked him to assist in the national reconstruction of the country. In February, after a visit by several Upper Volta Ministers to Accra, agreement was reached between Upper Volta and Ghana on transit trade and the free movement of citizens between the two countries. It was announced that a standing committee had been established and would meet every three months to implement the decision of June 1961 on the removal of customs barriers between Ghana and Upper Volta.

Yaméogo himself does not appear intimidated by the more powerful political figures around him, threatening and cajoling him into competitive alliances. He believes that the division of Africa into different groups has been largely exaggerated. He maintains:

> It is mostly a matter of words and gestures and striking attitudes. And the press plays its part in exaggerating differences and bandying slogans. Take 'positive neutralism'. It is a meaningless term because

it implies that there are two kinds of neutralism, positive and negative. What nonsense! Everyone must take up a position. Ours is that we want to be friends with everyone, but with the West in particular. That is the position of all of us – including the Casablanca group. We have the same interests.

Yaméogo, of course, frankly admits that lack of money is the principal reason why countries like Upper Volta have to maintain their links with the West. The nearer he moves to the Ghana-Guinea-Mali alliance, however, the more clearly he is likely to be shown that, even if there are not different kinds of neutralism in Africa, there are different kinds of emphasis that the policy of neutralism can bear.

Yaméogo remains a political lightweight, negotiating now with one, now with the other of his powerful neighbours. But he is not altogether his own master, for Upper Volta's chronic poverty creates political pressures increasingly difficult to evade. Sooner or later he may be forced to choose between Ghana and the Ivory Coast; it is by no means certain that Houphouet-Boigny or Nkrumah will allow him forever to enjoy the best of both worlds. And in the event of an economic tug-of-war, he may well be pulled to Accra rather than to Abidjan by the sheer involvement of Upper Volta in the economy of Ghana. Either way his country is unlikely to escape the pressures around it. Yaméogo may believe that the division of Africa has been exaggerated; it none the less exists. And a country geographically situated between the conflicting groups in their most expansive political and economic forms is certainly not in the most permanently comfortable of positions.

17 A Family Affair: Tubman's Liberia

President Tubman has helped to settle a strike involving more than 1,000 workers, and led by his son, Mr Shad Tubman, who is head of Liberia's trade union organization. The strike halted building on a new Executive Mansion for the President. Columns of strikers, who stopped work for a wage increase, demonstrated with placards reading 'we are human workers, not machines'. The police arrived with a brass band, and escorted the strikers in procession to Mr Tubman's house, where the President promised immediate action over the claim. The strikers said they would return to work.

Mr Shad Tubman this week married Miss Wokie Tolbert, daughter of Vice-President William Tolbert.

So reported *West Africa* in August 1961.

Liberia, with an area of 43,000 square miles and an estimated population of some 1,500,000, has been governed for over 100 years – with the exception of a brief period, from 1871 to 1877, when a Republican Party rudely intervened – by the True Whig Party, established in 1860 as the Whig Party and later renamed for emphasis. Opposition groups have been fragmentary, and none has ever persisted for long. The party itself is largely confined to the Americo-Liberian oligarchy, the descendants of those freed slaves from the United States who established their interpretation of American democracy on the west coast of Africa. Political groups led by tribal Liberians, the backward peoples of the hinterland, have either been suppressed or have wilted under the heat of the President's personality. The party has perpetuated itself in power by a system of extensive patronage and is the main source of employment outside of the Firestone Rubber Company, which in 1925 leased some one million acres – or four per cent of the country–at six cents an acre, to become a considerable economic influence.

For good or bad, Liberia is President Tubman, his family and friends, and the history of the past twenty years or so is largely the biography of Tubman himself.

Born in November 1895 at Harper, Maryland County, in the east of Liberia, WILLIAM VACANARAT SHADRACH TUBMAN comes from an old Americo-Liberian family; his father was the Reverend Alexander Tubman, a Methodist minister and one-time Speaker in the Liberian House of Representatives. He himself was educated at the Methodist Cape Palmas Seminary, which he left in 1913 to begin his career as a teacher. Descended as he was, however, from the select group which expects and is expected to hold high office in Liberia, he read Law meanwhile, as a stepping stone to politics. Called to the Bar in 1917, he soon enjoyed a successful practice, and in 1922 he entered government service as a recorder in the Monthly and Probate Court, to become Collector of Internal Revenue and Country Attorney.

Civil servants in Liberia were not forbidden to participate in politics, and in both 1923 and 1929 Tubman was elected as Senator for the True Whig Party, the youngest Liberian ever to have been admitted to the country's ten-man upper house. In 1928 he became a lay preacher in the Methodist Church and visited the United States to represent Liberia at a Methodist conference in Kansas City.

A scandal over the export of slave labour from Liberia led to international protests and an inquiry by the League of Nations in 1930. Both President King and Vice-President Yancy were compelled to resign, and Tubman, who was compromised as one of Yancy's lawyers and himself a Senator, resigned from the Senate and stood successfully for re-election in 1934. From 1937 to 1943 he served as Deputy President of the Supreme Court and in 1943 was the successful candidate for the Presidency of Liberia, having stood with the support of the out-going President, Edwin Barclay.

Barclay may well have thought that he could manipulate his

successor, wielding the real power himself while permitting Tubman to enjoy the ceremonial. Certainly, if he did, as several of his associates believed, he was soon enough to find himself mistaken. Tubman intended governing Liberia himself. As President-Elect he visited President Roosevelt in 1943, and on his return from the United States took the reins of government firmly into his own hands.

On taking office in 1944, he at once began to assault the encampments of the Barclay administration, almost entirely confined to Americo-Liberians, and to spread opportunities to members of the indigenous Liberian people in the hinterland. While carefully preserving his own power and influence, he extended the vote, reformed the fiscal and legal systems, and travelled widely throughout the country, attempting to weld the various elements of the population together. In 1951 his eight-year term of office – only two four-year terms were permitted to the President – came to an end, but the constitution was amended to allow him to stand again. Dihdwo Twe, leader of a Reformation Party, opposed him and lost calamitously, to be subsequently charged with sedition. Re-elected in 1955 and 1959, Tubman seems likely now to continue his Presidency for as long as he lives.

During his administration, education facilities have been extended, and the standard of living gradually if imperceptibly improved. Women have been given the vote, and many of them today play an important part in the government, while Tubman has deliberately encouraged investment from countries other than the United States in an attempt to make the Liberian economy more independent. In 1953, indeed, he even imposed a twenty-five per cent income tax on the profits of the Firestone Company, in order to finance internal development. Swedish financial interests are now heavily invested in iron ore mining, and the economy is no longer entirely dependent upon rubber production. The value of mineral exports for 1961 has been estimated to have topped £14 million, exceeding for the first time receipts from rubber exports themselves, at some £12 million.

In 1959–60 Tubman stepped on to the Pan-African stage,

participating in the Sanniquellie Conference with President Nkrumah of Ghana and President Sékou Touré of Guinea. Though he refused to join the Ghana-Guinea Union, he expressed himself in favour of a loose confederation of West African states, bound by practical forms of cooperation like the removal of all customs barriers.

In May 1961 a conference of independent African states took place at Monrovia under the sponsorship of Liberia, the Republic of Cameroun, Nigeria, and Togo, and since Liberia was the host country, Tubman was elected chairman of the meeting. Twenty of the twenty-seven independent African states sent delegations, and fifteen of them were represented by their Presidents or Prime Ministers; only the Sudan, together with the militants of the Casablanca bloc – Ghana, Guinea, Mali, Morocco, the United Arab Republic – and the formerly Belgian Congo Republic, which had not been invited, did not attend.

There were four major items on the agenda – the promoting of better understanding and cooperation among African states; threats to peace and stability in Africa; the establishing of special machinery to which African states might refer in the event of disputes amongst themselves; and the possible contribution of African states to world peace.

Opening the conference, President Tubman said that economic ties constituted 'the best road to political unity', and that he hoped to see concrete proposals for economic cooperation among the African states. On the whole issue of African leadership, he was engagingly frank. He said that there were those who thought Ghana should lead, because she was physically more developed than other states and was a large country; but more than development and physical size would be needed to assume leadership. Some thought it should be Egypt, because of her rich tradition and antiquity; but it would require more than tradition and antiquity. Others would prefer Liberia, because she was the oldest African Republic and was 'riper in political experience'. But he thought that the leadership of Africa would require an aggregate of all three qualifications – 'and more besides', an aggregate of the best in all. And he added:

> This conference is not intended to hinder conclusions of previous conferences; neither will we fail to support and endorse such decisions of other conferences as we know to be in the best interests of Africa and the world. ... Decisions of other conferences, including the Casablanca conference, should be studied.

He called upon all African leaders 'to reason together', to set the climate for building 'a new Africa and a new world order'.

In detailed resolutions, the conference condemned the policy of race rule in South Africa, backed independence for Algeria (though nothing was said to embarrass negotiations between France and the Algerian nationalists), affirmed loyalty to the United Nations, pledged all possible assistance to the Angolan nationalists, and condemned all nuclear tests. On the Congo, the conference contented itself with urging that outsiders should not interfere and with promising full support to the United Nations operation there.

It was agreed that nothing likely to split the conference should appear on the agenda, so that neither the dispute between Nigeria and the Republic of Cameroun over the Northern Cameroons, nor the Somali Republic's border quarrel with Ethiopia, was discussed. The published resolutions referred in friendly fashion to those states which had not attended the conference and expressed the hope that they might find it convenient to attend later meetings. The resolutions also claimed that the unity it was aimed for the moment to achieve was not the political integration of African states but a unity of aspirations and actions. Meanwhile certain principles were laid down as the basis for a permanent association of the Monrovia countries: freedom to accept or reject political unions; respect for the territorial integrity of all states; non-interference in the domestic affairs of other states, though national movements in colonies should be given every assistance; and recognition by all independent African states of their political equality.

Tubman announced that he was as happy as 'a bug in a rug' about the results of the Monrovia summit conference, maintaining that he was quite content to watch the Nigerian Federal Prime Minister, Sir Abubakar Tafawa Balewa, and Félix

Houphouet-Boigny, the Ivory Coast President, emerge as the leading figures. 'We do not seek leadership or notoriety; it matters not to us whence unity comes and who is responsible for it, as long as it is achieved.' His own policy of African co-operation in all fields, as opposed to political unification, had been unanimously endorsed and vindicated by the conference, and he added: 'We must have unity in such a way that each nation retains its sovereignty.'

The Monrovia conference was certainly a success for Tubman. Liberia lacks the wealth of countries like Ghana and the Ivory Coast, the force of populous states like Nigeria and the United Arab Republic, the influence of an experimental society like Guinea. Monrovia, with its social atmosphere compounded of Victorian dress and Bible Belt Protestantism, its dollar trade and brass band air, makes easy enough game for more sophisticated capitals like Cairo and Rabat, more proudly African ones like Accra and Conakry.

Certainly Tubman's claims to guide democracy in Liberia are mocked by the still profound backwardness of the indigenous peoples, the great gulf between them and the dominant Americo-Liberian class in Monrovia, and the monopoly of politics by his True Whig Party. His famous yacht, by which he travels to other countries and criticism of which the Liberian government meets by claiming that it is essential for coastal communications, cannot dazzle the labourers in the rubber plantations who earn the equivalent, in cash and subsidized rice, of two or three shillings a day.

A flamboyant personality, with a sharp intelligence beneath his sense of fun and his pleasure in good living, Tubman has set out to accommodate Liberia a little closer to the contemporary world. The Monrovia conference established him as a not inconsiderable force in African politics. But the closer Liberia is drawn to developments in the rest of the continent, the more urgent will a solution to its internal problems of poverty, illiteracy, and administrative casualness become.

William Vacanarat Shadrach Tubman has served now as President for eighteen years. Changes there have certainly been, but hardly those considerable or various enough to mark his régime as much of a contribution to 'a new Africa and a new world order'. Outside of Monrovia, most of Liberia has not yet been drawn into the twentieth century. Tubman's venture into the exterior may well carry the twentieth century into his own hinterland.

The capital is no longer carefree. On 11 September 1961 some 15,000 strikers in Monrovia tried to march on the presidential palace and had to be dispersed by police. The strike, which brought all commerce and industry in the city to a standstill, had begun a week before when employees at a garage had walked out in support of a wage claim. The grass must have been very dry to catch fire at such a spark. On 12 September Tubman asked the Legislature for drastic emergency powers to establish special courts; suspend *habeas corpus* for a year; arrest without a warrant and detain without bail for ninety days all persons considered dangerous to public safety and the security of the state. The President claimed that world developments were reflecting themselves in Liberia and that 'there are infiltrating into the nation organized, underground experimental movements designed at subversion, sedition, and treason, with intent to undermine and overthrow the government by craft, artifice, and subversive anti-Liberian activities'. Such activities were being 'instigated and supported by a small dissident group of malcontent citizens and certain foreign traducing agencies'.

Liberia seems unlikely long to remain a family affair.

18 Sékou Touré and the Guinean Experiment

Writing in *L'Éveil de l'Afrique noire* in 1948, Emmanuel Mounier reported on his journey through Africa:

> On arrival in Guinea you search for the Guinean problem. You find nothing. . . . You look there for a sign of the political eddy, at this period when all Africa is in tumult. . . . There is no social agitation, no political agitation . . . elections take place with a tedious absence of incident. Unassuming Guinea is neglected. . . . The capitals have forgotten it, they have left it to sleep in its African fold. . . . A Guinea developed, prosperous, a harmony of its different resources and the temperament of its people, could well become Africa's centre of equilibrium, even the brain or the living flame.

Mounier would have written differently three years later, for industrialization was raising a new society on foundations of iron and bauxite. With the development of a vigorous proletariat, and one strongly influenced by the French Communist trade union movement, the Confédération Générale des Travailleurs (C.G.T.), Guinea had ceased to be a political stillness in the breaking storm of French West Africa. And the man who was to change it even further, who was to become the symbol of militant African independence, was a product alike of Guinea's nationalist past and contemporary aspirations.

SÉKOU TOURÉ was born at Faranah in 1922 of poor Moslem peasant farmers, his father a Soussou and his mother a Malinke, and himself a grandson of Almamy Samoury, the almost legendary leader who fought the French forces long after the rest of Guinea had been overcome. More than fifteen years younger than Félix Houphouet-Boigny, President of the Ivory Coast, and Léopold Senghor, President of Senegal, and more than ten years younger than Hubert Maga, President of Dahomey, he belongs to the third generation of African leaders, the first of which, more or less privileged by wealth or university education, founded the political movements in Senegal and the Ivory Coast, and the second of which scaled political barriers through the secondary schools of French West Africa. He himself came up the third way, the hard climb of trade unionism and revolution, arriving at manhood during the Second World War, when France itself had suffered military defeat and succumbed to foreign domination.

A Moslem, his relationship to the empire of Samoury quickening in him the Islamic faith and respect for traditional law, he began his studies at a village Koranic school and was sent at the age of ten to primary school in Faranah, before entering in 1936 the French technical school at Conakry. Expelled in the following year for leading a food strike at the college, he continued to educate himself and completed his secondary schooling by correspondence. So equipped he gained employment in 1940 with the Compagnie du Niger Français, a commercial firm, and in 1941 passed an examination qualifying him for work in the post and telecommunications organization. In his new employment he showed considerable ability and a vigorous interest in the labour movement, becoming in 1945 the Secretary-General of the P.T.T. Workers' Union and helping to form the Union Cégétiste des Syndicats de Guinée, of which he became Secretary-General in 1946. But if he frightened the French administrators – he soon lost his job and in 1947 spent a brief period in prison – he clearly interested the leaders of the largest French trade union federation, and in March 1946 he attended the C.G.T. Congress in Paris.

Introduced to the core of left thought in France, he is rumoured to have visited Prague at this time and to have studied there for a short while. In 1946, he was a founder member of the Rassemblement Démocratique Africain, formed at Bamako under the leadership of Félix Houphouet-Boigny of the Ivory Coast. Entering Guinea's Treasury Department, he soon afterwards became Secretary-General of the Treasury Employees' Union, but he was dismissed for political activities, and, turning his energies to the trade union struggle, became in 1948 Secretary-General of the C.G.T. in Guinea and in 1950 Secretary-General of the Coordinating Committee of the C.G.T. in French West Africa and Togo.

There is no doubt that Sékou Touré saw in trade unionism an effective instrument of power, a method of acquiring control over the masses comparable to that enjoyed by the intellectual Senghor or the aristocratic Houphouet-Boigny. Equally, there can be no doubt of the important part which trade unionism played in forming him both as a man and as a leader, in establishing his aspirations and strategy. In an interview with Fernand Gigon, published in *Guinée, État-pilote*, he stated, with the intellectual passion that was to become the hallmark of so much he was to write and say:

> Trade unionism is a faith, a calling, an engagement to transform fundamentally any given economic and social régime, always in the search for the best and the beautiful and the just. To the degree that trade unionism is an apostleship, a choice, an engagement, it implies action against that which is contrary to the interests of the workers.

He soon extended his scope, however, beyond mere trade unionism, and in 1952 became Secretary-General of the Parti Démocratique de Guinée (P.D.G.), the Guinea section of the R.D.A., to build it up into a powerful mass movement. In 1953 he was one of the organizers of a general strike, from which he emerged as the idol of the Guinean workers; after seventy-three days, Paul Béchard, Governor-General of French West Africa, was forced to submit. All eyes turned to Sékou Touré, and the young Africans, irritated by the modest reformism of their leaders – Houphouet and his colleagues had broken all links with the French Communist Party and formed an alliance with the prudent U.D.S.R. – saw in him the leader of the radical opposition.

In the same year he successfully fought a by-election for Beyla to the Territorial Assembly, and in June 1954 he contested the seat of Guinea Deputy in the French Chamber, vacated by the death of Yacine Diallo; but he lost to his opponent, Barry Diawadou, amid violent popular protests against open electoral rigging by the administration. His reputation for courageous radicalism increased and, when in the same year he was called to membership of the Coordinating Committee of the R.D.A., he had already become a figure of considerable significance in French West Africa. The administration at last recognized that it was far more dangerous to hurl such a man into permanent opposition, even defiance of the law, than to permit him entry into the councils of the Republic, where he might be soothed by power into a more moderate approach. He was elected Mayor of Conakry in 1955 and Deputy in the election of 2 January 1956.

Several of his political friends began accusing him of treating with the enemy, of allowing himself to be tricked by the administration. Certainly he had grown dissatisfied with the affiliation of Guinea's trade unions to the Communist C.G.T., holding that the Marxist doctrine of the class struggle was irrelevant in the stage of history through which Africa was passing, and that an African trade union movement could not but be weak when divided among three rival European ideologies. He accordingly founded in April 1956 the Confédération Générale du Travail Africaine (C.G.T.A.), which broke all affiliation with the C.G.T. and its international counterpart, the World Federation of Trade Unions. There were mutterings that he had followed the advice of the administration in Dakar and was about to lend his prestige to an anti-Communist offensive. His motives, however, could hardly have been more different. The absence of trained administrators and adequate local funds had initially forced the trade union leaders to associate their African movements with the C.G.T., but the development of militancy, together with the growing differences between local and metropolitan problems, encouraged a structural change. After having attacked Sékou Touré for deviationism and even betrayal, the local C.G.T. leaders were finally forced to fuse with the C.G.T.A. at its Cotonou Congress in January 1957, to create the Union Générale des Travailleurs d'Afrique Noire (U.G.T.A.N.). This was to be free of all metropolitan and international affiliations, and planned 'to unite and organize the workers of black Africa, to coordinate their trade union activities in the struggle against the colonial régime and all other forms of exploitation . . . and to affirm the personality of African trade unionism.'

Sékou Touré became first Secretary-General and then President, while the new movement succeeded in absorbing the vast majority of workers in French West Africa. It was perhaps this very breakaway from the C.G.T. which symbolized the real independence movement of French Black Africa. For if the African workers had different needs and aspirations from the metropolitan workers, how long could their leaders feel that they had a place in the Paris parliament? The establishment of the U.G.T.A.N. generated a current of ideas in direct contradiction to those of Houphouet-Boigny and Senghor, who remained loyal to the image of an African France.

Although his connexion with the Communist Party had been close, Sékou Touré had not hesitated to enter into conflict with the C.G.T. and so with the Communist Party of France in order to affirm his Africanism, his belief in an Africa with its individual personality and aspirations. Though he was a Deputy in Paris, it was to Guinea itself that he continued to devote his time and talents, in the organization of the P.D.G., in the advancement of the trade unions, and in an attack upon all the old tribal and village structures which sustained the powers of the Chiefs. While most of his colleagues from French West Africa concentrated their energies upon increasing their influence in Paris, he recognized that it was in Africa that the foundations of real power were to be laid.

The legislating in June 1956 of the *loi cadre* established internal autonomy in the various territories of French West and Equatorial Africa, creating an Executive Council in each, the President of which was to be the Governor, but the Vice-President of which was to be the elected political leader of the territory. In Guinea, the position of the second-in-command was peculiarly strong because of the control that the P.D.G. itself possessed over the political life of the country, not only in the capital and amongst the intelligentsia, but in the smallest villages, where the power of the chiefs had already been substantially reduced. In the March 1957 elections, Sékou Touré led the

P.D.G. to an overwhelming victory, and he himself became Vice-President of the territory. Three operations seemed necessary to assure autonomy – Africanization, industrialization, and the final destruction of traditional rule. Africanization admitted exceptions, and the first Guinean Cabinet formed in May 1957 contained two European Ministers. In March 1957 the structure of the aluminium industry was established, and the economic development of the country accelerated with the construction of railways, bridges, and roads. Though the traditional chiefs had agreed to partial agrarian reform in August 1956, Sékou Touré was not satisfied, and he used all the power of his position to establish peasant cooperatives and village councils, destroying the last vestiges of chiefly authority.

He continued, however, to emphasize his attachment to France. In a speech before the Governor in July 1957, he claimed:

> France wants, with the territories of Africa – it is our common wish – to build not for France alone but for a new community, where all the peoples will stand on an equal footing. . . . We have made our choice, and even when there has been misunderstanding between our movement and those who represent the administration, it has never been the intention of the leaders of this movement to injure France as a nation.

His willingness to cooperate with France was regarded as a betrayal of African nationalism by the more radical of the African intelligentsia, and he was attacked, from time to time, in the pages of *L'Étudiant d'Afrique noire*, the organ of the Federation of Students from Black Africa in France (F.E.A.N.F.). In December 1957 a correspondent described Sékou Touré's trade union report to a congress at Bamako as 'demagogic and pseudo-analytical', denouncing 'the hypocrisy, the demagogy as much as the treason that characterize our African parliamentarians'. In May 1958 the same journal published an even more scathing attack. 'To identify M. Sékou Touré with the African working class is a monstrous swindle that ought to be denounced. . . . Sékou Touré and company speak of "liquidating the colonial system", of "the struggle for emancipation", of decolonization", but they altogether avoid the clarion call of our times, "independence".'

In May 1957 Sékou Touré became a member of the Grand Council of French West Africa, but his association with the French government was to be short-lived. After the *loi cadre* election of March 1957, open conflict raged within the R.D.A. over whether the political growth of French Africa should be towards a federal structure, linked as a community with France, or towards individual sovereignty, with each territory linked to France separately and directly. A passionate advocate of the first approach, in opposition to Houphouet-Boigny, Sékou Touré revealed his strength in the September 1957 Conference at Bamako; but a split was avoided, a compromise resolution was passed, and he was elected Vice-President of the R.D.A. Differences, however, continued to develop, and a break seemed inevitable when, at its March 1958 meeting, the Grand Council of French West Africa passed a resolution, under pressure from Sékou Touré and in the absence of delegates from the Ivory Coast, recommending the creation of a federal executive.

The break came when the de Gaulle government suddenly offered the French African territories a choice between autonomy within a new French Community and complete independence from France. Nearly all French African leaders, fearful of the economic consequences that might attend a real rupture with France or reluctant to sever political ties, called for a vote of 'yes' – acceptance of the French Community – in the referendum of 28 September 1958. Sékou Touré, however, stating – 'We prefer poverty in freedom to riches in slavery' – called for a vote of 'no', the choice of complete independence, and was immediately expelled from the R.D.A. In the referendum itself, Guinea voted 'no' by 1,136,000 to 57,000, and the break between the territory's leadership and the R.D.A. was complete.

General de Gaulle, on his visit to Conakry at the end of August, had promised: 'I say here, even louder than elsewhere, that independence is available to Guinea, she can have it; she can have it on 28 September by saying 'no' to the proposition that is put to her, and in saying this I guarantee that Paris will raise no obstacle to it.'

On 2 October Guinea officially became an independent republic, with Sékou Touré as its President, and the new government made immediate approaches to Paris. All overtures, however, were rejected by France, French administrators were swiftly withdrawn, and capital equipment removed by departing personnel. By the first week of November, less than twenty French administrators remained of the 4,000 technicians, teachers, doctors, judges, who had been in the territory at the time of the September vote, and Guinea's trade with France had dwindled drastically. The determination of the new Guinea government to consolidate independence, however – in December the opposition parties fused with the P.D.G., and Barry Diawadou, leader of the largest, joined the Cabinet – made a recovery possible. Ghana offered Guinea a £10 million loan, and soon afterwards another loan was made by the Soviet Union, while Senegalese teachers helped to keep the schools functioning. In November 1958 Sékou Touré himself visited Ghana and in December signed an agreement establishing a union between the two countries as the basis for a union of West African States. This 'project for union' was joined by Mali in December 1960, when it was decided to hold quarterly meetings of the three heads of state and establish committees to explore economic and political cooperation.

In November 1959 Sékou Touré visited the United States and several Eastern European countries, making trade agreements with the purpose of diversifying as far as possible Guinea's trading pattern, and in 1960 he visited China, where he received a loan of some £9 million, interest-free and repayable by 1979. Basing his foreign policy upon African neutralism and the rejection of alliances with any of the power blocs in the Cold War, Sékou Touré established relations with the Communist States probably more friendly than those of any other African leader, but he persistently made clear his willingness and wish to cooperate with the West as well.

He reportedly advised Patrice Lumumba, first Premier of the

Congo Republic, to call in the assistance of the East when the West refused to help in expelling Belgian mercenaries and forcibly ending the secession of Katanga. Certainly he gave unwavering support to Lumumba throughout the Congo crisis, and in October 1960 delivered a two-and-a-half hour speech to the General Assembly of the United Nations, in which he attacked the Secretary-General for his policy in the Congo. 'Those who fear that Africa will fall to a bloc and that they will lose their ancient privileges', he stated, 'are wasting their time. Africa is no longer booty or a bone of contention.' In January 1961 he attended the Summit Conference at Casablanca of heads of state from Ghana, Guinea, Mali, Morocco, and the United Arab Republic, together with the President of the Provisional Government of the Algerian Republic, the Foreign Minister of Libya, and Ceylon's Ambassador to Cairo. The Casablanca States – as they came to be called – attacked 'neo-colonialism' and launched committees for economic, political, and cultural cooperation.

A determined and dynamic Pan-Africanist, whose speeches and writings reveal a coherent and radical philosophy both eloquent and imaginative, Sékou Touré has become perhaps the single most influential and significant figure on the continent for the younger, more radical African leaders. They see in his career the symbol of an African nationalism that challenged a colonial government head-on and yet survived without capitulating to the dominion of the Eastern bloc. It is in this sense that he has become a more spectacular apostle of Pan-Africanism than the man by whose ideas he was himself influenced, President Nkrumah of Ghana. It would be difficult to imagine a more calamitous response to contemporary Guinea than the assumption, made in so many Western capitals, that Sékou Touré himself is a Communist and that Guinea emerged from its clash with France as a Soviet satellite.

The assumption, indeed, was revealed in all its absurdity during December 1961, when the Guinea government expelled Danil Solod, the Soviet Ambassador. In the previous month, the reportedly Communist-dominated Teachers' Union had distributed a memorandum criticizing the government's policies and demanding equal pay for equal work, regardless of academic qualifications. The memorandum had been rejected, while on 20 November two of the union leaders had been sentenced to ten years' imprisonment, and three of them to five years, on charges of activity against the state. When trouble broke out in various parts of the country, Sékou Touré had visited the affected areas to reassert the government's authority and, having returned to Conakry on 11 December in order to address a meeting of party activists, had used the occasion to accuse those responsible for the disturbances of having supplied embassies of the Eastern bloc with information. Then, on 15 December, Sékou Touré had summoned the heads of Communist missions to the Presidency, and on the following day the Soviet Ambassador had left for Moscow.

Early in January Anastas Mikoyan, Soviet First Deputy Prime Minister, visited Guinea at the invitation of the government. At the opening of a Soviet trade show, in the presence of Mikoyan, Sékou Touré reminded the world that Guinea had no intention of committing itself either to the Soviet bloc or the West. While Guinea would accept aid from any country, he continued, 'she refuses to be drawn into choosing sides in a power struggle between two blocs'. That is why, he continued, she had affirmed that 'revolutions cannot be imported or exported, but . . . are the fruits of the people's will'. He recalled that the Soviet Union had been amongst the first to grant disinterested aid to Guinea. Such cooperation, he maintained, should be a force for progress and peace in the service of humanity and should continue to be based on non-interference in each other's internal affairs, on reciprocal loyalty and friendship.

West Africa of 13 January 1962 reported that Mikoyan was expected to offer increased aid to Guinea and 'give guarantees that Communist diplomats would cease political intrigues'. Early in February 1962 it was announced that West Germany had granted a 25 million mark loan to Guinea and a further 5 million to the Guinea State Bank for use in providing pure water supplies and extending roads. On 24 February the government of Guinea withdrew the world's biggest bauxite concession from Bauxites du Midi, the French subsidiary of Canada's Aluminium Limited. A presidential decree announced that the company had failed to establish a processing plant in Guinea, despite government policy that all Guinean minerals should be processed in the country itself.

France forced Guinea to turn to the East for aid in order to survive. A precedent now exists. Certainly the form of economic blackmail in which France engaged in order to bring Guinea to its knees can only result in establishing ties between Communism and militant African nationalism. There can be no doubt that such ties exist in Guinea today – Conakry is crowded with technicians from Eastern Europe, the Soviet Union, and China – but Guinea itself still remains an independent socialist society, climbing the rocks of rapid industrialization between the breakers of East and West. A West which persists in seeing such independence as covert Communism may well succeed not only in making this true, but in persuading all militant African nationalists of its inevitability.

19 An African Presence: Léopold Sédar Senghor of Senegal

We delighted, my friend, in an African presence:
Furniture, from Guinea and the Congo, heavy and polished,
dark and light.
Primitive and pure masks on distant walls yet so near.
Tabourets of honour for the hereditary hosts, the princes
from the High-country.
Wild and proud perfumes from the thick tresses of silence,
Cushions of shadow and leisure like quiet wells running.
Eternal words and the distant alternating chant as in the
loin-cloths from the Sudan.
But then the friendly light of your blue kindness will soften
the obsession of this presence in
Black, white and red, O red like the soil of Africa.[1]

Senegal's relationship with France is the oldest in all of what was once French Black Africa, and the first African deputy ever elected to the French National Assembly came from the territory in 1914. The whole policy of 'assimilation', to which French colonialism was overtly committed, had been first engendered by the French Revolution of 1789 and its belief in the brotherhood of man. By the 16*e Pluviose*, *Ann. II*, and its restatement by the Second Republic in 1848, citizenship was extended to the four Senegalese communes of Dakar, Saint Louis, Rufisque, and Gorée, and in 1848, as well as from 1875 onwards under the Third Republic, Senegal citizens could vote for one member in the Chamber of Deputies. In the early days of the Third

1. 'For Khalam (a guitar with three strings)' by Léopold Sédar Senghor, translated by Miriam Koshland for *Africa South* (Vol. 2, No. 4, July-September 1958). The original appears in *Anthologie de la nouvelle poésie nègre et malagache de Sédar Senghor* published by Presses Universitaires de France.

Republic, the four Senegalese communes were created '*communes de plein exercise*', with their own elected mayors and municipal councils, and apart from the introduction in the 1930s of laws enabling a few highly educated Africans from other parts of French Black Africa to become citizens, the inhabitants of the four communes were the only beneficiaries of the assimilation policy. All others were 'subjects', with no right of representation, no access to higher posts in the civil service or universities, and little chance of secondary school education. They could be drafted into forced labour brigades and under the legal code could be tried and sentenced on the spot by French administrators. They resented the privileged status of the citizens, whom they tended to identify with the French administration, and this resentment partly explains why after the Second World War Africans in other territories resisted attempts by the sophisticated Senegalese to take the lead in French African politics.

LÉOPOLD SÉDAR SENGHOR was born in October 1906 at Joal, outside of the four citizenship communes and consequently a 'subject' in status. His prosperous Serer family remained Catholic in a predominantly Moslem country, and he was educated at the Catholic school in N'Gasobil. Proceeding to the lycée in Dakar, he did brilliantly at his studies and left Senegal for Paris, where he was the first African ever to win an 'agrégation', qualifying him to teach at a lycée. In 1935 he joined the staff of a lycée in Tours and then transferred to another in Paris, studying African languages at the Ecole des Hautes Etudes.

At the outbreak of the Second World War he joined the French army, but he was soon captured, and though he was approached by the Germans to desert the French cause, he refused and instead organized resistance amongst his fellow prisoners. In 1943 General de Gaulle's Provisional Government resumed control over French West Africa, with an awareness of the great share that the Africans had had in accomplishing this victory. On 30 January 1944 the Brazzaville Conference, called by the Colonial Commissioner, René Pleven, set out to define the future relationship between France and its overseas territories; and on the advice of the Conference, France's African possessions were later invited to send representatives to a Constituent Assembly in Paris. In 1945 Senghor formed the Bloc Africain with Lamine Guèye, a Senegalese 'citizen', as a socialist party in Senegal connected to the S.F.I.O., the socialist party of France. Together they were elected the two deputies for Senegal to the First and Second Constituent Assemblies, and Senghor himself played an important part in the framing of the constitutional changes which resulted.

The First Constituent Assembly included many colonial reforms in the April 1946 draft constitution, but this constitution was rejected in a referendum, and the October 1946 constitution which emerged from the Second Constituent Assembly was considerably less liberal. The new Fourth Republic established an indivisible French Union, with the overseas territories firmly within a unitary republic, and by Article 72 all power over legislation in matters of 'criminal law, the organization of public freedoms, and political and administrative organization' belonged to the French parliament alone. The constitution gave to each territory in French West Africa, however, its own General Council, renamed a Territorial Assembly in 1952, and an increased number of deputies in the French parliament.

Regarding the new constitution as utterly inadequate, the African deputies agreed to meet at Bamako in French Soudan during October 1946 to discuss the formation of a mass party. The leaders of the S.F.I.O. were afraid that this meeting would be dominated by the Communists, however, and persuaded those Africans associated with them, including Léopold Senghor and Lamine Guèye, not to attend, so that the important Rassemblement Démocratique Africain (R.D.A.) was established without them. The decision of Senghor and Laime Guèye to absent themselves, though it seemed relatively insignificant at the time, led to a rift between the popular leaders of Senegal and those in the rest of French West Africa which lasted for some twelve years and was only bridged by the de Gaulle referendum of September 1958 and the events that followed it.

In November 1946 Senghor was re-elected as a deputy, but he was growing deeply dissatisfied with the policies followed by Lamine Guèye and the S.F.I.O. At the S.F.I.O. party conference he pressed for greater decentralization and canvassed the claims of the 'subject' Africans, demanding the organization of a mass political movement to further their complete emancipation. He started his own journal, *Condition Humaine*, in which he attacked Lamine Guèye and the whole organization of the Bloc Africain. Finally, in October 1948, he formed his own party, the Bloc Démocratique Sénégalais (B.D.S.), and leaving the S.F.I.O., he joined the Indépendents d'Outre Mer (I.O.M.), a group of deputies from France's overseas possessions who rejected affiliation to any metropolitan political party.

Passionately interested in African culture himself and already a poet of considerable reputation, he established with Alioune Diop in 1947 *Présence Africaine*, the magazine which is still published in Paris as a common African front against cultural colonialism. More than any other African perhaps, he focused attention on the great accomplishments and continuing energy of African art, underlining in his own poetry the beauty of image and rhythm that was so much a part of Africa's literary inheritance. His whole philosophy of 'Negritude' was a reaction to the assimilationist assumption of France that African culture was essentially inferior to the French. The growing African élite responded by devoting themselves seriously to becoming writers, students of African legend, history, and language, to developing a specifically African idiom and standpoint. They sought in this way to demonstrate that African culture was as valid and exciting as any other, and they succeeded as a result in making a far more vital artistic contribution than the British-educated Africans who were less exposed to cultural attack.

In 1951 the Bloc Démocratique Sénégalais, very efficiently organized on regional lines and revealing exceptional strength in the rural areas, defeated Lamine Guèye and his supporters, to win both the seats in the French Chamber of Deputies. Senghor himself was elected to one of the seats and became the undisputed leader of the I.O.M.

In November 1952 the I.O.M. deputies influenced the adoption by the French parliament of an Overseas Labour Code, which gave rights of collective bargaining and substantial welfare benefits to workers in African territories. The I.O.M. itself then attempted to extend its influence at its Congress in Bobodioulasso, Upper Volta, in February 1953, by proposing the formation of an African federal republic within the French Union. This federal proposal was elaborated by Senghor in the following year, when he suggested dividing French West Africa into two federations, one with its capital at Dakar in Senegal and the other with its capital at Abidjan in the Ivory Coast. The conflict between the federalists and the particularists that resulted was to become one of the principal policy issues on which French Africa was to divide.

Though the B.D.S. grew irresistibly stronger within Senegal itself and easily won the territory's two seats again in the elections of January 1956, the R.D.A. – under the leadership of Félix Houphouet-Boigny of the Ivory Coast – resoundingly defeated the I.O.M. in the rest of French West Africa. In November the strength of the B.D.S. within Senegal was again confirmed in municipal elections, and Senghor himself became Mayor of Thies.

Passionately committed to the unity of French West Africa, Senghor bitterly but unsuccessfully opposed the new constitutional changes of the *loi cadre* – which gave universal suffrage and an Executive Council to each territory in French Black Africa – since he felt that this was likely to balkanize the whole region. In 1956 he founded the Bloc Progressiste Sénégalais (B.P.S.), a coalition of the B.D.S. with other smaller parties, which became the Senegalese branch of the Convention Africaine, a new inter-territorial party formed by the I.O.M. deputies. Then, in 1957, the Convention fused with the Mouvement Socialist Africain (M.S.A.) of Lamine Guèye, in an effort to turn the growing inter-territorial strength of the R.D.A. Nothing, however, availed, though within Senegal itself Senghor's influence remained supreme, and in the March 1957 elections, held in terms of the *loi cadre*, the B.P.S. won forty-seven seats out of sixty and formed the government. Finally, in March 1958, all leaders outside the R.D.A. combined to found the Parti du Regroupement Africain (P.R.A.), as a federalist movement.

In July, at the P.R.A. Conference, Senghor outlined his concept of an African-type socialism, stating that it was more a question of 'modifying and out-growing colonialism than of suppressing it'. Believing strongly in a federation of all French West African states, linked as a unit with France, he claimed – 'we must have an African community before a Franco-African community'. In 1958 he joined with his old enemy Lamine Guèye to form the Union Progressiste Sénégalaise (U.P.S.) as the Senegal section of the P.R.A., and he showed his hostility to the way that de Gaulle had come to power in France by going on holiday when the General visited Senegal in August. The U.P.S. however, voted 'yes' in de Gaulle's September referendum, choosing limited autonomy within the French Community rather than complete independence from France, though it did so with manifest reluctance, and only because it judged this the best way towards federation and an unbalkanized independence.

In December 1958 a Congress was held at Bamako by leaders from Senegal, Soudan, Dahomey, and Upper Volta to discuss a federation of the four states. In January 1959 Senegal became a republic, and in the March elections to its Legislative Assembly, the federalist U.P.S. won all eighty seats. Meanwhile, however, Upper Volta and Dahomey had withdrawn from the proposed Mali Federation under pressure from the government of the Ivory Coast and its leader, Houphouet-Boigny. The Federation of Mali, established in March, was therefore only an association of Senegal and Soudan, and Senghor himself became, in April, first a member of the Mali Federal Assembly and soon afterwards its President.

Differences, however, rapidly developed between the Federation's leaders from Senegal and those from Soudan over the precise form of government that Mali should adopt; those from Soudan desired a unitary system while those from Senegal, especially Senghor, demanded a federal form. Soudan had been brutally colonized, and it wanted visible signs of its emancipation; its leaders demanded a complete separation between past and present – Africanization of the civil service, the expulsion of French armed forces, and the taking over of all public services by the Soudanese themselves. Senegal's response was somewhat more tranquil; it had suffered relatively little from colonization, had had Senegalese technicians for some time, and feared the financial consequences of a complete break with France. There were, too, considerable differences in economic development. Senegal was at the beginning of real industrialization, with the assistance of French capital. Soudan, on the other hand, had no industry, and capital investors in Senegal were suspicious of the Marxist socialism projected by the Soudanese leaders. In June 1960 Mali became fully independent; but in August the differences between the Senegalese and Soudanese leaders finally came to a head over the election of a President, and on the night of 19 August 1960 the Federation collapsed. Since then relations between the two states have been extremely strained, and railway traffic between Bamako and Dakar has come to a complete halt.

In October 1960 Senegal attended the meeting of former French African states called by Houphouet-Boigny at Abidjan, and then in December the further meeting at Brazzaville which resolved on a common foreign policy and economic cooperation. With Senegal now one of the twelve states constituting the 'Brazzaville bloc' and one of twenty states which met at Monrovia in May 1961, Senghor is at last – after many years – working again in association with Houphouet-Boigny, though the firmness of their alliance is yet to be ascertained. Senghor himself stands mid-way between the radicalism of Sékou Touré, President of Guinea, and the conservatism of Houphouet-Boigny; equally, his own brand of federalism is mid-way between the unitary theories of Casablanca and the staunch particularism of many in the Brazzaville bloc.

Amongst the young intelligentsia of Senegal, the close association with France and the refusal of the Senegalese government to take a more militant Pan-Africanist line are undoubtedly unpopular, and pressures within Senegal are likely to grow for a swing to the left by Senghor's administration. In November 1961 Assane Seck, the opposition leader with a substantial following in the Casamance area, who had parted political company with Senghor by advocating a vote of 'no' in the 1958 de Gaulle referendum, was arrested after the alleged discovery of a secret arms dump. Later in the month the government announced that it would impose censorship on all news dispatches leaving the country. The Senegalese Information Minister, Obeye Diop, explained: 'In a young and developing country trying to build itself up, journalists have special duties of which they should be aware. They must impose a particularly severe ethical code upon themselves which, without disturbing the objectivity that is their first duty, invites them to watch carefully for consequences of the news they diffuse, lest they hinder the progress of young African states, progress without which there will surely be no freedom in the world of tomorrow.'

During December most of the students at Dakar University went on strike after the government banned a conference of the General Union of West African Students to which a number of opposition personalities had been invited. Several student leaders were arrested and others expelled. In March 1962 the Senegalese Information Minister announced the discovery of a planned *coup d'état* for which commandos had allegedly been trained in Mali, a spy network established in Senegal, and opposition parties within Senegal approached. The Information Minister further reported 'strong presumptions' that Morocco had participated in preparations for the *coup*. The Moroccan Embassy in Dakar later issued a statement denying the accusation as 'a product of the purest imagination'. The Embassy said it was difficult to see what motives could have stimulated Morocco to attack the security of an African country to which it had been linked by close contact over centuries. The Foreign Minister of Mali also denied that his country was being used as a base for aggression against any African state. He pointed out that Mali had not restricted the entry of Senegalese citizens, though Senegal had restricted the entry of citizens from Mali.

Ultimately, of course, the future of Senghor himself must lie in the progress of his 'African Socialism', in his ability to use the developing wealth of Senegal for the benefit of its whole population. In February 1962, Mamadou Dia, President of the Council of Ministers in Senegal and Assistant General Secretary of the ruling Union Progressiste Sénégalaise, announced that the most significant socialist policy carried out to date had been the government's decision to 'take over the entire production of groundnuts'. He said that it was wonderful to think that private enterprise should have agreed to such a measure without constraint.

Senghor still doubtless believes in the closest possible association among African states, and within the alignment of moderates established at Monrovia, he is likely to exert his influence towards the development of ever closer ties. Whatever his political contribution to the shape of contemporary Africa, however, his intellectual one has already been considerable, and he must rank high amongst those who have given to the continent a confidence in its cultural accomplishments and aspirations.

20 The Moroccan Monarchy

Contemporary Morocco, with its population of 10,556,000 in an area of 153,870 square miles, is largely the political creation of its monarchy and the resistance of that monarchy to French dominion. Since the end of February 1961, a new king, Hassan II, has been on the throne, in absolute control of the country's political life, while, in the depths, below the swells of trade union and left-wing opposition, a crisis between tradition and modernism, autocracy and popular government, appears to be approaching. The defeat of the monarchy would be speedy and inevitable were its prestige less substantial or its function less organic. That it should have survived so long and seem able to survive for some time yet to come is a reflection of the part it has played in producing independent Morocco.

In 1912 the Sultan of Morocco, a member of the Alouite dynasty which had ruled in north-west Africa since the middle of the seventeenth century, signed the Treaty of Fez that turned Morocco into a protectorate of France, and then abdicated. Moulay Youssef, the Sultan's brother, succeeded to the throne, to rule until 1927, when his third son, Sidi Mohammed Ben Youssef, the late Mohammed V, succeeded him.

Born in 1910, Mohammed V was educated by French tutors and was permitted to mount the throne only, it is generally believed, because the French considered that he would be politically manageable. A Regency was proclaimed, but in 1930 the new Sultan began suddenly to assert himself, concluding the Regency and showing himself hard-working and intelligent, profoundly attached to Islam though with a mind receptive to new ideas.

Compelled to accept Vichy rule in 1940, he welcomed American forces in 1942, and in January 1943 he met President Roosevelt and Winston Churchill at the Anfa Conference in Casablanca. Meanwhile nationalist sentiment was fast developing within Morocco, and in January 1944 nationalist forces there defined their claims, founded the Istiqlal or Independence Party, and addressed a manifesto to Mohammed V and the French Residency in which they demanded the abrogation of the protectorate treaty and the recognition of Morocco's right to independence.

In 1947 the Sultan, in a famous speech at Tangier, proclaimed the affiliation of Morocco with the Arab World and demanded that her legitimate national aspirations be immediately recognized, so associating himself with the nationalists and making open conflict with the French inevitable. The only means of resistance open to him was to refuse his royal seal to decrees drafted by the French, and in this way he frustrated all attempts made by the French authorities to ban the Istiqlal.

Nationalism in the country was speedily consolidated around the throne, spreading from the middle class and the intellectuals to the proletariat and the traditionalist peasantry, while international opinion began at last to stir in its favour. The French reacted by encouraging a number of the Sultan's rivals, under the leadership of Thami Al-Glaoui, to organize a vast march of rural nobles, who demanded that the Sultan be deposed. Using the demand as its excuse, the French government on 20 August 1953 deposed and exiled the Sultan together with his family, first to Corsica and then to Madagascar. The people of Morocco, however, were infuriated rather than cowed, and they responded by rallying overwhelmingly to the throne as the symbol of Moroccan nationalism. Considerable unrest broke out, culminating in the formation of the Army of Liberation and widespread acts of violence.

The French government found it necessary to negotiate with the Sultan, and in November 1955 he returned to the throne amidst great popular acclaim and with France's agreement to the principle of independence. A government was formed under an army colonel, Si Bekkai, who was himself an independent in politics, with representatives from the Istiqlal and the Democratic Party of Independence. This government negotiated terms with the French, and Morocco at last became independent on 2 March 1956, while a corresponding agreement was reached with the Spanish government over the northern zone of the country.

The coalition government now faced enormous problems – the Moroccanization of the civil service, the re-establishment of order with the absorption of the Army of Liberation, the form of future relations with France, and the Algerian war, already in its second year. In internal politics the Sultan remained the dominating figure, but around him tensions were speedily developing.

In November 1956 a Cabinet reshuffle eliminated those Ministers representing the Democratic Party, which soon disappeared, and the new government was almost entirely drawn from the Istiqlal. A Consultative Assembly was nominated by the Sultan, with the majority in general support of the Istiqlal and with representatives of the powerful trade union, the Union Marocaine du Travail (U.M.T.), and in May 1958 an entirely Istiqlal government was formed under Ahmed Balafrej. The Sultan then announced the grant of a Royal Charter, which declared that national sovereignty was embodied in the King and that government would take the form of a constitutional monarchy, with advances by gradual stages towards a fully elected National Assembly.

Conflict was developing within the Istiqlal itself, however, between the conservative and the radical elements, and in December 1958 the Balafrej administration fell. The King issued a vigorous appeal for unity and eventually formed a new caretaker government, drawn from the left wing of the Istiqlal under Abdullah Ibrahim, which he charged with holding elections. A clash between traditionalists and the new militants seemed inevitable none the less, and in September 1959 those radicals who had left the Istiqlal because of its conservative policies, its gradualist approach to reform, and its close links with the palace, established the Union Nationale des Forces Populaires (U.N.F.P.) under the leadership of El Mehdi Ben Barka and with the support of the Secretary-General of the U.M.T., Mahjoub Ben Seddik.

In May 1960 the King dismissed the Ibrahim administration, considering it too sympathetic towards the U.N.F.P., and established a new government with himself as President and his eldest son, the Crown Prince, as Vice-President. Local elections held in the same month revealed considerable popular support for the U.N.F.P. in the major cities of Casablanca, Rabat, and Tangier, though little following in the traditionalist rural areas.

In January 1961 Mohammed V was host at Casablanca to a Summit Conference of Ghana, Guinea, Mali, Morocco, and the United Arab Republic, with the Foreign Minister of Libya, Ceylon's Ambassador to Cairo, and Ferhat Abbas, as President of the Provisional Government of the Algerian Republic, also attending. This conference of the Casablanca states – so named to distinguish them from the less militant, pro-Western countries in the Brazzaville bloc – supported Morocco's claim to Mauritania and Algeria's demand for self-determination, as well as resolving to establish an African Consultative Assembly, committees for political, economic, and cultural cooperation, and an African High Command to coordinate action against foreign intervention.

However conservative his domestic régime might be, the King was shrewdly blunting radical criticism within Morocco by the militancy of his foreign policy. He still retained great personal prestige for the part he had played in the independence struggle, and he seemed able to secure the monarchy against serious attack for many years to come. Then, on 28 February 1961, he died suddenly while undergoing an operation, leaving his son as Hassan II to face the struggle between traditionalism and the forces of reform in Morocco.

Born in July 1929 at Rabat, HASSAN II received under private tutors both an Arabic and a Western education, to qualify as a lawyer. On 20 August 1953 he was exiled together with his father, first to Corsica and then to Madagascar, returning with the triumphant Sultan to Morocco in 1955 and assisting him with the negotiations in Paris which resulted in Morocco's independence. On 9 July 1957 he was proclaimed Crown Prince and his father's heir, a necessary step since succession within the Moroccan Royal House is not automatically linked to the eldest son.

Appointed Commander-in-Chief of the Moroccan Army, he was responsible for its complete reorganization and took an increasing share in the political life of the country, exercising considerable influence over his father and becoming – with his appointment as Vice-President in May 1960 – the effective head of the new government. Widely held to be rigidly conservative, he disarmed many of his critics, however, by continuing his father's militant foreign policy and by unexpectedly announcing on 5 March 1961 that all French forces would leave the country by October, two years ahead of schedule.

The Moroccan monarchy has given sufficient proof of its vigour by the passing of the throne from Mohammed V without any of the popular disturbances which had been so widely predicted. Yet tensions within the country clearly exist, increased in June 1961 by the promulgation of a 'fundamental law', dyed in all the colours of conservative Islam. Jean Lacouture commented in *Africa South* (Vol. 6 No. 1, October–December 1961):

> Hassan II has little time for the political and worker organizations of his country. In his view, Morocco needs for many years more a 'responsible leader', surrounded by 'a small team of competent and devoted men' who will establish a régime of direct contact – free of the 'intermediaries' so joyfully denounced by General de Gaulle – with a trusting and submissive people.

Criticism, however, is not silent. On 5 August 1961 the French-language trade union journal *L'Avant-Garde* denounced 'the exploitation of the people by foreigners and their lackeys ... of a clique thirsting for dictatorship and *lettres de cachet* ...'

About the same time as the article in *L'Avant-Garde* appeared, a Students Congress at Azru passed a series of resolutions which strongly condemned the 'personal power' and diplomacy of the King and severely censured the economic policy of his régime.

Supported by a loyal army and the traditionalists still so strong in the rural areas, Hassan II seems at the moment unassailable, whatever threats he will in the future have to face from the industrial workers in the west of the country. And threats he will certainly have to face, for the urban masses increasingly flock to the banners of the Union Nationale des Forces Populaires, drawn by a manifesto which promises to consolidate independence and remove all vestiges of colonialism, particularly in the economic and military spheres; to reform the agricultural system in order to raise the peasantry's standard of living; to install in Morocco full democracy, with the King as a constitutional monarch; to help the Algerian people in their struggle for independence; and to work towards the unity of the Maghreb.

Morocco is not two countries; a constant current of political ideas flows between city and village. And the Moroccan throne is only as strong as the prop of the Moroccan peasantry, which constitutes the vast bulk of the population. The rural areas still represent a great deal of loyal capital on which Hassan II is able to draw. Such capital is none the less limited, and the monarchy will have speedily to improve the condition of the impoverished peasants if it is to continue counting upon their support. This task has been made all the more difficult, however, by a calamitous harvest in 1961, which produced only half the average cereal yield and is severely straining the budget by imports of food.

The King's first year of rule has registered several successes. In a crash programme conducted by the army, hundreds of one-room schools, with attached living quarters for teachers, have been built, enabling far more Moroccans to receive a basic education. Two million hectares of religious, state, tribal, and settler land are to be consolidated into cooperatives in which the peasants will hold titles to the use but not the ownership of the land, so preventing the fragmentations of inheritance. Above all, the King has followed his father's lead in giving open support to the Algerian struggle for independence. Indeed he was personally active in negotiating with the French government over the prison conditions and then the release of Mohammed Ben Bella, the F.L.N. leader who was arrested with four of his colleagues in November 1956, when the plane they were travelling in from Morocco to Tunis was brought down at Algiers. The Moroccan government has also given unequivocal encouragement to the concept of a Maghrebin federation, though Hassan II could hardly be unaware of the likely consequences for the Moroccan monarchy of an association with the militantly socialist F.L.N. government of an independent Algeria. Certainly, within Morocco itself, the gulf between rich and poor remains dangerously great. The anniversary celebrations of the King's accession to the throne on 3 March 1962 were conducted with an intricate opulence that emphasized the bleak daily life of most Moroccans by contrast. The palace in Rabat is too near to the mud-and-stick huts in which four out of every five Moroccans live not to foment frustration and anger by the differences it displays.

All commentators agree in acknowledging that the new monarch has a sharp intelligence, a strong will, and a subtle, complex personality. His father established the political unity of the country. It is his own task to create an economic and social unity as well. If he can commit himself to the demands of contemporary Morocco, throwing off the influence of the conservative middle class, he may yet secure for many years to come the throne which has already played so organic a part in establishing Morocco's independence. If he cannot, he is likely to be swept aside, and the whole Alouite dynasty together with him.

21 From Reform to Revolution in Algeria

Within an area of 855,077 square miles, Algeria contains a population of 10,288,000, of whom 9,255,000 are Moslem and 1,033,000 non-Moslem mainly European settlers. Technically, the territory is governed as an integral part of France, and it is indeed in pursuit of complete independence that Arab nationalism has fought a war with the French army and government since 1 November 1954. Since September 1958 a provisional nationalist government, the Gouvernement Provisoire de la République Algérienne (G.P.R.A.), has existed with headquarters in Cairo and Tunis, recognized by Ghana, Guinea, Indonesia, Liberia, Libya, Mali, Morocco, the Sudan, Tunisia, and the United Arab Republic within Africa, and by a number of Arab States, the People's Republic of China, and the Soviet Union. The history of a nationalism which has struggled so bitterly for so long against French rule may best be personified in the careers of Ferhat Abbas and the new President of the G.P.R.A., Youssef Ben Khedda.

The origins of Algerian nationalism in its present form date back to 1925, when Messali Hadj founded the Étoile Nord-Africaine (E.N.A.) among North African workers and intellectuals in Paris. The return to North Africa of the movement's leaders during the thirties led in 1937 to the foundation of the Parti Populaire Algérien (P.P.A.), which was banned in 1939 but continued to develop illegally – around a militant group of students and workers – under the Vichy régime during the war.

FERHAT ABBAS was born in October 1899 at Taher in Constantine, the son of a local administrator, and was educated first at primary school in Djidjelli and then on a state bursary at a lycée in Constantine. In 1923 he went to Algiers University in order to study pharmacy and there was elected, in 1926, President of the Algerian Moslem Students Union. The law of 4 February 1919 had eased the admission of Moslems to French citizenship and opened to them the doors of various assemblies, giving to their elected representatives in the municipal councils a say in the selection of mayor and subordinate officials. These years were accordingly tranquil ones, and Abbas, excited by politics and literature, reflected a spirit of optimism in his writings. In a book of his various articles and essays, entitled *Le Jeune Algérien*, he referred to his military service, making the first of many declarations on what he believed the relationship between France and Algeria to be. 'I served with the forces because I am French and for no other reason. We are Moslem and we are French. We are natives and we are French.'

His studies concluded and his political reputation established by *Le Jeune Algérien* and his activities as President of the Algerian Moslem Students Union – he presided in 1929 over a Congress of North African Students – he decided to set up as a pharmacist at Sétif, opening his shop in 1933. Starting at once on his political career, he became during 1933–6 a councillor general in Constantinois, a municipal councillor in Sétif, and a financial deputy to Algiers – the climb to success envisaged by all the bourgeois Moslems of Algeria. In 1933 he founded a weekly publication, which appeared until 1939 under the title of *L'Entente*, a symbol of his beliefs in the advance of Moslem Algeria through Franco-Algerian cooperation. And on 23 February 1936 he unfolded in *L'Entente* his political ideas, in a now famous passage:

> If I had discovered an Algerian nation, I would be a nationalist and I would not blush for it as though it were a crime. Men who die for a patriotic ideal are daily honoured and regarded. My life is worth no more than theirs. Yet I will not die for the Algerian homeland, because such a homeland does not exist. I have not found it. I have questioned history, I have asked the living and the dead, I have visited the cemeteries; no one has told me of it.... One does not build on the

wind. We have once and for all dispersed the storm clouds of fantasy in order to tie for ever our future to that of the work of France in this land. . . . No one, moreover, believes in our nationalism. That which is worth fighting for behind that word is our economic and political emancipation. . . . Without the emancipation of the natives of Algeria, French Algeria cannot endure. . . .

Abbas was stating his faith, but also his conditions.

With the outbreak of the Second World War, he enlisted at the age of forty and volunteered for a combatant unit, calling upon the readers of *L'Entente* to 'dedicate themselves altogether to the saving of the nation on which our own future depends. . . . If democratic France ceases to be powerful, our ideal of liberty will forever be buried. . . .' Future leaders of the Algerian revolution, like Mohammed Ben Bella and Belkacem Krim, also took to the colours. Abbas was demobilized in August 1940 and, profoundly shaken by the defeat of France, returned to his pharmacy in Sétif. On 10 April 1941 he addressed a memorandum to Marshal Pétain, the signatories of which, he stated,

have sworn an oath to struggle and agitate under all circumstances . . . until the law in Algeria is the same for all and privileges have been abolished. They demand from France reforms capable of improving the lot of their race, of facilitating their evolution, of correcting the social inequalities and preparing a real rebirth of the country.

He followed with a plan for bold and radical agricultural reform, including the expropriation from the great agricultural cartels of land for the peasantry and the creation of a 'peasant's fund' to assist small proprietors. The memorandum was the work of an intelligent reformer, and its dismissal by Marshal Pétain was the dismissal of all the policies of moderation and their submergence in revolution.

Abbas was angered by the vague and delayed reply of Marshal Pétain. On 8 November 1942 he met Robert Murphy, Special Envoy of the United States to the authorities in Algiers, and their conversations appear to have had considerable influence upon Abbas, who read the Atlantic Charter with rising excitement and began to have second thoughts about the moderation he had so assiduously exhibited. On 22 December 1942 he dispatched to the French authorities a message from influential Moslem Algerians, demanding a conference to establish a new political, economic, and social statute for the territory. The administration rejected the new approach as well, and on 10 February 1943 the famous *Manifeste du Peuple Algérien* appeared. In it, Ferhat Abbas and other influential Moslem moderates demanded a specifically Algerian constitution, guaranteeing: (1) the complete liberty and equality of all Algeria's inhabitants, without distinction of race or religion; (2) the suppression of feudal ownership by a programme of agrarian reform; (3) the recognition of the Arab language as official and equal in status with French; (4) liberty of the press and of association; (5) free and compulsory education for children of both sexes; and (6) freedom of worship for all Algerians, with the separation of Church and State. The Manifesto also required 'the application to all countries, large and small, of the right of peoples to self-determination', the immediate and effective participation of Algerian Moslems in the government of their country, and the liberation of all those condemned and imprisoned for political reasons, regardless of the party to which they belonged.

It was a demand for internal autonomy, a clear break with the support which Abbas and his colleagues had given before to the concept of Algeria as an inseparable portion of France. The government rejected the Manifesto, and Abbas, to mark his solemn rupture with the régime, refused to attend the September 1943 session of the Financial Council in Algiers. On 14 March 1944, he founded at Sétif the 'Amis du Manifeste et de la Liberté', with the support of Messali Hadj and his Parti Populaire Algérien.

This high point of harmony in the history of Algerian nationalism was not, however, to be long sustained. The revolutionaries of the P.P.A. were uncomfortable under the leadership of Abbas, and the spectacular growth of the Amis du Manifeste et de la Liberté, which claimed 500,000 adherents by the end of 1945, drew the leadership further and further into the hands of the radicals. At the congress in March 1945, Messali Hadj himself was proclaimed 'the uncontested leader of the Algerian people', and those who had initiated the movement experienced the defeat of their own motion – that a future Algeria should be associated federally with France – for one proclaiming that any future Algerian State should freely choose its international associations.

On 1 May 1945 nationalist fever began to mount throughout the territory and when, one week later at Sétif, the news of the armistice was received, columns of young Moslems formed behind banners and the green-and-white flags of Algerian nationalism. The police fired upon the flag-bearers and an explosion of fury followed in which several Europeans were killed. News of the riot spread rapidly throughout the country, lighting similar disturbances elsewhere, and 108 Europeans lost their lives in the course of the three days from 8 to 10 May. The repression that followed was swift and relentless. Against the Algerian nationalists, two forces addressed themselves, the *colons* and the army – the *colons* setting themselves up as judges with a promptness and efficiency rivalled only by the savagery they showed, while the French air force and navy assisted the army in its campaign of re-establishing French authority. Jean Lacouture of *Le Monde* was to write in his *Cinq Hommes et la France:* 'Never perhaps has a French force struck a colonial people with such brutality and on a scale so vast as in the time of the European armistice.' Official figures admitted to 1,500 Moslem dead, while tracts of the P.P.A. claimed a figure of 45,000. A semi-official estimate, reproduced in many publications and on several occasions quoted in the French parliament, settled upon 15,000. It was not, however, the number which was significant; it was the sheer passion of embitterment engendered by the repression. The revolution that suddenly sprouted in 1954 was planted during the days and nights of May 1945.

Paris, however, soon recognized the dangerous character of its violence. It had not succeeded in erasing Algerian nationalism; everywhere cells of the P.P.A. were spreading, everywhere the followers of Ferhat Abbas were increasing. While the Algerian people lay prostrate, brooding a bitter revenge, representation in the French Assembly was at last given to elected Moslems. Though limited to two seats, this symbolic gesture might at one time have made Abbas hesitate. It was now too late. Ten years earlier, Maurice Violette, a former Governor-General of Algeria, had said to the French National Assembly:

> These Moslems, when they protest, you become indignant; when they approve, you become suspicious; when they are silent, you become afraid. Gentlemen, these men have no political country of their own. . . . They crave to be admitted to yours. Should you refuse, you may well fear that they will soon create one.

While Messali Hadj, deported to the French Congo, then to France, and finally detained in a suburb of Algiers, remained the leader of the Algerian masses, Abbas thrust himself with boldness and with skill into the world of legal action. He founded the Union Démocratique du Manifeste Algérien (U.D.M.A.) in the spirit of Habib Bourguiba and the leadership of Tunisia's Neo-Destour, propagating modernism, a Western commitment, and a policy of dynamic compromise. A party of the middle classes and the intelligentsia, the U.D.M.A. speedily acquired prestige amongst the masses as well, and in its first electoral attempt achieved a triumph which even the great reputation of Abbas could not have promised; on 2 June 1946, in elections to the Second French Constituent Assembly, it obtained seventy-one per cent of the votes polled and eleven of the thirteen seats reserved for Algeria. Meanwhile the militants of the P.P.A. organized themselves in October 1946 into the Mouvement pour le Triomphe des Libertés Démocratiques (M.T.L.D.), out of which the Algerian revolution was to spring some eight years later. The M.T.L.D. did not fight the 1946 elections, and Abbas became, with Messali Hadj, the great figure of Algerian nationalism.

On 9 August 1946 the U.D.M.A. parliamentarians placed before the French Assembly a projected constitution for an Algerian Republic, associated with France along the general lines that had been proposed in the 1943 Manifesto.

> Article 1: The French Republic grants to Algeria its complete autonomy . . . an Algerian Republic, an Algerian government, and an Algerian flag.

Article 2: The Algerian Republic is a member of the French Union as a federated state. Its diplomatic relations and national defence are common with those of the French Republic and lie within the powers of the Union, in the exercise of which Algeria will be associated.

Article 5: All the inhabitants of Algeria, without distinction of race or religion, except for those under foreign jurisdiction, are declared Algerian citizens and proclaimed equal.

Article 6: Every French citizen will enjoy in Algeria the status of an Algerian citizen. Reciprocally, every Algerian citizen will enjoy in France the status of a Frenchman.

Article 9: The official languages of the Algerian Republic are French and Arabic.

Article 30: Immovable property, French and Moslem, will be respected ... the agrarian, political, and social reform of the peasantry will take place within the framework of the public good.

Paris would have none of it.

On 23 August, during a debate on Algeria, Abbas addressed the French Assembly in terms very different from those in which, ten years before, he had described Algerian nationhood.

The Algerian personality, the Algerian fatherland, which I did not find in 1936 amongst the Moslem masses, I find there today. . . . The change that has taken place in Algeria is visible to the naked eye, and neither you nor I can or have the right to ignore it. . . . We are called, Moslem Algerians and French Algerians, Algeria and France, to live together. Let us learn to respect each other, to support each other and love each other. We will then have realized the great ideal of democratic France.

The French parliament, however, had become an arena of irreconcilable conflict. In 1947 the U.D.M.A. representatives lost their parliamentary seats as the result of a new election notable for the dishonesty with which it was conducted. The M.T.L.D. was from then onwards the dominant nationalist force in Algeria, and those French deputies who had cried out furiously against the proposals of Ferhat Abbas, had to make the political acquaintance of Messali Hadj and his associates instead.

The years from 1948 to 1954 marked a period of brazen

electoral manipulations, of fumbling attempts to shatter Algerian nationalism, and of a gathering crisis within the M.T.L.D. itself. Abbas, leading a much weakened U.D.M.A., remained loyal to legal action but was all the while shedding his faith in the French people. Each attempt at reaching an understanding with France was rejected with casual brutality, while unremitting electoral fraud eliminated all nationalist representation from the French Assembly.

Though Messali Hadj was still widely revered as the leader of the M.T.L.D., the organization was beginning to weaken through an internal conflict, which split its leadership into three clashing groups. The Centralists believed in encouraging the liberal spirit in France and upholding the paramountcy of group decisions taken by the Central Committee. The Messalists were loyal to the increasingly authoritarian leadership of Messali Hadj, and though they believed in revolution, made little effort to get down to organizing one. The third group, small but vigorous, believed in an immediate recourse to violence as the only way of accomplishing Algerian independence, and it was the members of this who in 1947 formed the Organisation Secrète to build – and in March 1954, the Comité Révolutionnaire d'Unité et d'Action to launch – the revolution, with its united call in the Front de Libération Nationale (F.L.N.).

Under the title 'The Inevitable Choices', Abbas wrote in *La République Algérienne*, his new journal, on 8 October 1954:

> Our people, tired of indignantly pleading without success its cause before a tribunal which is ruled by racialism alone, is silent. This silence and this calm have been interpreted as an expression of adherence. In reality, fury is at its height, and the silence is one of contempt and of rebellion.

On 1 November 1954, between one and two in the morning, the rebellion broke out at a dozen different points in Algeria. Police stations, garages, and gas works were attacked, while fifteen dead marked the beginning of a war that was to take many years and kill in the hundreds of thousands.

Despite the tone of his editorials, Abbas clearly shared in the stupor exhibited by all the publicly known national leaders. The conspiracy had been mounted in shadow by men like Mohammed Ben Bella and Belkacem Krim, and the French authorities had caught no suspicion of it. All the major nationalist organs denounced the insurrection. Ferhat Abbas himself wrote in *La République Algérienne* on 12 November: 'We continue to be persuaded that violence will settle nothing.' The mouthpiece of the M.T.L.D., *L'Algérie Libre*, denounced some days later 'this dangerous attempt at using force', as did the journal of the Algerian Communist Party, *Liberté*. Most of the Centralists hesitated for a long time, though Mohammed Yazid, one of their leaders and now Algerian Minister of Information, left at once for Cairo to join Ben Bella and the other leaders of the rebellion. Youssef Ben Khedda, a young man of twenty-four, who had been Secretary-General of the M.T.L.D. and amongst the most influential of its leaders, was arrested on the morrow of the rebellion before he could openly associate himself as well.

If Messali Hadj, the 'father of independence', was lost to the insurgents, was it not perhaps an opportunity for the U.D.M.A. to reinstate itself at last as part of the revolutionary movement? A revolution requires a figurehead, and the revolutionaries must have been aware of this. Certainly, from the beginning of 1955, contact was maintained between the men of the maquis and Abbas. Though the exact date of his adhesion to the F.L.N. remains unknown, many believe that Abbas actually joined in May 1955, though it was only on 26 April 1956 that he made a public statement of his allegiance to the Front at a press conference in Cairo.

In April and August 1955, and again in April 1956, Abbas visited Algiers and Paris to gauge the possibilities of legal action and the concessions Paris might be prepared to make. Everywhere disappointed, he became more and more sure that force alone was capable of making France see reason. On 23 April 1956 the news leaked out to correspondents of the French press in Egypt that Ferhat Abbas had flown to Cairo, and three days later, addressing himself to some 100 journalists, he announced his open support of the F.L.N. Speaking soon afterwards with members of the French press, he explained:

They know in Paris that I am honest, that I work only for a return to peace. Today I can do nothing inside my own country or in France. I have knocked on all the doors, I have spoken to all the politicians able to understand me, to understand us. Those who have really understood can do nothing. I cannot continue any longer to stand bail for a situation of which I entirely disapprove. My departure will show at last to my fellow citizens that I have withdrawn from ineffectual politics.... The U.D.M.A. no longer exists, no more than do any Algerian parties.... I am simply joining here the organization which struggles for the liberation of Algeria, because there is no other way.

Between April 1956 and September 1958 Abbas was based in Switzerland, supervising F.L.N. publicity throughout Europe and travelling far afield on behalf of the movement – to Latin America (1957), the Arab States (1958), and South East Asia (1959). At the end of April 1958, as head of the F.L.N. delegation to the Tangier Conference, he met in secret session with leaders of the Moroccan Istiqlal and the Tunisian Neo-Destour, who subsequently committed themselves to 'total support' for the Algerian people 'in the war of independence'. On the last day of the meeting, Abbas held a press conference at which he announced: 'We prefer to be ten million corpses rather than ten million slaves.' Settler and French army opinion within Algeria hardened. In May Pierre Lagaillarde, a young Algerian settler leader, led an assault on the government buildings in Algiers, the Fourth Republic collapsed, and on 1 June General de Gaulle took over the government of France.

On 18 September 1958, the F.L.N. formed in Tunis the Gouvernement Provisoire de la République Algérienne, the Algerian government-in-exile, and Ferhat Abbas was elected its president. The moderate had become the acknowledged leader of the revolutionaries. But under de Gaulle, the French government too was undergoing a change. On 16 September 1959, in a radio and television address, de Gaulle made his historic offer of 'self-determination', and though he was characteristically vague about the details, the Algerian settlers and elements in the French Army itself reacted with fury. De Gaulle had to discipline his own forces, and in January 1960, with the failure of the uprising in Algiers, he made clear that he would permit no opposition to his policies within the army or submit, as so many successive French governments had done, to settler pressure in Algeria itself. As Edward Behr wrote in *The Algerian Problem*,[1] however:

> The failure of 'Barricades week' left General de Gaulle in a stronger position than at any time since his return to power. But then, as later, he was to display a contempt for the time factor in politics which was to delay preparations for an Algerian settlement. . . . Each step forward was accompanied by a half-step back. . . . In the eyes of the F.L.N. each 'positive' statement on Algeria was accompanied by unacceptable qualifications.

The war continued.

In April 1960, after an Algerian delegation had visited the People's Republic of China, Abbas stated in an interview with *El Moudjahid:*

> The West tries to convince us that it is better for us to be killed by the weapons of the West than to defend ourselves with the weapons of the East. The Algerian people, knowing that they are in the right, will make friends with all those who help them in the struggle.

Negotiations between the French government and an emissary from the F.L.N. took place in the middle of 1960 at Melun, but broke down because, as Abbas later explained, the status to be given to the F.L.N. representatives was that of political prisoners. In September Abbas denounced the North Atlantic Treaty Organization and all countries which allowed their troops and weapons to be turned against Algeria, while in October he visited Peking and showed himself willing to accept aid from China. On 1 November he announced that a union of Tunisia and Algeria, proposed by President Bourguiba of Tunisia, 'can be achieved and will be the best way of obtaining the independence of all'.

Demonstrations supporting the F.L.N. in Algeria on 11 December, in which Moslem crowds waved Algerian flags and shouted 'Abbas to power', together with massive French approval in the January 1961 referendum for de Gaulle's declared policy of

1. Penguin Books, 1961.

eventual Algerian self-determination, opened the door to serious negotiations. In January Abbas attended the Casablanca meeting of African States, called to launch a programme of cooperation among the 'militants' of the continent and formulate a common policy towards the crisis in the Congo and the Algerian war. Attending the funeral of King Mohammed V of Morocco at the beginning of March, he consulted with President Bourguiba of Tunisia and Hassan II, the new King of Morocco, over the latest moves by the French government to end the Algerian war. On 15 March the French Council of Ministers announced its desire for 'discussions' with the Algerian nationalist leaders, and two days later the G.P.R.A. agreed to send an official delegation to meet the French. Peace negotiations at Evian, however, finally broke down on 28 July over the refusal of the French government to recognize Algerian sovereignty over the Sahara or support the political integration of all Algeria's peoples in an independent State. The F.L.N. refused to concede any special status for the European community or to yield up any of the Sahara, which it claimed as an integral and recognized part of Algerian territory.

While the war continued within Algeria itself, and right-wing French groups within both France and Algeria engaged in a campaign of terrorism, differences were developing within the Algerian leadership. On 27 August the F.L.N. announced, after the meeting of its 'parliament' in Tripoli, a number of changes in the G.P.R.A., the most important of which was the replacement of Ferhat Abbas as President by Youssef Ben Khedda. Though the Western press reflected delicate degrees of shock in its reports, Aziz Maarouf wrote in *Afrique Action:* 'For Algeria the change symbolizes the return of the Algerian revolution to its initial homogeneity and logic.'

YOUSSEF BEN KHEDDA was born at Berrouaghia and was educated first at Blida and then at the University of Algiers, where – like Ferhat Abbas before him – he studied pharmacy. By the age of twenty he had joined the Parti Populaire Algérien of Messali Hadj, and in 1943 he was arrested and detained for eight months. In 1946 Messali Hadj and his colleagues decided to substitute for the banned P.P.A. a new mass movement, the Mouvement pour le Triomphe des Libertés Démocratiques, and Ben Khedda, surrendering his plans for a pharmacy at Blida to a life of nationalist politics, became Secretary-General of the M.T.L.D. With Saad Dahlab, now Algerian Minister of Foreign Affairs, and Mohammed Yazid, Minister of Information, he belonged to the Centralist section of the movement, opposing the authoritarian leadership of Messali Hadj and upholding the ultimate authority of the Central Committee, while generally still trustful of political reform within Algeria. The three men were, however, the most radical within the group, and throughout 1954 kept in contact with the extremists of the Comité Révolutionnaire d'Unité et d'Action (C.R.U.A.), who launched the insurrection of 1 November 1954. With the oubreak of the rebellion the M.T.L.D. disintegrated, and Mohammed Yazid escaped to Cairo, where he joined the insurgents. Ben Khedda himself, however, was arrested and detained until April 1955, when he was released 'for reasons of health' on repeated representations by the more liberal advisers of the then Algerian Governor-General, Jacques Soustelle.

Joining the F.L.N. at once, he soon became one of the dominant leaders within Algeria itself and, together with Abane Ramdane, organized the Soumman Congress in August 1956, which established the legislative and executive structure of the revolution – a Conseil National de la République Algérienne (C.N.R.A.) of fifty members and, at its centre, a five-member Comite dé Coordination et d'Exécution (C.C.E.). To this last, he was elected,[1] together with Abane, Saad Dahlab, Belkacem Krim, and Ben M'hidi. Ben M'hidi was responsible for organizing military offensives, and Abane was the theoretician, while Belkacem Krim, from the mountains, and Dahlab, the peasant, developed and supervised the combatants in the interior. Ben Khedda was responsible for the liaison between the six organized zones (wilayas) within Algeria and the Moslem population of Algiers itself. Constantly changing his identity, at all times appearing as inconspicuous as possible, he passed unperceived through the

1. *Afrique Action*, the Tunisian weekly, 2–8 September 1961.

European sectors and maintained contact with the various centres of insurrection.

The Moslem quarter of Algiers was at that stage under the complete control of the F.L.N. and became, under Ben Khedda's leadership, the most active area in the whole rebellion. On 27 January 1957 French paratroops, under the command of General Jacques Massu, set out to destroy the power of the rebels within the city by eradicating the leadership, just as the F.L.N. was about to stage an eight-day 'insurrectional strike'.

It is estimated that out of the 80,000 Moslems in the Kasbah, between 30 and 40 per cent of the active males were, at some time or other, arrested for questioning, and questioning came increasingly to involve the use of torture as a means of obtaining rapid results. What became known as the 'battle of Algiers' was won by the French, but the shape of the struggle rallied the Moslems of Algeria to the F.L.N. as never before. Within a month M'hidi was arrested and subsequently reported to have committed suicide. The four survivors of the C.C.E. left Algeria, Ben Khedda and Krim for Tunisia, Abane and Saad Dahlab for Morocco. Abane was to be killed by French forces in May 1958, leaving only three of the original five to see their committee grow into a government.

In September 1957, at the second meeting of the C.N.R.A. in Cairo, a clash developed over whether the F.L.N. should concentrate upon diplomatic pressures, establishing a fixed headquarters and a virtual government-in-exile, or sustain a mobile leadership, assuring the greatest liaison with the actual combatants inside Algeria. Abane, Ben Khedda, and Dahlab, partisans of the second policy, failed to sway the bulk of the Council, and the C.C.E. was enlarged to fourteen members as a first stage towards the creation of a provisional government, established exactly one year later in Cairo. Ben Khedda, a member of the enlarged C.C.E., represented the F.L.N. in Syria, Indonesia, and Yugoslavia, and with the establishment of the G.P.R.A., became Minister of Social Affairs. In 1957 he became the first influential F.L.N. leader to visit the People's Republic of China, and he received the nickname 'Chinois'.

The election of Ferhat Abbas as President of the G.P.R.A. in September 1958 reflected the whole course of policy that the F.L.N. had decided to follow. With his reputation as a moderate and his enormous standing among the Moslem middle-class of Algeria, Abbas had given to the F.L.N. in 1956 the character of a united Algerian front, committed to emancipation rather than set revolutionary aspirations. The movement accordingly concentrated upon diplomatic pressures and the possibility of a negotiated settlement with France. At the third meeting of the C.N.R.A., in December 1959 and January 1960, Ben Khedda expounded his opposition to this policy: his belief that the structure of the nationalist government had become too static and ornate, that it was essential to create an organic link between the leadership in Tunis and the combatants within Algeria itself, and that the leadership should specify the social, economic, and political aspirations of the revolution. Persuaded that negotiations with the de Gaulle government in France looked more probable than ever before, a majority of the Council rejected his views, and though his authority remained great – he directed Algerian lobbying at the United Nations General Assembly and headed a F.L.N. mission to the capitals of Latin America – he was relieved of his post as Minister of Social Affairs. Negotiations with the French government, however, finally broke down in July 1961, and the fourth meeting of the C.N.R.A. at Tripoli during August dismissed Ferhat Abbas from the Presidency of the G.P.R.A., together with the policy he embodied, and elected Ben Khedda in his place. With Belkacem Krim made Minister of the Interior and Saad Dahlab the new Minister of Foreign Affairs, the three surviving members of the original C.C.E. were placed in absolute control of the Algerian revolution. The Tripoli meeting issued as well a communiqué which emphasized unequivocally the socialist objectives of the revolution ('an economy at the service of the people'), neutralism ('the politics of non-engagement'), and the various measures taken to draw the government of the revolution much closer to its combatants, while simplifying the structure of administration.

Meanwhile, the French government was accommodating itself

to the necessary terms of a peace settlement with the F.L.N. The speed with which the revolt of the four generals on 22 April 1961 had collapsed made it clear that the armed forces would not support a putsch against de Gaulle in the cause of *Algérie Française*. Generals Challe and Zeller gave themselves up to the French government, faced trial, and were imprisoned. Generals Jouhaud and Salan went into hiding. While the French government moved in slow and careful steps towards a negotiated cease-fire, a united settler front led by General Raoul Salan, which had announced its formation in April as the Organisation de l'Armée Secrète (O.A.S.), attempted to disrupt all administration in Algeria and erode the authority of the de Gaulle régime by largely indiscriminate acts of terrorism. While its support in France appeared small enough – estimates varied from 500 to 8,000 members – its hold over the white settlers in Algeria was revealed time and again as almost absolute. On 14 January 1962 French military officials in Algiers admitted that 228 people had been killed and 489 injured in acts of violence throughout the territory in the two weeks since the beginning of the year. And the violence convulsively increased till on 1 March officials estimated that 65 people had been killed, 55 of them Moslems, and 93 injured, 82 of them Moslems, in the terrorist activities of the previous day alone.

In December 1961 secret talks between representatives of the G.P.R.A. and the French government took place, and on the twenty-ninth de Gaulle announced that two French divisions and several air formations would be withdrawn from Algeria during the coming month. On 5 February 1962, in a broadcast to the nation, he stated that the outcome of self-determination for Algeria would certainly be a sovereign independent state, and that it was necessary to establish an understanding between France and Algeria over cooperation and the protection of France's essential interests. On 11 February negotiations to end the Franco-Algerian war began at Évian, with Louis Joxe, Minister for Algerian Affairs, leading the French delegation, and Belkacem Krim, Minister of the Interior in the G.P.R.A., and Saad Dahlab, Minister of Foreign Affairs, the chief Algerian delegates. On 18 February the talks were reported to have ended in agreement, and the details were presented for ratification to the Conseil National de la République Algérienne, meeting at Tripoli in Libya. On 28 February the general terms of the proposed cease-fire agreement, disclosed to officials by the French Delegate-General in Algeria, were reported in the press.

The French army would remain in Algeria for three years, during which time a provisional executive would be established and the Algerian people provided with an opportunity for full self-determination. Should Algeria choose – as seemed inevitable – its independence, a number of mutual guarantees would operate. At the end of three years, French citizens, while permitted to retain their French nationality, could opt for Algerian citizenship. France would recognize Algerian sovereignty over the Sahara, but French interests in the petroleum and natural gas fields there, with French property rights throughout the country, would be acknowledged by the new Algerian Republic. The naval base at Mers-el-Kébir and the atomic testing ground at Reggane in the Southern Sahara would be leased to the French government for specified periods. France would continue to assist in agricultural and industrial development, while Algeria would stay in the franc zone. On 6 March truce negotiations were resumed at Évian, in what clearly seemed to be a settlement of final differences before the declaration of a cease-fire.[1]

The war which had cost France more than £2,500 million was ending. The figures of the dead will doubtless never be precisely known, as the extent of suffering can never be measured. On 8 March military authorities in Paris announced that total French casualties during the seven years of the war to the end of 1961 had been 17,250 officers and men killed and 51,800 wounded, while rebel losses were estimated at 141,000 killed. F.L.N. leaders have estimated their dead as more than one million, many of them killed in concentration camps, in the torture cells of Algiers, and in the strategic transfers of population.

In the twenty-six years since Ferhat Abbas had denied the

1. On 18 March the cease-fire was signed and came into force at noon on the following day.

existence of an Algerian homeland, Algerian nationalism had grown into one of the most formidable forces of the contemporary world. It had developed from petition to protest, from protest to struggle, from struggle to war. And its objective had changed from reform to revolution. The Algeria of the future is now committed to a policy of militant socialism within and positive neutralism without. France has willed it so herself.

22 The Politics of Compromise: Habib Bourguiba of Tunisia

> Bourguibism may well prove one of the casualties of the battle of Bizerta. The name of the Tunisian President – who can combine fiery Arab oratory with the bargaining skill of a Mediterranean merchant – had become a symbol. Bourguibism stood not only for skilful diplomacy and the art of compromise; it also stood for moderation and collaboration with the West. Habib Bourguiba used to be opposed to Abdul Nasser as the other pole of the Arab world. He never concealed that his great ambition was to sponsor a North African federation and keep the Arab West, the Maghreb, within the western world through association with France.

So the Paris correspondent of the *Economist* wrote, on 29 July 1961, the epitaph on Bourguibism.

The death rattle of Tunisia's friendship with France had sounded suddenly. On 27 February 1961 Bourguiba had met President de Gaulle at Rambouillet for talks on a settlement of the Algerian conflict and had expressed himself confident of de Gaulle's personal good faith. Less than five months later, on 7 July, Bourguiba wrote to de Gaulle demanding the surrender of the Bizerta naval base – under a French control that Tunisian independence had questioned but never interrupted – and threatening demonstrations in response to any French refusal. The French government rejected the demand, Tunisian volunteers dug themselves in around the base, and on 19 July – the day set by Bourguiba as the deadline for French evacuation – Tunisian troops launched an attack to which the French forces replied with extravagant force. Soon afterwards Tunisian casualties were provisionally estimated at 670 dead and 1,155 wounded, while the French lost thirty killed and fifty wounded. Tunisia broke off diplomatic relations with France, to arraign it soon afterwards before a special session of the United Nations General Assembly, and that bridge between France and North Africa, between Africa and the West, that had been the policy of Bourguiba, lay in rubble at the feet of the two Presidents.

Born in August 1903 at Monastir on the east coast of Tunisia, HABIB BOURGUIBA was the last of eight children, son of an officer in the Tunisian Army. His father, like many of those in straitened circumstances – the family had suffered a series of severe reverses – possessed a great regard for the advantages of a substantial education and sold the family olive trees to send his children to school.

Enrolled as a boarder at the Sadiki College in Tunis, he was eight years old when, in 1911, events first jolted him into politics. The building of the Zaghouan road had bitten into ground belonging to the Djellaz cemetery, and a riot had exploded in protest at the sacrilege. Three years afterwards the First World War broke out.

In an interview with Jean Lacouture,[1] Bourguiba reminisced:

Amongst us, everybody had taken the side of Turkey. She was Islam, she was the enemy of the colonizer. Our nationalism wore a peculiar dress. . . . I began to be conscious of such issues. And an incident took place that revealed I was already on the road of Bourguibism – a primitive form of Bourguibism though it was. . . . On one of my school exercise books, I wrote the slogan: 'Up with France – with Turkey. . . .' 'Down with Germany, Italy. . . .' Curious, isn't it? Turkey was certainly my favourite, but I felt that it was France who had the power. And so in order that the 'Up with Turkey' should come to pass, I wrote also 'Up with France' – though the two countries were of course in opposite camps, as were Germany and Italy.

The Sadiki College, caught up in the wide demands of the war, made economies in the food and clothing given to the students. At the end of 1919 Bourguiba caught cold and developed a primary infection of the lung. Admitted to the hospital

1. Jean Lacouture, *Cinq Hommes et la France* (Éditions du Seuil, 1961).

at Sadiki, he brooded over the state of his country, reporting later that on 1 January 1920 a friend had brought him a pamphlet by Sheik Taalbi, *La Tunisie martyre*, and that he had crept under his blankets to read it surreptitiously, strongly stirred by what he felt to be the humiliation of the colonized.

As soon as he was well, he went to convalesce with his eldest brother Mohammed, a medical assistant in the hospital at Le Kef, and in October 1921 returned to Tunis. Reluctant to go back to Sadiki and repeat his classes with younger boys, he went to stay with his one unmarried brother Mahmoud, a minor civil servant in the Department of Justice, and entered the Carnet Lycée.

> I was terrified. I did not feel at home as at Sadiki. I was a little lost amongst the French, the Italians, and the Jews. I threw myself into work with passion, as with everything I did. I wished my brother, who had devoted himself to me, to be proud of me. To be first, never to be anything but first, that was my objective. And then I had to show that Tunisians were better than foreigners.[1]

In 1922, he involved himself directly in politics for the first time. The Resident-General had banned *Al Sawab*, the Arabic organ of the Destour, which was the nationalist movement founded in 1920 under the leadership of Sheik Taalbi to secure Tunisian emancipation. Bourguiba addressed a telegram of protest to the Resident General – 'We energetically protest against the banning of *Al Sawab*.' Bourguiba was later to recollect:

> I had employed the plural. But when I tried to obtain the support of my fellows, I stumbled upon those who had civil servants as their fathers, who had relations to look after – it was my first experience of political cowardice. I was forced to experience it again and again! But it was from then onwards that I considered myself a Destourien.[2]

In 1924 he was awarded the French *baccalauréat*, and he had to resolve upon a profession. His eldest brother wished him to be

1. ibid.
2. ibid.

a doctor, but he considered the practice of medicine too specialized and restricted. Wishing to serve his country, he chose law, with the object of climbing into public life, and with a loan from his brother Mahmoud and a small purse from the head of Sadiki College, he arrived in Paris during the autumn of that year. Studying psychology, literature, and political science, he threw himself at once into the political life of the city.

> I saw men of colour, those who had come from far horizons, Africans, Indo-Chinese, and West Indians. I saw too that there were Frenchmen who supported the claims of the colonized people, and this made me think – these men struggled for the liberty of their country, and here were Frenchmen who understood them and helped them. . . .[1]

While in Paris, he met a war widow, whom he married soon afterwards. Though he fell ill just before his final examinations, and much of his thoughts were on the imminent birth of his first child, he passed them successfully and left for home.

> We left Paris, my wife, child, and myself, to a final misfortune: at the moment of our departure in August 1927, there was a strike of taxis, a protest against the execution on that day of Sacco and Vanzetti![2]

Tunis in 1927 offered more closed doors than open ones for the Moslem decorated with diplomas and home from his student days in Paris. Student life in Paris, where all lived on terms of a careless equality, was painfully different from the colonial reality. The years from 1927 to 1930 were, in addition, years of social transformation, heady with the changes that industrialization was bringing. Bourguiba himself rapidly acquired a reputation as a brilliant lawyer, while becoming increasingly involved in active politics.

Though he was angered by the crude inequalities of colonialism, he established a number of friendships with Frenchmen – some, whom he found intellectually exciting and sympathetic, in the administration, and others, like the publisher of *Tunis-*

1. ibid.
2. ibid.

Socialiste, who fortified the influence of his former teachers in Paris and turned him further towards contemporary and secular liberalism.

Though he had registered as a member of the Destour soon after his return from Paris, he soon saw that the movement was merely vegetating. Its leaders, representatives of the urban bourgeoisie, protected themselves by a complacent intransigence. They rejected any middle way between independence and non-cooperation, and since there could be no question of independence without a prolonged struggle, they simply refused to recognize the existence of the French protectorate.

Their doctrinal purity provoked the youth, who refused to resign themselves to a sterile disdain. Bourguiba demanded a new analysis, a re-examination of Tunisian thinking as well as French. He needed a newspaper, and he persuaded one of the young leaders of the Destour, who was ambitious and rich, to turn the weekly, *La Voix du Tunisien* (*The Voice of the Tunisian*) into a daily. Bourguiba himself soon became the new organ's moving force, making it widely known throughout the country. Despite the newspaper's mood, however, which would today seem tranquil enough, some of those responsible for producing it were soon prosecuted for inciting hatred between the races. The association between Bourguiba and the newspaper owners could not survive for long, and in November 1932 Bourguiba founded a new journal, *L'Action Tunisienne*. In it he unfolded a doctrine, revolutionary for that time in its modernistic and secular tones. 'The Tunisia that we mean to liberate will not be a Tunisia for Moslem, for Jew or for Christian. It will be a Tunisia for all those, without distinction of religion or race, who wish to have it as their country and live in it under the protection of just laws...'

On 31 May 1933 the administration suspended publication of the journal, and the new Resident-General, M. Peyrouton, set out to split the Destour by driving the older leaders and the more militant Bourguiba group apart. Hearing of negotiations between the leadership and the Residency, the youth were disquieted and then furious, certain that emancipation would never be acquired through collaboration or sheer inactivity. Bourguiba resigned from the Executive Committee of the Destour on 9 September 1933, and on 2 March 1934 at Ksar-Hellal, close to the birthplace of Bourguiba himself, the youth gathered under the chairmanship of Dr Materi and publicly proclaimed their rupture with the older leadership by forming the Neo-Destour. Theirs was the rebellion of the provincial petty bourgeoisie against the passive nationalism of the urban professionals and shopkeepers. A new movement had been born, and Bourguiba became its Secretary-General.

The party developed rapidly, its leaders taking to the road and enlisting the peasantry. The administration, however, did not long delay its reply. On 3 September 1934 Bourguiba was at home in Monastir when he was arrested. For twenty months he was interned at Bordj-Leboeuf, where he suffered acutely from attacks of dysentery, but he continued to pursue his cause, writing letters which he occasionally succeeded in having smuggled out of the camp. At the beginning of 1936, under the influence of the new Popular Front, the French administration decided to review the case of the detainees, and at last, on 23 May 1936, the new Resident-General set the leaders at liberty. Bourguiba and his associates began at once to propagate the policies of their movement again. With the old Destour in ruins and Bourguiba's party widely acknowledged as the organized force of Tunisian nationalism, Bourguiba went to Paris to plead for an end to Tunisia's protectorate status. In August 1936 he demanded specifically 'the replacement of the despotic régime by a constitutional régime which permits the people to participate in power.'

Though the Neo-Destour itself remained officially banned, the period which followed the first detention of its leaders constituted a high point in the party's development. Hallowed by their detention, the leaders enjoyed complete ascendency over the masses; everywhere their orders were obeyed. Within three months the number of party cells had increased tenfold, reaching some 400 by the end of 1936.

A fierce struggle broke out between the nationalist and

European trade unionists within Tunisia. The Tunisian nationalists wanted an indigenous movement separate from the French, broke with the Communist-dominated Confédération Generale des Travailleurs, and, under the leadership of Ferhat Hached, founded the Union Générale des Travailleurs Tunisiens (U.G.T.T.) as a workers' movement to help in the struggle for national emancipation. This conflict between the French and the Tunisian trade unionists embittered relations between the Neo-Destour and the Popular Front government in France, relations already strained by the French refusal to surrender their protectorate. The second conference of the Neo-Destour in September 1937 expressed its distress at the deterioration and rejected responsibility for any rupture.

During the six months that followed, tension ceaselesly mounted. In an article, Bourguiba announced that 'the people are ready for the struggle', and though his menacing language frightened many of his associates, the National Council of the Neo-Destour passed a resolution in March 1938, expressing 'confidence in the Political Bureau and the Secretary-General, whose writings and speeches have faithfully traced the political line of the party'.

The storm broke early in April. On Tuesday, 5 April, two Neo-Destour leaders, Dr Ben Slimane and Salah ben Youssef, were arrested. Strikes broke out, and the whole Tunisian intelligentsia was in ferment. On Friday, 8 April, a large procession marched to the Resident General in order to demand the liberation of the arrested leaders, and in the afternoon the governing council of Neo-Destour summoned a meeting for Sunday, the 10th. It was on Saturday, the 9th, however, that the explosion took place. The police fired upon a crowd of demonstrators outside the civil court a little after three o'clock. A throng poured out of the Medina and overflowed the square, overwhelming the guards. By five o'clock the riot had been crushed, at the cost of some 100 dead. Only one French soldier had lost his life. More than a thousand militants were detained, while Bourguiba and those of his principal lieutenants who had not yet been taken into custody were arrested, imprisoned, and hauled before a military court on a charge of threatening the security of the state.

For the second time, the Tunisian leader was in the hands of the French authorities. The judicial inquiry dragged on while the nationalists remained, unforgotten, in military gaol. On 27 May 1940, together with eighteen of his fellow prisoners, Bourguiba was taken to Marseille and lodged in the prison of Haut-Fort St Nicolas, where he stayed until 18 November 1942. Transferred to Fort Montluc at Lyons and then to Vancia, he was on 12 December 1942 taken by the Germans to a camp at Chalon-sur-Saône, on 8 January 1943 to Nice, and finally to Rome.

It was during this long period of imprisonment that he wrote and smuggled out of gaol one of his most significant texts – his letter to Dr Habib Thamer, the young doctor who had taken over the political control of Neo-Destour after the arrest of its leaders.

> Since the armistice, I have been visited by several compatriots of different backgrounds, students, businessmen, lawyers. In discussions with them, I have acquired a conviction that all, or nearly all, people believe firmly in the victory of the Axis. . . . I say that it is an error, a serious error. . . . The truth which stares one in the face is that Germany will not win the war. . . . Our rôle is to act in such a way that at the end of the war the Tunisian people, and more especially the Neo-Destour, will not find itself in the camp of the vanquished. . . . Under these circumstances, this is how you ought to proceed. Give to the militants, on my responsibility and over my signature if necessary, the order to enter into relations with the French Gaullists of Tunisia – there must be some: certain of our socialist friends for example – with a view to joining our own clandestine activities with theirs, leaving on one side until after the war the problem of our independence. . . . Our help to the Allies must be unconditional. . . . It is a question of life or death for Tunisia. . . . It is an order I give you. Do not question it.

The release of Bourguiba, together with Mongi Slim and Salah ben Youssef, by the German government was an attempt by the Axis to use the North African nationalists as weapons in its struggle against the Allies. On 9 January 1943 the leaders of the Neo-Destour were received in Rome as men of high rank and installed at the Piacentini Palace, not far from the residence of the Grand Mufti of Jerusalem.

Mellini, chief of the African Section in the Italian Ministry of Foreign Affairs, proposed to Bourguiba the formation of a Tunisian government-in-exile, but Bourguiba retreated behind the authority of the Bey and declined all offers made to him. The Italians repatriated his colleagues, but retained Bourguiba himself, in order to extract from him a declaration to the Tunisian people which might serve their own political propaganda. Bourguiba resigned himself to a broadcast on 6 April, and although his speech did not bear the tone of his letter to Dr Thamer, it contained no call for any collaboration with the Axis.

> The national cause is too lofty and noble to be influenced by the pleasures, adversity, intimidation, or temptations experienced by the individual.... Our country is passing today through one of the most difficult periods of its history. It is the theatre of terrible, of fatal events, a prey to colonial greed and the object of foreign covetousness....

The speech could hardly have pleased his Italian hosts; but after three months of unsuccessfully tempting him to collaboration, they permitted him to leave for Tunis. With the Allies very close to Tunis, the German authorities placed an aeroplane at his disposal and invited him to retreat to Germany, but he refused and with increasing boldness exhibited his hostility to the Axis.

He made contact with the Gaullists and wrote *For a Franco-Tunisian Bloc*, which was clandestinely distributed by supporters of the Neo-Destour to the Allied forces as they entered Tunis. 'A new world will come the day after this victory. The Allied nations have solemnly promised it. Our first duty is to aid them in winning the war, and the best way of helping them is to form a bloc with struggling France . . .' When Tunis at last fell to the Allies, General (later Marshal) Juin took over interim control as Resident-General and ordered an inquiry into Bourguiba's wartime activities. As a result of reports from the police, who had encountered Bourguiba during his imprisonment and discovered his hostility to the Axis, Juin at long last closed the prosecution instituted in April 1938 against Bourguiba and his companions.

A period of considerable hardship for the Tunisian leader and his colleagues ensued none the less. As he himself reported: 'The Tunisian people have probably never known a stage more sombre in their history than that which followed the arrival of the Allies. Everyone was catalogued as having been sympathetic to Hitler and had to pay the consequences.' He found himself faced by a French authority which seemed even less well disposed to him than that of the Third Republic had been, and many of his friends reminded him of how different his experience of an Allied victory was from what his expectations had been. Making up his mind that there was nothing he was likely to attain from victorious France, he changed his whole strategy and resolved to seek help throughout the world, and above all from the Arab countries. In March 1945, the month in which the League of Arab States was formed, Bourguiba left in secret from a beach close to Sfax, taking a smuggler's boat to Faroua, a small beach in Tripolitania, and from there fled sometimes on foot, sometimes on camel, over the desert of Libya to Cairo, which he reached on 26 April. The period that followed – from April 1945 to September 1949 – was one of the most unhappy in his life. Though he established himself in Cairo, he travelled widely, to the United States, Switzerland, and Belgium, as well as throughout the Middle East, but everywhere he felt himself alone and his aspirations misunderstood. His experience undoubtedly had a strong impact upon his subsequent views of the Arab world, and he was to speak bitterly afterwards of the sterile effervescence that he had encountered amongst the Arab leaders at that time.

His moderation, however, persisted. In July 1946 he wrote of 'an honourable compromise with France' in a message sent to Ferhat Abbas, then the leader of the Union Démocratique du Manifeste Algérien, who was campaigning for the creation of an Arab republic federated with France. He continued to demand the establishment of a sovereign state in Tunisia, joined to France by a treaty freely negotiated, the election of a constituent assembly, and the establishment of a democratic government. He added, however, that 'all this will not happen in a day', and that 'a dramatic gesture by France . . . creating a climate of confidence, will facilitate the solution of all the secondary difficulties. . . .'

In the summer of 1949 he decided to return to Tunisia, though, having left the country illegally, he was aware of the risk that he would be running. The Resident-General, Jean Mons, considered Bourguiba less dangerous in Tunisia than outside, however, and hoped that his return would provoke an open conflict within the Neo-Destour between Bourguiba himself and Salah ben Youssef, who had become Secretary-General of the movement in Bourguiba's absence.

It was a triumphant return. On 9 September 1949 he was greeted by throngs in Tunis, and six months later he was in Paris, cajoling and threatening. On 15 April 1950 he announced a 'seven-point programme' of Tunisian demands, chief amongst them the election by universal suffrage of an assembly to determine a constitution and resolve Franco-Tunisian relations.

On 1 June, M. Louis Périllier replaced M. Mons as Resident-General, and on 11 June M. Robert Schuman, Minister of Foreign Affairs, announced: 'M. Périllier's mission . . . is to conduct Tunisia to the full flowering of its riches and to lead it to the independence which is the ultimate objective of all the territories in the French Union.' Bourguiba excitedly proclaimed that 'with independence accepted as a principle, there are no more problems', and on 19 July Schuman announced that he would put an end to direct administration and turn Tunisia towards internal autonomy. Bourguiba returned home and on 4 August presided at a meeting of the National Council of the Neo-Destour which agreed to participate in a new Tunisian government, with Salah ben Youssef, Secretary-General of the movement, as its representative in the administration formed on 17 August by M. Chenik. The Resident-General then announced that Chenik would negotiate the constitutional modifications which, by successive stages, would lead Tunisia to internal autonomy.

Resistance to the reforms, however, was organized by the French community in Tunisia and supported by the Governor-General of Algeria, who was deeply disturbed by the effect that Tunisian independence might have on the Moslem population across the border. Having returned from a short visit to France, M. Périllier announced on 7 October a political 'pause'. Bourguiba remembered the 'pauses' of previous years, and his confidence at once evaporated. The Neo-Destour, he emphasized, 'has been the first to hold out its hand; it will be the last to withdraw it . . .' After various interviews with the Resident-General he left at the beginning of February 1951 for Asia and was in Karachi when on 8 February the Resident-General announced a plan of reform which maintained the principle of co-sovereignty and ultimate French control.

Bourguiba began to prepare himself for what he now spoke of as a trial of force, though he continued to announce his willingness to reach a possible settlement with France if the French government would only reveal sufficient good will. On 15 December 1951 the French government, having refused to set up a Tunisian parliament, announced that it was unable to proceed further with reforms, and Bourguiba, summoned from Cairo by his friends, returned to Tunis on 4 January 1952. He decided to take the issue to the United Nations, and on 13 January Salah ben Youssef secretly left Tunis in order to confer with Arab and Asian leaders over the placing of the Tunisian case before the Security Council.

On 16 January the Congress of the Neo-Destour, called for the following day, was banned, and in the early morning of the 18th Bourguiba was arrested. He was sent first to Tabarka, near the Algerian frontier, where he enjoyed relatively liberal treatment and was permitted to receive friends and journalists.

Tunisia exploded into protest and violence. The U.G.T.T. called a general strike, and on 26 March the Resident-General arrested M. Chenik and four of his colleagues. Bourguiba himself was transferred to Remada in the Sahara. International opinion began to swing in favour of Tunisian emancipation.

In May Bourguiba was again transferred, this time to the

La Galite island, where he stayed for two years, often suffering from the effects of the humidity there. Meanwhile the resistance of the Tunisian people grew, and groups of terrorists formed in the south. It became clear that the French government would have to return to direct colonial rule or appeal to those who enjoyed the confidence of the Tunisian masses.

In May 1954 France decided to make its first gesture and on the 21st of the month transferred Bourguiba to Groix in France, where he was permitted to receive journalists, friends, and politicians. On 17 July, during the last stages of the Geneva conference on Indo-China, he was again moved, this time to Amilly near Paris, and on 30 July he was informed that the Premier, M. Mendès-France, would visit Tunisia with Marshal Juin to proclaim internal autonomy for the country. Bourguiba declared that the announcement constituted 'a substantial and decisive step along the road to the restoration of complete Tunisian sovereignty. But the journey to that ideal should in future not assume the character of a struggle between the Tunisian people and France. It must proceed by adjustments and arrangements . . . in reciprocal confidence and refound friendship. . . .' It was the triumph of Bourguibism.

Compromise, however, could only further widen the existing breach between Bourguiba and Salah ben Youssef. Since March 1952 the Secretary-General of the Neo-Destour, who had escaped to Cairo, had been subject to the more radical influences of the Nasser-Neguib régime, established by the successful army revolt of 23 July 1952. At the beginning of 1955 he denounced the proposals of Mendès-France and proclaimed a nationalism closely united to Pan-Arab, Afro-Asian militancy, and Moslem traditionalism.

On 1 June 1955 Bourguiba returned to Tunis in triumph, where he was welcomed by cheering crowds, lining the quayside and the avenues leading to the residence of the Bey. Then, on 3 June, the agreements were finally signed which granted internal autonomy to Tunisia.

On 13 September Salah ben Youssef returned to Tunisia and delivered an attack upon the Franco-Tunisian agreements, claiming that they were 'a step backwards'. Bourguiba attempted for some three weeks to avert a rupture, but on 8 October he had the party expel its Secretary-General. At the Neo-Destour Congress in Sfax on 15 November, 1,000 delegates gave a crushing majority to Bourguiba and against Salah ben Youssef. Guerilla resistance broke out and was suppressed by the government with the strongest measures.

In November 1955 Morocco was promised complete independence by France, and Tunisia asked for the same, receiving it at last on 20 March 1956. A Constituent Assembly was elected, and on 9 April Bourguiba was voted its Chairman, to become on 12 April 1956 the first Premier of an independent Tunisia. Then on 25 July 1957 a solemn meeting of the Constituent Assembly abolished the monarchy, proclaimed a republic, and conferred on Bourguiba the office of President of Tunisia.

Bourguibism appeared to have succeeded. Absolutely dominant within Tunisia itself, and genuinely revered as the founder of modern Tunisian sovereignty, Bourguiba took active steps to modernize the judiciary and raise the status of women. His friendly relations with France, however, could not long survive the demands of Maghrebin unity. From the outbreak of the Algerian war on 1 November 1954, he was drawn ever increasingly into the conflict, and he finally allowed the Algerian army, with the leaders of the Front de Libération Nationale (F.L.N.), to operate from Tunisian territory. In January 1960 he appeared on the Pan-African stage when the second All-African Peoples Conference was held at Tunis; and though he consistently took a more moderate stand than Dr Nkrumah of Ghana or Sékou Touré of Guinea, believing that countries should establish their stability before engaging in political union, he repeatedly expressed himself in favour of a Maghrebin association. His refusal to support Morocco's claim to Mauritania, however, led to increasing tension between Tunisia and Morocco, and he did not go to the January 1961 Casablanca Conference of African 'militants' attended by Ferhat Abbas for the F.L.N. and King Mohammed V of Morocco.

At the beginning of March 1961 he met Ferhat Abbas and King Hassan II of Morocco at a Maghreb summit in Rabat, mainly to discuss his contacts with de Gaulle and the chances for a negotiated end to the Algerian war. He seemed sure of the French President's goodwill and hopeful of an early North African peace. Yet soon a crisis was to break that would threaten not only Maghrebin union, but Tunisia's political and economic relationship with France and the whole efficacy of Bourguibism in contemporary Africa.

The negotiations at Evian between the Algerian nationalists and the French government stalled over the demand of the Algerians for sovereignty over the Sahara and their refusal to concede any separate communal status to the French settlers in the territory. In July Bourguiba laid claim to a substantial stretch of the disputed Algerian Sahara, and simultaneously demanded the evacuation of French troops from the Bizerta base. It is difficult to resist the conclusion that he was balancing his demand for expansion – to territory which would include the prosperous oil field of Edjeleh, 175 miles south of the southern tip of Tunisia – by a campaign against a foreign base, hoping in that way to rally support to himself throughout the Afro-Asian world. The timing of the July assault by Tunisians upon the French base at Bizerta certainly seemed to suggest an attempt at neutralizing Algerian hostility to any demand for a part of the Sahara, which the Algerian nationalists passionately claimed as their own.

On 26 August the United Nations General Assembly declared that the presence of French troops in Tunisia and by implication the maintenance of the naval base at Bizerta violated Tunisian sovereignty. It asked the French government to heed the Security Council and begin 'immediate negotiations' with Tunisia over the withdrawal of French troops from Tunisian soil. The French delegates boycotted the debate. Sixty-six nations, however, encompassing the whole of the Communist bloc and the overwhelming majority of Afro-Asian States, including the former French colonies of Senegal, Gabon, and the Malagasy Republic, voted for the resolution, while no votes were recorded against, and the United States and Great Britain abstained.

Talks between French and Tunisian officials over the future of Bizerta, initiated in December 1961, broke down during January 1962 because of the refusal by France to set any date for withdrawal from the naval base. The Bizerta crisis could only remain a constant call to further armed collision, while having calamitous effects on Tunisia's economy. In the six months since the three-day battle, almost one-third of the 95,000-strong French community had left, and thousands of Italians, with their virtual monopoly over the mechanical trades, had packed their bags in fear of further trouble and its consequences for all European settlement. The country's adverse balance of trade reached the startling total of £31 million in the first ten months of 1961, £16 million of it with France, while foreign currency reserves fell steadily to £18 million by the end of the year. During 1961, despite the battle for Bizerta, France alone supplied 55 per cent of Tunisia's imports and took 56 per cent of her exports. An economic break with France would have drastic consequences on Tunisia's agricultural base.

Partly as a result of the heightened nationalism which the battle of Bizerta aroused, partly as a step towards disengaging the Tunisian economy from foreign control, all foreign businesses in the country, with the exception of banks and petroleum distributing concerns, have been given one year in which to admit at least 50 per cent Tunisian participation in capital and management. Yet, any effective economic planning must itself wait upon an end to the Bizerta crisis. For as long as French forces remain in the country, the Tunisian government is compelled to devote an excessive portion of its budget to defence. As George Leather reported in the *New Statesman* of 12 January 1962:

> In the last financial year – that is before the fighting this summer – five times as much money was spent on defence as on education, eight times as much as on health, and twice as much as on agriculture. Yet this is a country where 42 per cent of all deaths occur in the first year of life, where there are still only 2.5 hospital beds for every 1,000

people, and where a population increase of 66 per cent in twenty-five years has been accompanied by an increase in food production of a mere 25 per cent. Agriculture, which occupies three-quarters of the active population, receives only 40 per cent of the national income.

The Bizerta crisis has placed Bourguibism in the perspective of the sixties. Bourguiba himself discovered in de Gaulle's resolute refusal to evacuate Bizerta that French colonialism was by no means dead. He discovered too that, whatever the rights of the issue, neither Britain nor the United States would associate itself with the condemnation of France. When the votes of the United Nations General Assembly came to be counted, it was those of Africa and Asia that upheld the right of Tunisia to complete sovereignty over its territory. The Bizerta crisis may have exploded upon an unsuspecting world; the materials for the explosion had been long in preparation and experiment. Bourguibism assumed the possibility of compromise between colonized and colonizer. And even if such a policy had patently failed in Algeria, it appeared to have succeeded in Tunisia. Its final test was the great naval base at Bizerta. It failed. As the *Economist* commented:

> The Bourguibist doctrine that there is a third way between colonial subservience and intransigent nationalism has been undermined. And this may rapidly have repercussions throughout French-speaking Africa. . . . If the Western powers do not help the Tunisian leader to stage some spectacular recovery, the bullets of Bizerta will have written an epitaph on Bourguibism that Western statesmen may not enjoy reading.

Bourguibism posed an alternative to neutralist African resurgence, in the face of the pressures embodied by Guinea or the United Arab Republic. It rested fundamentally upon a belief in compromise and cooperation between the West and the continent that the West had colonized. If Bourguibism died with Bizerta, so too did the belief which gave it birth. In its place there is likely to grow in Tunisia too, as there has grown all over the continent, a belief that only a united Africa, strong in itself and free from Algiers to Cape Town, can sustain itself in the contemporary world. If Bourguiba accommodates himself to this continental longing for a final freedom from the centuries of intervention and possession, he will survive the death of the policy that he originated. If he refuses, his power is unlikely long to outlive his trust.

23 The Desert Kingdom of Libya: Idris I

It is impossible to remain in Libya for long without realizing that the country is in the middle of an oil boom. The hotels are packed with oilmen from seven or eight different countries, oil concession maps are on sale at news-vendors' stalls, and with so many new Libyan companies being registered, plans are being made for the establishment of a bourse to facilitate the buying and selling of shares. All this adds a new dimension to those familiar incongruities of Middle Eastern life also present in Libya: the brand-new buildings on unpaved, undrained streets, the air-conditioned cinemas showing the latest Hollywood films, and the mini-buses full of Bedouin tribesmen.

So Roger Owen introduced his article on Libya in *Africa South* (Vol. 5, No. 3, April–June 1961).

Libya, with its 679,343 square miles of territory and its estimated current population of 1,200,000 was until recently, as it had been for more than 100 years, the battlefield of stronger nations, with Turkish rule giving place first to Italian conquest and colonization and then to the Second World War. The struggle between the Axis and the Allies raged fiercely over the area for possession of the approaches to the Suez Canal, and even when Libya gained independence in December 1951, it was as a weak country, artificially created out of three areas with substantially different histories and social organizations. Indeed, it is only the King himself who has held the nation together so far and who threatens to disrupt it with his passing.

IDRIS EL-SENUSSI I, King of Libya, was born in March 1890 at Djaghaboub, a desert oasis in the south of Cyrenaica, of a family claiming descent from the prophet Mohammed. His grandfather, Mohammed Ali el-Senussi, had founded the Sanusi sect for the purification and propagation of Islam – a religious movement to which all the Arabs of Cyrenaica and many of those in Eastern Tripolitania now belong, so giving some degree of local unity to the country. He himself was given a traditional Koranic education – to this day he speaks no Western language – and in 1915 became spiritual leader of the Sanusi.

In 1911 the Italians attacked and conquered both Cyrenaica and Tripolitania, despite considerable resistance from the Sanusi. Relations between Italy and Cyrenaica, however, gradually became easier, and Idris was recognized in November 1920 as Emir. Then, with the coming to power of Mussolini in Italy, the submission soured, Idris left Cyrenaica for Egypt, and the Sanusi took up again their struggle against the Italians. Italian rule denied all political rights and economic advancement to the indigenous inhabitants, but it did unite the three territories of Tripolitania, Cyrenaica, and the Fezzan – the constituents of modern Libya – and initiate a building programme of roads and harbours.

During the Second World War, Idris assisted the Allies by recruiting scouts and guerilla fighters for use as guides in the desert campaigns, and he finally returned to his country in 1943 when the Italian army was routed in Cyrenaica. The British forces took Tripolitania and Cyrenaica, while the French took Fezzan in the south, and considerable dispute ensued over what would happen to the three territories at the end of the war, ranging from proposals for United Nations Trusteeship to suggestions that they be returned to Italian rule. Independence for all three territories was first proposed by Ernest Bevin, the British Foreign Secretary, in 1946, but the idea received little international support. Then in 1949 Britain recognized Idris as Emir of Cyrenaica, and the United Nations finally agreed that all three territories should become independent, with a United Nations Commission under Dr Adrian Pelt of the Netherlands established to frame the constitution. In 1950 a national Constituent Assembly of the three territories together pronounced Idris King of Libya, though the country itself did not formally exist, and in December 1951 the new independent United Kingdom of Libya at last came into being.

Elections were held, but not along party lines except in Tripolitania, where a National Congress Party (N.C.P.) in opposition to Sanusi dominion had been organized by Beshir El Saadawi, a returned exile who had served as an adviser to King Ibn Saud of Saudi Arabia. The N.C.P. was, however, defeated, riots ensued, the party was dissolved, and Beshir himself was deported. The second general election of January 1956 was not conducted on party lines at all but on grounds of personality and family influence. In May 1957 Abdul Mejid Coobar became Prime Minister, and in the middle of 1960 a scandal broke over the building of the Fezzan Road, when the Libyan construction company concerned had exhausted the money provided for the whole project with only one-third of the work actually completed. In October a vote of no confidence in the government was carried by parliament, and Coobar was forced to resign.

It was the first occasion on which parliament had successfully challenged the Libyan cabinet, on which, moreover, Tripolitanian and Cyrenaican deputies had been able to sink their provincial rivalries in a reasonably stable political alliance. The Coobar cabinet was replaced by one under Mohammed Othman Al Said, a Fezzanese, but the new cabinet contained a majority of members who had served in the old one, so ignoring the principle of collective cabinet responsibility explicitly laid down in the constitution. It was only on 7 May 1961 that the resignation of five ministers was announced and a new cabinet again formed, with Mohammed Othman Al Said remaining Prime Minister.

A shrewd and experienced statesman, very learned, the King has had to face the difficult task of uniting three entirely different provinces, despite a tradition of strong rivalry between two of them, Cyrenaica and Tripolitania, and the serious deficiency in educated administrators. Presiding over a federal form of government, with an elected House of Representatives and Senate, the King is Head of State and appoints the Prime Minister, on whose advice he nominates and dismisses other ministers. He directly appoints the provincial governors and senior civil servants, and though he cannot constitutionally veto legislation, he may delay it. In theory he is a constitutional monarch with more than customary powers; in practice, he is the hinge of Libyan unity and independence.

His most formidable problem remains the lack of an unquestioned heir. He married his cousin Emira Fatima in 1933, but has had no son. The uncertainty of the succession has inevitably led to feverish palace intrigue, which culminated during October 1954 in the assassination of the Minister of Palace Affairs, Ibrahim El Shelhi, by one of the royal princes. This forced the King's hand. He divested almost all the members of the royal family of their titles and privileges, had the assassin executed, and named his own brother Mohammed El Rida as his heir. Mohammed died soon afterwards, and his son Hassan Rida was appointed by the King as Crown Prince and heir to the throne of Libya.

A number of factors have combined to prevent the emergence of any strong political parties since the banning of the National Congress in 1952. The great distances between centres of population inhibit the coordination of political activity and the rapid dissemination of ideas, while parochialism makes it very difficult for anyone to achieve a hearing outside of his own town or district. Above all the King disapproves of parties; political clubs are banned by law, meetings forbidden, and the press is subject to licence and control. The only programme for which there may be sufficient popular enthusiasm to create a national party – the abolition of the treaties which give Britain and the United States the right to establish military bases in the country, and the pursuit of a more dynamic and pan-Arab foreign policy – is one which neither the King nor successive Libyan governments have shown themselves prepared to tolerate. The vigilance and efficiency of the Libyan police make a final contribution to limiting or eliminating the activities of illegal political parties. The once-powerful Omar Mukhtar group in Cyrenaica, dissolved as a political organization some time before independence, now exists as an association with few political aspirations, while the Libyan Communist Party did not survive the expulsion of seven of its leaders in November 1951. Sports clubs act as covers for a limited amount of political activity, as do trade unions, though it was only in 1960 that the rivalry between the officially recognized Libyan General Workers' Federation and the Libyan Federation of Labour and Professional Union, till then confined to union matters, became overtly political.

On 3 February 1962 a Tripoli Court sentenced eighty-seven people to imprisonment, on charges of 'forming in Libya cells of the Arab Socialist Ba'ath Party and carrying on subversive activities aimed at overthrowing the political, economic, and social system'. The prison terms ranged from six months to two years and eight months, and the Court ordered the dissolution of the party cells, and the confiscation of their funds, papers, and books. Most of the defendants were young Libyans, but a few came from other Arab states and were issued with deportation orders.

Until oil in great quantities was first discovered in June 1959, Libya seemed destined to remain forever a poor country, the majority of its inhabitants compelled to rake a meagre living from the raising of livestock and the cultivation of arid land. Now the oil boom is bringing changes in its wake, though not all of them beneficial. The arrival of the oil companies, with their staffs and their families, has stimulated a huge demand for consumer goods which the country has been unable to produce; there are at present 30,000 vehicles registered in Tripolitania where there were only 6,000 five years ago. Practically nothing industrial is locally produced, and businessmen have concentrated simply on purchasing abroad and selling to the ever-growing market at home. Real estate, of course, has been among the first sectors of the economy to be swept by the oil boom, and prices of office accommodation and flats have risen to very high levels. All consumer articles, especially fresh fruit and vegetables, have rocketed in price with the sudden surge in demand. The *Financial Times* commented in November 1961:

> Heavy demand for imported goods at high prices, combined with the disastrous effects of drought on home agricultural production, have produced ludicrous trade figures for Libya. Imports (even if those

brought in directly by the companies are excluded) have shot up from £11 million in 1954, through £28 million in 1959, to £43 million last year. Exports, which reached £4.7 million in 1957, dropped to only £2 million in 1960. But in the country's overall payments balance the 'gap' is more than covered by invisibles. The spending of the oil companies on capital goods and services and of their employees, both Libyan and foreign, on everyday purchases increases steadily. To this is added the revenue from foreign aid (totalling about £10 million from Britain and the U.S.).

The use of the income from royalties on oil for development projects is the obvious answer to Libya's present poverty. A country that possesses an infant mortality rate of some 300 out of every 1,000, with many of its hospitals and schools and roads destroyed during the war, requires a massive investment programme, efficiently utilizing all the capital it can get. Whether the Libyan government is prepared to secure its future by using its sudden surge in income, or whether it will squander its prosperity in a temporary spree, will be answered only when the figures for actual investment appear. Of the royalty money from oil, seventy per cent is to be channelled into the newly formed Development Council, at the moment in the process of preparing a five year plan. Over ten million pounds are to be spent on improving transport and communications, a further six million on unspecified 'public utilities', and three and a half million on agriculture; the remainder is to be divided among industry, trade, education, and other items.

In October 1961 King Idris signed a decree increasing the Libyan government's share of oil profits, at present on a fifty-fifty basis, for all future agreements. The decree also made the oil companies responsible for much of the expense involved in development and threatened the refusal of further concessions to those companies which objected to the terms. The King, it seems clear, intends to make as much out of the oil bonanza as he can. His problem, however, remains the almost complete absence of professional experts, technicians, and trained efficient civil servants.

So far Libyans with access to capital have made a great deal of money out of the discovery of oil, but the gap between rich and poor has only increased. This is spectacularly obvious in the suburbs of Tripoli and Benghazi, where smart new villas built by wealthy Libyans and foreigners are sometimes only a few hundred yards from the shanty towns of wood and discarded-tin shacks, where live the many thousands who have come in search of a regular wage. Problems of health and housing and employment, brought by these new immigrants, will have to be solved, and solved with speed. There are countries not far from Libya where the discovery of oil has enriched only a small aristocracy, to make the surrounding poverty even more dreary and desperate. Libya would do well to learn from their example, or its government may find the discovery of oil something more than a sudden stroke of luck.

24 The Socialist Pharaoh: Gamal Abdel Nasser

On 23 July 1952, a group of officers in the Egyptian Army, known as the Free Officers Movement and dominated by Colonel Gamal Abdel Nasser, seized power and destroyed a royal régime that dated back, through a variety of different despotisms, to the first Pharaoh. Theirs was an assault upon the politics of corruption conducted by the Court and the roundabout of Wafd and Saadist Parties, a revolt against the ever-increasing decadence of the Egyptian government and the ever widening abyss between a landless peasantry and the opulent Cairene landlords. In a Cairo of over two million people, more than 100,000 males were officially admitted to be unemployed, and most families existed on some seven pounds a month. The democracy that the country displayed was no more than a lucrative form of commerce for the great landowners and merchants. Less than twenty per cent of the voters were literate, and the vast majority of votes were bought and sold at the polls by a few very wealthy men.

The army revolt was a revolt too against foreign dominion. Since long before the opening of the Christian era, Egypt had been ruled by foreigners; and even when the British permitted a paper independence in 1936, foreign control, directly economic and covertly political, held the country as subject as it had ever been. What Nasser and his colleagues rose up, therefore, to acquire was not only the power to stop the slide of Egypt's masses into ever-greater poverty and wretchedness, but the power first to ensure the rule of Egypt by Egyptians. They believed, as nationalists everywhere believe, that economic advance is finally inseparable from political independence.

GAMAL ABDEL NASSER was born in January 1918, son of a post office employee, at Beni Morr, a small town in the Assiut Province of Upper Egypt. Educated at Cairo, he was from an early age embittered by the decadence of Egypt and determined to liberate it from British rule, concerning himself with the theory of revolution and ways of accomplishing his objectives. In 1937 he entered the Military College and, after graduating, joined the Third Rifle Brigade. Sent to Assiut Province, where he met several of those who were later to be his close political colleagues, he was transferred to Alexandria in 1939. There he first encountered and formed a friendship with Abdel Hakim Amer, who later assisted him in the organization of the revolution and was to become Second Vice-President and Minister of War in the United Arab Republic.

In 1942 Nasser served at El Alamein and in the Sudan. Appointed a teacher at the Military College, he continued his studies and graduated from the Army Staff College. He was sent to Palestine to fight against the Israeli forces in 1948, and he was deeply disillusioned and embittered by the casual cruelty of the Egyptian government in sending its troops into battle with inadequate and even faulty ammunition. He himself fought with considerable courage in the Faluja area and, at this time, wrote much of his book *The Philosophy of the Revolution*, which was published in the United States in 1955.

For some years he had been collecting around him a group of officers – later known as the Free Officers Movement – which was organized in complete secrecy and which exercised a wide influence within the Army. In 1951 the group showed its strength by electing General Neguib, in open opposition to the nominee of King Farouk, as President of the Committee of the Officers' Club. Then on 23 July 1952, by a *coup d'état* in which Nasser himself was indisputably the moving force, the army seized power from King Farouk, forcing him to abdicate in favour of his son and go into exile. Though Nasser himself had been the architect of the revolution, he advanced the appointment of General Neguib – an older man and a widely respected soldier – as the first Chairman of the military junta, later called the Revolutionary Command Council, which took power, while he himself became the Deputy Chairman.

In September 1952 Neguib became Prime Minister, and when in June 1953 Egypt was declared a republic, Neguib became President and Prime Minister, with Nasser as Deputy Prime Minister and Minister of the Interior. The first act of the revolutionary government was to shatter the power of the large landowners, by setting a maximum land holding and redistributing the excess among the landless. Two rival forces, however, still faced the new régime – the Communists and the Moslem Brotherhood. By the end of May 1954, 252 influential Communists had been imprisoned, and the remainder were being relentlessly pursued. The Moslem Brotherhood, however, was far less easy to crush; it was much more powerful, with strong support even among the army officers, tightly organized, fanatical, and accustomed to the use of terrorism as a political instrument. The Brotherhood had fully supported the revolution, but in the belief that it had been forging a weapon to cut its own path to power. When it at last recognized beyond doubt that Nasser intended the revolution to be a secular one and under his ultimate control, it turned upon the régime, attempting first to play off Neguib against Nasser and so split the army.

Stresses were, in any event, beginning to appear within the Revolutionary Command Council between the growing authoritarianism and political conservatism of Neguib, who demanded more personal authority and a gradual return to party political rule, and the radical temper of Nasser himself, who believed that military rule was essential to accomplish the objectives of the revolution and who was supported in his stand by the clear majority of the Council. To Neguib's demand for greater power, the Council responded by driving him even further from authority, through a policy of deliberate neglect. On 23 February 1954, convinced of his unassailable popularity in the country at large, Neguib challenged the Council by resigning. The Council, however, instead of surrendering to the threat and granting Neguib the authority he wanted, accepted his resignation. The cavalry officers demanded Neguib's immediate restoration, despite an appeal from Nasser. The Moslem Brotherhood organized demonstrations in favour of Neguib. And on 28 February, the President was reinstated, this time with Nasser as Prime Minister.

Nasser resolved to act with greater circumspection. On 9 March he relinquished the two posts he had assumed, resigning as Prime Minister and as President of the Revolutionary Command Council. To Neguib's persistent demand for a democratization of the whole régime, he replied on 25 March by steering through the Council a resolution which announced its own abdication on 24 July, restoration of the political parties, and free direct elections for a constituent assembly. The gamble succeeded. The army and the trade unions rallied to Nasser and made clear that they would not permit the revolution to collapse before its objectives had been achieved. On 17 April Neguib reinstated Nasser as Prime Minister, and Nasser reimposed censorship, cancelled the decision of 25 March, and put on trial the cavalry officers who opposed him.

The power of the Brotherhood remained. On 26 October, while Nasser was addressing a meeting in Alexandria, a member of the Brotherhood attempted unsuccessfully to assassinate him. The police and army took to the streets, and before morning many of the leading members of the Brotherhood were in jail. On 14 November Neguib himself was put under house arrest, and there were no longer dissident cavalry officers or the Moslem Brotherhood to rally to his cause. The Presidency fell vacant.

In April 1955 Nasser, who had never before travelled beyond the Middle East, attended the Bandung Conference in Indonesia and played an important part in developing the concept of a dynamic neutralism expounded there. Meanwhile, however, Egypt's relations with Israel, Britain, France, and the United States were deteriorating. Foster Dulles, United States Secretary of State, withdrew an American offer of a loan to finance the Aswan High Dam project, and dependent loans from Britain and the World Bank were accordingly cancelled. The West, disturbed by Nasser's neutralism and the threat to its economic interests in Egypt, was putting the régime in an economic press, in the knowledge that the Aswan Dam was essential to Nasser's whole development plans for Egypt. On 26 June 1956, Nasser struck back. He nationalized the Suez Canal Company and claimed that the Aswan High Dam would now be built from Canal profits. France and Britain sharply protested and prepared for war, while the Arab League declared its support off Nasser.

On 29 October Israeli forces invaded Sinai, while France and Britain stated that they would intervene unless both Egyptian and Israeli forces withdrew immediately to a distance of ten miles from the Canal. Israel accepted the ultimatum, but Egypt naturally rejected it. Britain and France began bombing raids and three days later landed at Port Said in defiance of a United Nations resolution. International pressure forced Britain and France to withdraw, and a United Nations emergency force took over, confirming Egyptian control over the Suez Canal. It was a sweeping moral victory for Nasser and provided him in addition with an excuse to seize British and French assets in Egypt itself. In 1960 Nasser reached agreement with the Soviet Union over a loan for the construction of the Aswan Dam, and the economic pressure of the West, which had been aimed at keeping Egypt free from any Soviet influence, ended by driving the Nasser régime into accepting massive Soviet aid.

On 16 January 1956, at the end of the three-year transitional period that had been proclaimed by Neguib, Nasser announced a new constitution. While a National Assembly would have the right to overrule any Presidential veto by a two-thirds majority, a National Union, the precise form of which was to be determined by the President, would possess sole authority to present candidates for the Assembly. As Fathy Radwan, Minister of National Guidance, described it: 'The National Union is not a party, nor is it a one party system. As specified in the constitution, and as its name indicates, it is an all-embracing union of the Egyptian people.'

On 23 June Nasser was elected President, with only 5,267 votes out of some 5,500,000 registered against him. The Revolutionary Command Council was dissolved, and all but six of its members returned to civilian life. In May 1957 Nasser decided to proceed with the election of candidates for the Assembly and appointed three Ministers as a temporary Executive Committee of the National Union in order to conduct the selection. Most of Egypt's former politicians and all the leaders of the outlawed Moslem Brotherhood were effectively filtered away by a new law which excluded from candidacy those who had been arrested, tried, or sentenced at any time by the Revolutionary Command Council or any of its instruments. The filtering was not, however, yet complete. Of 2,508 registered candidates, the Executive Committee of the National Union, with the President's approval, accepted only 1,320, and these were not recommended but merely cleared of objection. In five districts no candidates were found to qualify. The 350 Deputies of the National Assembly showed themselves independent none the less, and many of them not only cross-examined but often vigorously criticized the Ministers.

In February 1958 Syria, with a population of four million and an area of 73,000 square miles, joined Egypt, with a population of twenty-six million and an area of 286,000 square miles, to form the United Arab Republic. Nasser became President of the new State, and adjourned the Egyptian National Assembly in order to constitute a new parliament, after a brief transitional period, from the members of the two territorial assemblies.

By the opening of 1961, the Nasser régime appeared to have destroyed any real opposition. The Communist Party had been shattered in both Egypt and Syria, though remnants – more noteably in Syria than in Egypt – remained active. The Moslem Brotherhood had been smashed altogether as a mass organization, and any activity was restricted to a few political cells which were destroyed as discovered. The only significant opposition seemed to come from the Pan-Arab Socialist Ba'ath Party, illegal but possessing some support in Syria and among a few influential members of the labour movement in both countries. It was in Syria that Nasser was to encounter his greatest trial since Suez.

On 19 July 1961, Nasser's revolutionary government took a series of steps which seemed likely at last to make good its claim to be creating a socialist society. A list of Presidential Decrees gave the State control – in whole or in part – over most major industrial and financial concerns in the United Arab Republic. The nationalization of banks and insurance companies was extended to Syria and completed in Egypt, while several large textile and mining companies were taken over by the government altogether. Some 300 industrial concerns were compelled to sell a half share of their capital to the government, while the State took a controlling interest in ninety-five other companies and acquired all individual and corporate shareholdings worth more than £10,000 in a further 158 enterprises, compensating for these seizures by government bonds carrying four per cent annual interest and redeemable in fifteen years. No man would be permitted to hold two directorships at once, the régime proclaimed, and new rates of income tax would be established, allowing a top net income from all sources of £5,000 a year. All company boards were to include two 'workers representatives' out of not more than seven directors, while workers – who would receive twenty-five per cent of all company profits, either directly or by way of social services, and enjoy a seven-hour working day – would be prohibited from holding concurrently more than one paid job each or from doing overtime. The maximum permitted land holding, formerly 200 acres, was halved, and some 3,000 farmers were forced to surrender part of their land.

In the *Guardian* David Holden reported:

As a result, in both Syria and Egypt, the chief means of production and transport, the agencies of international trade – including the entire operation of the cotton market, which provides two-thirds of the United Arab Republic's foreign earnings, – the means of finance and exchange, and some of the internal distributive trades have been brought under virtually complete government control. Only the professions, the small workshops, landholdings up to medium size, and the bulk of the internal distributive trade remain available to restricted private enterprise. ... Nasser has spoken ... of socialism as 'an endless road', and ... what remains in the private sector probably soon will be reduced again.

The *Economist* of 19 August 1961 claimed:

President Nasser's revolutionary energy, which ran badly off course during the late nineteen-fifties, has now been redirected to the problems of social change in his own country. If the West, resenting the nationalization measures, sits back to enjoy a coming economic muddle, it may find itself sharing its smirk with the communist world. The reaction of the Arab communist parties, together with earlier warning grumbles from Moscow, indicates that the communists, at least, have recognized President Nasser's brand of socialism as one of the more formidable barriers to the Soviet Union's political penetration of the Arab world, and possibly of the African world too.

In August 1961 a single Cabinet was created for the United Arab Republic, instead of the three – Syrian, Egyptian, and Central – which had governed Syria and Egypt together until then. The National Union, it was announced, would meet only once a year in Cairo instead of once in both Cairo and Damascus, while the two Executive Committees of the National Union, one each for Egypt and Syria, were replaced by one committee. Then, in the second half of September, rumours began to appear in the press of Syrian discontent with Egyptian domination of the United Arab Republic, and in particular with the nationalization measures of July. On the 26th of the month, Colonel Abdel Hamid Serraj, the Syrian Vice-President of the United Arab Republic, with responsibility for Internal Affairs, resigned. Marshal Abdel Hakim Amer, U.A.R. Vice-President and Minister for War, was immediately sent to Damascus as President Nasser's special representative in Syria.

Suddenly, on 28 September, the First Army in Damascus revolted and seized control of the city. Nasser immediately broadcast from Cairo that the situation was more critical than in 1956 and stated: 'I have to guard the unity of the United Arab Republic and will not let this unity disintegrate in any circumstances. I have had many difficulties before, but this is the greatest of them all.' The following day, however, he admitted that all attempts to bring the Syrian rebels to heel had failed, and he announced in Cairo that he had cancelled plans for a full-scale assault after garrison commanders throughout Syria had joined in the revolt. Damascus Radio had meanwhile reported the formation of an eleven-man all-civilian Cabinet, headed by Dr Mamoun Kuzbari, Professor of Law at Damascus University, and containing a number of prominent bankers.

The Times, in its first leader of 30 September, commented:

> President Nasser must rue the day his delegate in Damascus, Field Marshal Hakim Amer, fell out with Colonel Serraj. It was the removal of the colonel, the efficient policeman and advocate of union with Egypt, that gave the signal for discontented elements in Syria to rise and, apparently, to triumph. Their reasons for discontent were numerous. Currency regulations and nationalization have hit hard the large and influential merchant class; drought and land reform have impoverished farmers at different levels. The main grievance, however, seems to have been simply that Egyptians are not Syrians, and that the Syrians, whether they were soldiers, civil servants, teachers, or anything else, disliked being, as they thought they were, told what to do by people whom they regarded, Arab unity or no Arab unity, as foreigners. . . .

At the beginning of October Colonel Serraj was arrested by the Army Revolutionary Command in Syria, 'in the interests of the safety of the revolutionary movement and public security', while Egyptian civilians in Syria began to be repatriated. On the night of 5 October President Nasser announced in a broadcast from Cairo that he would not oppose the Syrian application for membership of the United Nations, though he stated that he would not recognize any government in Damascus until the Syrian people had expressed their will and determined the road they would follow. 'I feel now that it is not inevitable that Syria be part of the United Arab Republic, but it is inevitable that Syria be part of the Arab nation.'

The *Economist* of 7 October commented:

> Beyond Egypt's immediate mortification, it is just possible, perhaps, to discern the foundations of a freer and sturdier association among Arab governments. What has happened is that Egypt, against its will,

has shed a discontented dependency; the shedding, in its initial stage at least, was quick and mercifully bloodless; the next stage could be long, awkward, and more dangerous. But even after being forced to retrace its steps, Egypt is still out in front of the other Arab nations. Egyptian influence still radiates far beyond that of any other Arab country. The U.A.R. was a false turning; yet, from its failure, a new and more viable path could be found in the end. It might not even be too far-fetched, though Egyptians may judge the British analogy to be in bad taste, to see a wider, friendlier commonwealth growing, eventually, out of the narrower colonial relationship.

In October the Egyptian government announced the names of forty 'reactionaries' who had been arrested to insulate them from 'any foolishness', while 167 capitalists had had all their property expropriated. It would seem, however, to have been a safety measure rather than any reaction to popular unrest. Within Egypt itself, the régime of President Nasser appeared if anything reinforced by what the Egyptian people saw as their President's Syrian martyrdom.

Nasser himself believes that democracy can only be profitably practised by a developed electorate, and that a return to party politics without educating the people who are to conduct it would be a return to the chaos and corruption of the pre-revolutionary epoch. To describe the National Union itself as a lethargic movement which has raised little mass response is not, however, to suggest that the régime itself, as personified by Nasser, is at all widely disliked or survives through popular listlessness alone. The nationalization of the Canal, the Egyptianization of British and French commercial interests after the 1956 Suez invasion and of Belgian assets during the 1960-61 Congo crisis, the nationalization or 'Arabization' of banks, insurance companies, and various individual concerns, have advanced Nasser's prestige enormously. The régime has destroyed the power of the hated land-owners and has got down to redistributing the land itself, while the introduction of rent ceilings and three-year leases has given the small farmers a new security and attachment to their holdings. An education programme aims at making primary school education available to all Egyptian children between the ages of six and twelve by 1964. Industrialization is proceeding, if sometimes wastefully, at a rate which promises some escape at least from the stranglehold of an agricultural economy. The Aswan High Dam will at last expand the amount of cultivable land available and provide a basis for the industrial growth so essential to meet the chronic problems of over-population and unemployment. Though the revolution may have fallen far short of its promises and popular hopes, it has extricated Egypt from the economic apathy and political corruption that had imprisoned it for centuries.

On 4 November 1961, Nasser announced a new attempt at guiding the Egyptian people towards democracy. Emphasizing the need to protect the revolution 'against the conspiracies aimed at making it crumble', he established a special committee to define the 'popular forces' in the country. On 19 December this committee recommended the calling of a National Congress of Popular Forces with some 1,500 members, 25 per cent of whom would be peasants and small farmers, 20 per cent industrial workers, 15 per cent trade-unionists, 10 per cent businessmen, 9 per cent civil servants, 7 per cent teachers, 7 per cent students, and 7 per cent women. This Congress – elected in nineteen days during February 1962 – was to debate a draft 'National Charter' presented by Nasser himself, which would then form the basis for the election of a new General Congress of the National Union, destined to be the supreme popular authority. It is impossible, from the vague outline so far presented, to discover whether Nasser intends to popularize government itself to any substantial degree. A more evident effect of Syria's withdrawal from the United Arab Republic has been the change in his whole approach to Arab unity. In March 1958, five weeks after the establishment of the United Arab Republic, a Union of Arab States had been formed with the Red Sea Kingdom of Yemen, providing for a unified foreign policy and military command. On 23 December 1961 Nasser strongly attacked conditions in the Yemen, which he said were against the 'law of justice and the law of God', and three days later the Egyptian government announced that it was severing its links with the Kingdom, to dissolve the Union of Arab States. Clearly the image of Egypt that Nasser now proposed to project was of a socialist society prepared to unite only with those Arab states of similar economic character and objectives. The old largely middle-class nationalism, which had formed the basis of Nasser's first Pan-Arab project, had given place to socialism as the new criterion for unity.

It is perhaps in the field of Pan-Africanism that Nasser himself has until now made his most significant mark. In *The Philosophy of the Revolution*, he wrote of Egypt as an African as well as an Arab State, and with the assistance of Dr Fouad Galal, his adviser on African affairs, he has engaged increasingly in the struggle for the emancipation and the unity of the continent, providing facilities for opposition movements from the colonies and white-dominated territories and vigorously espousing their cause on international platforms.

He consistently supported the claim of Patrice Lumumba to represent the Central Government of the Congo Republic as its only constitutionally elected Premier during the Congo crisis of 1960-61, and in January 1961 he attended the Summit Meeting at Casablanca of Ghana, Guinea, Mali, and Morocco, together with the President of the Provisional Government of the Algerian Republic, the Foreign Minister of Libya, and Ceylon's Ambassador to Cairo. The Conference resolved to form a joint African High Command in order to protect African States from aggression and, if necessary, take action independently of the United Nations; to assist the Algerian forces in the war with France; to pursue a policy of international non-alignment; and to establish committees for cultural, economic, and political cooperation. It is a reflection of Nasser's continental identification and his retreat from Pan-Arab preoccupations that the All-African People's Conference should have decided to hold its third meeting at Cairo in March 1961. No doubt the failure of his experiment in Arab unity will turn his face more than ever towards an African commitment.

A member of the Casablanca bloc, as the more vigorous neutralists of Africa have come to be known, the United Arab

Republic refused to attend the Conference of Independent African States at Monrovia in May 1961, or its successor at Lagos in January 1962, while Nasser himself was one of the sponsors of the conference of twenty-five non-aligned nations (Algeria represented by its provisional government) which took place in Belgrade at the beginning of September 1961.

Nasser's influence throughout Africa is considerable, particularly among the Moslem populations, while his principal Arab antagonist within the continent, Habib Bourguiba, has made peace with him since the Bizerta conflict of July. In the words of *The Times* Special Correspondent: 'Cairo today is the most important town in Africa – a sort of political Tangier, a free port for politicians and political ideas (so long as they keep within strictly anti-colonial lines, of course).'

The distraction of continuing Israeli-Egyptian hostilities, however – the two countries are technically still at war – cannot but handicap Nasser, not only in his relations with several African States which are on friendly terms with Israel, but in the economic development of Egypt itself. Until real peace has been established in the Middle East, Egypt must spend on armaments what might otherwise be devoted to the development of the country. It is therefore hardly an exaggeration to claim that Israel is the real test of Nasser's statesmanship. He cannot hope to fulfil the promise of his leadership while he fails to make every effort to heal the ulcer that is his relationship with Israel.

Certainly he emerged from the Syrian crisis with his reputation for statesmanship much enhanced. He could so easily have attempted at all costs to crush the military revolt which had severed Syria from his experiment in Arab unity. He paused to consider the consequences, and he accepted the break. He may yet accept the existence of Israel and bring into his foreign relations a new security. Were he to do so, and concentrate all his resources on building Egypt into a strong and fast-developing society, he might yet go down in the history of his country as the socialist pharaoh who left behind him a great human monument.

Index

Hereditary rulers appear under the names of their territories.